RUN EVERY STREET:

MANCHESTER

Exploring a city's history in the least efficient way

Neil Scott

For all who go anyway...

4

A Journey from Eh to Why?

The man turned off his lawnmower and I welcomed in the sinking chill of awkwardness.

'It's a dead-end pal, you want the next street over!' He beamed helpfully from his front garden.

I look from him to the end of the cul-de-sac. As one of the 6275 roads in Manchester, I had somehow vowed to run, I must go to the end to tick it off my list. Over the last few months, I had discovered no pacifying reply to my friends and family's bewildered questions, let alone explain it to a complete stranger. I didn't want to return, but every fibre of my body was at Defcon cringe.

I opened my mouth, mind buffering as I pointed down the dead-end like a simpleton. 'I'm running all the...I'm running...every single...street...'

He stared blankly, any words but plain gratitude too ludicrous to register, his smile fading as I stiffly stepped away...in the wrong direction.

I never wanted to run all the streets of Manchester, it's plainly a ridiculous undertaking and as nonsensical as the man who licked cathedrals or the chap collecting chips from Wetherspoons. I am not an elite athlete, nor a great adventurer. I am apathetic to Everest's existence and disinterested in the two frozen wastes atop and beneath our planet. Yet on one particular run close to home, my curiosity got the better of me...

My running story to that point had been a fairly typical jaunt of endless loops of the park, a dozen races and long mindful runs around Manchester. At forty-two, I knew I'd probably gone as fast as I ever would and as far as I ever could, I needed something new to refresh my interest and pitch me out in all weathers. I'm no longer sure why my curiosity stepped up, but I did start wandering and wondering about the side streets I often passed while out on a run...what's down there?

As it turns out, *down there* were some more houses, different cars and a belligerent youth mistakenly encouraging me to run like a forest. Undeterred, I started running different routes through South Manchester, deliberately getting lost and then finding my way back. I was like Lassie speeding home with an important message about some mistakenly belligerent youth, who'd accidentally and anonymously been pushed down a well. Yet, I'd also seen old buildings and peculiar street names, Victorian parks and repurposed mills, abandoned heritage and dilapidated grandeur hiding amidst the houses.

What other fragments of the city's history survived today, hiding in plain sight down these Mancunian streets. What other stories and tales once shocked and titillated the gossiping neighbours of a community, but now faded as the years pass and memories quieten. Was I an amateur runner with a history problem or an amateur historian with a running problem? There was only really one way to find out.

Serendipitously, I then discovered the niche running hobby of City-Striding: Collecting streets by running their full length. Before I could resist, I had a map of all the runs I've ever done, my runs radiating out from my house like the disorganised web of a bohemian spider. More importantly I had a figure, a total number of 313 roads, streets, avenues *and* cul-de-sacs I'd run around Manchester. Beside it was a list of the 40 runners who'd run more roads in Manchester than me.

No one had been stupid enough to run all 6275 of them.

Not yet...

The man in the cul-de-sac with the dormant lawnmower was still staring when I returned past him in the other direction.

'I told you it was a dead end!'

Thursday 6ᵗʰ February 2020 – 15.50km – The other side of the road.

On this day, in 1836, HMS Beagle arrived in Van Diemen's Land (Tasmania), with a 26 year-old Charles Darwin stepping ashore to explore the islands natural secrets. Nearly a century later in 1935, the board game Monopoly with its collectible streets and stations went on sale for the first time in the U.S.A. On the 6ᵗʰ February 1952, a young, inexperienced Queen Elizabeth II succeeded King George VI to the British throne and looked out upon her new kingdom. In 1971, Astronaut Alan Shepard travelled a long way from home, simply to do something ridiculous; play golf on the Moon. Then, in 2020, I stepped out of my front door for a run into the unknown. I then proceeded to step back inside again for my gloves as despite the blue skies, it was only 2C.

Once begloved, besnooded and behatted, I stepped boldly outside once more into the low winter sunshine for a run to go places I'd never been before, to traverse ground my feet had never touched, to see sights...I *could* actually imagine. A daunting, fanatical, obsessional journey around every single street, road and avenue of Manchester could naturally only start in one place – a local park in South Manchester near my house, where there are precisely zero streets on my list.

Alexandra park is a Victorian jewel in Whalley Range. Built in 1870 and named after the royal celebrity at the time; Princess Alexandra, it retains the sweeping pathways, flower beds and a half-mile tree-lined lime walk that would have been a joy for sauntering and promenading Victorian couples and families. But back in time, past the coffee pavilion and the small lake festooned with hungry ducks, the park was also a venue for the working classes in their hunger for socialist reform. In 1892, the Independent Labour Party (forerunner of the Labour Party) held their first May Day rally here. It was organised by the party's leader Keir Hardie – for whom current leader Keir Starmer is named – and was attended by a colossal 60,000 people.

The park also staged important historical steps in the Women's Suffrage movement. Emmeline Pankhurst was born close by in Moss Side and with other campaigners organised a Grand Demonstration march of thousands of suffragists from Albert Square in the centre of Manchester to this park on October 24th 1908. Five years later in November 1913, amidst a nationwide suffrage campaign of more direct action, a homemade bomb wrecked the park's cactus house - with its £50,000 plant collection – with an explosion strong enough to blow out many of the windows. Such were the ripples of outrage amongst the male-dominated establishment and media, the cacti atrocity was even reported in brief in the New York Times under the headline: 'Havoc By Militants'.

After the reassuring balm of a couple of laps of the familiar park, I crossed one of the main arteries leading into the city centre into an area of much local contention, brow furrowing and furious letters to the local paper. Until 2011, an odd looking, but iconic building stood on the corner of Bowes Street, looking like a row of offices with a high bricked-up archway and small clock tower at one side. Built in 1909, this was the huge Princess Road depot that housed trams and buses as the Manchester Corporation expanded its growing fleet of public transport. Despite its modest frontage – partially hidden by some trees - the building was a colossal size, reaching back almost 350 metres from Princess Road. This brick hangar of exhaust and oil fumes, dust and grime could house 300 trams and buses in a building so large it could hold three football pitches!

Bricked up for years before demolition, new blocks of apartments are now springing up beside this busy dual carriageway, but the controversy centres on a large chunk of streets moving out of the Moss Side ward to become a Whalley Range postcode. Cue much local outrage and accusations of gentrification. Into this hotbed of ire and social injustice I ran, moving as swiftly round these unknown streets as a bus conductor chasing a ticket-less scamp or a park keeper with a splintered prickly pear in their behind. Up and down the streets and around the building sites I went, painting some wonky lines on the map on my phone and avoiding women eyeing me suspiciously from behind their pushchairs. Crossing Wilbraham road to the bottom of the estate and coming back up the other side, I returned to the park for a celebratory lap of this arboreal haven away from the ghosts of oily mechanics and sputtering omnibuses. Safely running home with tall tales of foreign undiscovered lands across Princes Road, I congratulated myself on such a daring expedition into the unknown.

31 streets collected in one day. I wrote on my Strava "Maniac!" with little concept of what lay ahead...

Wednesday 12th February 2020 - 11.24km - Chorlton Green where men were mean

With the weather still frosty, a new pair of shoes on my feet and the Wednesday morning news full of some far-flung disease in China they'd now labelled Covid-19; I shrugged and headed off for the wholesome, leafy environs of Chorlton Green. There's something rather pleasing about bounding along beside the rush hour traffic, the air full of plumes of exhaust fumes and the purr of idling engines. Weaving in and out of commuters shuffling along swathed in woollen hats and scarves, their heads bowed and shoulders tense was somehow liberating as I imagined their burdens of meetings, spreadsheets, emails and the banal anecdotes of Kev in Accounts. I was free to breathe in that crisp - and only slightly polluted - morning air, pump my arms and bathe in the imagined curses of the hugely indifferent masses at that carefree runner in his brilliant, trendy, amazing, new shoes.

Bouncing south from Chorlton, down Barlow Moor Road from the traffic lights, I turn onto Beech Road and zigzag my way up and down the adjoining streets until I reach the Horse & Jockey Pub. This black and white timbered pub sits opposite the triangular patch of grass at the heart of the old village, this is where the locals stocks used to stand and also a pound for stray animals, known as the 'Lord's pound'. The release fee for unattended livestock was a shilling to the local constable – proof that even before traffic wardens, there were farm traffic wardens. The Green gives off an atmosphere of permanence, an area infused with layers of everyday history, a place where people have laughed, fought, gossiped, played and moaned for centuries. A focal point of the village where villagers made declarations and settled matters.

Yet not all is as it seems, many buildings claim long histories, but little of the original remains. The pub claims to date back to 1512, yet the timber frontage only appeared in 1908. The Bowling Green Hotel dates back to the 17th century, but the current building – the third on the same site – proudly boasts a 1908 plaque on its front. At the other end of the green is a cemetery for the Church of St Clement, which unlike its cockney namesake couldn't say Oranges and Lemons even if it wanted to as it was replaced by a larger church 400m away on Edge lane in the late 19th century, before becoming dilapidated and finally being dismantled in 1949. A fantastically strange gatehouse entrance to the churchyard remains though. A black and white timbered bell-tower, looking like a bloated dovecote, towers over a simple brick archway. Built in 1888, it was a gift from English barrister, banker and Conservative MP: Sir

9

William Brooks. A parishioner in Chorlton, he objected to the church's relocation and seemingly erected the turret as an architectural protest, with bells on. It is one of only two listed buildings in the area, the other being the early 19th century Higginbottom Farmhouse, which also looks out onto the green.

Chorlton Green was always something of an oddity in Manchester, even up to the beginning of the 20th century. Somewhat isolated from the industrial shockwaves turning much of the rest of Victorian Manchester upside down and inside out, this village on the outskirts looked the other way. Facing south to the clean Cheshire horizon rather than that dark pall of smog to the north, it retained the outlook and spirit of a rural farming community. With surrounding fields and meadows stretching down to the river, it was a place where over half of the population was involved in hard agricultural labour and with several pubs in the area, hard agricultural drinking. Like a very English version of a wild-west frontier town, the high-spirited locals revelled in 'sports' such as Bull-baiting and cockfighting, until they were outlawed in 1835. Undefeated, the locals instead renewed their passion for bare-knuckle fighting and disorderly horse and running races around the meadows. When the authorities and village constable came to break up the commotion, the locals would simply flee across the Mersey into Cheshire and carry on their revelry unabated on the other side.

The protected Chorltonville estate now covers some of those same meadows; a lovely garden village built in 1910 in the style of much larger garden cities such as Wells or Letchworth. Full of semi-detached houses with gardens, open spaces and curving roads, they were a move away from the stark terraced streets that covered much of the rest of the city. Interestingly, all the pairs of houses were built in an Arts and Crafts style, but all slightly differ from one another in design. It was also the last residence of writer, actor and gay-rights activist Quentin Crisp, who died at his Claude Road home in 1999.

Running along these avenues and round the odd little grassed circles, much to the bemusement of one or two people rounding their kids up into their cars for the school run, was a nice way to add some roads to my total and honour those sturdy farm workers who ran on this ground before me. Although I wasn't half-cut on ten flagons of ale, nor rolling up the sleeves of my smock to impress the Blacksmith's daughter, it's the thought that counts.

With counting being the aim, I managed 23 completed streets and almost as many blisters. Stupid, unfashionable, ridiculous new shoes. I wonder if Nike does a hob-nailed boot...

Sunday 16th February 2020 – 21.81km - Half Flying, Half Dead.

Setting off early in the murky February morning twilight, I stuck once more to familiar territory with a run southeast from Chorlton-Cum-Hardy into the neighbouring electoral ward of Chorlton Park. This is not to be confused with Chorlton Park, which is a spacious green park within Chorlton Park; the electoral ward, not the park. Nor is it to be mistaken for Chorlton Water Park, which is a park with water in Chorlton Park, the electoral ward, not the park. Chorlton brook is a watercourse that runs through Chorlton Park in Chorlton Park, but not through Chorlton Water Park in Chorlton Park. Chorlton-Upon-Medlock is right out. Thankfully, none of these places were included on this run and all possibilities of confusion were therefore thankfully avoided.

Heading down the bottom of Withington Road on familiar territory, I plod up one of those deceptive gradual climbs to a bridge over a disused railway line. Another traffic-less running haven I used to plod relentlessly before this challenge runs beneath – the amazing 10km cycleway and footpath of the Fallowfield Loop. Also affectionately known as the F'Loop – the railway line used to connect southern Manchester in a loop through Old Trafford to Manchester City Centre. With a station nearby and lots of flat open fields to the south, where Hough End Playing Fields are now, this site was chosen in 1917 by the War Office for the Alexandra Park Aerodrome. Parts of Biplanes and Bombers built in Old Trafford came here for final assembly and testing before flying off to war. After the Armistice, the field had five years as a civil aerodrome before closure and the land around the hangars and accommodation transferred to the Manchester Police, who remain on site today. They train and look after all their Police dogs, handlers and Police horses here. The evidence of their training in traffic often poses yet another hazard for a street runner in the surrounding streets, but the local rose growers are probably not complaining.

Heading west along the F'loop, I meander sleepily towards Chorlton Green to snag a few pesky side streets and cul-de-sacs I'd missed from the last run. An all too easy occurrence that was teaching me all new useless map-reading skills, albeit slowly. Stop starting all the time to make sure I was grabbing the right roads and not missing any more, I eventually circled south east, across the tramlines on Hardy Lane and into the rather bland 1960's council estate between Barlow Moor Road and Chorlton-Cum-Hardy golf club. At least this early on a Sunday morning in February it was blessedly empty. With the roads empty, I made short work of the meandering curves and looping avenues so loved of town-planners of the period, including two roads that hold particular interest in popular culture.

At number 8 Grindley Avenue, a certain Alan James Clarke grew up. Originally from Oldham, he would leave Barlow Hall Secondary school at 15 for a job at the Manchester Evening News as a copy boy, before finding his feet as a budding actor. Changing his name, as his girlfriend of the time loved Warren Beatty, he would go on to star in countless movies and television shows as a successful character actor with a gruff northern appeal. Warren Clarke is perhaps most famous for starring in Kubrick's A Clockwork Orange or as the grumpy detective in eleven series of Dalziel and Pascoe, but for me he will always be the Bob, the crazed pub landlord in the football hooligan film I.D. His last appearance was on Poldark in 2014 playing a man on his deathbed. He would sadly pass away in his sleep just a few weeks later, aged 67

Meanwhile, just as Clarke was finishing school, a 15-year-old Belfast lad had arrived to stay at number 9 Aycliffe Avenue under the watchful maternal eye of Mrs Fullaway. His employers wisely strictly forbid single men to choose their living arrangements. Living in this family home with Mrs Fullaway's son Steve and a fellow trainee (David Sadler), this shy young boy would blossom into one of the most talented players in the game. For Mrs Fullaway was employed by Manchester United, the game was football and the young Irish lad was George Best. Staying at these humble digs for eight years, long after he was earning luxurious wages and still happy to play football and cricket in the street with the local boys, he eventually had a grand house built for himself in Bramhall. Yet after his drink problems escalated and he disappeared for a week in 1971, Manchester United sent him back under the watchful eye of Mrs Fullaway, the 25-year-old football superstar returning to his small bedroom on Aycliffe Avenue.

Of course, much like Chorlton Green, this estate used to be fields and meadows on the outskirts of the City, except for one rather large exception. On the other side of Barlow Moor Road, away from these homes of life, laughter and sporting prowess is quite the opposite. Southern Cemetery, opened in 1879 and still owned by Manchester City Council, is the largest municipal cemetery in the UK. Famous people buried here include: Manchester's first industrialist millionaire, John Rylands with the finest memorial in the graveyard, Sir Matt Busby of Manchester United and Busby Babes fame, L.S Lowry, renowned painter of matchstick men in urban Manchester and Tony Wilson, founder of Factory Records and responsible for the Manchester bands New Order, Joy Division and the Happy Mondays. It's also the final resting place of

Irish sculptor, John Cassidy (a name that passed me by until June this year, when a certain statue of slave owner John Colston was pulled off its plinth and pushed into Bristol harbour as part of an anti-racism demonstration. Cassidy created the statue back in 1895).

Tiring, but thankful that my healing feet were tolerating the looser fit of my running shoes, I cut through the peace of the Cemetery and headed for home. Despite never travelling more than two miles or so from my house, by the time I stopped I was amazed to find I'd done more than a Half Marathon and clocked up a new run record of 51 streets. Not bad for half a morning's work.

Wednesday 19th February 2020 – 15.50km – The Gone, the Bad and the Ugly

Searching for the forgotten delights, awkward mistakes and unseen horrors hidden in plain sight amongst the genteel streets of Chorlton and Chorlton Park.

Stepping out into the mid-morning rain, I headed for the south of Barlow Moor Road once more having realised I'd missed a whole slew of swirling, meandering roads close to Chorlton Water park. On the way there, I took in familiar ground, heading down Withington Road, ignoring the F'loop this time and heading on to Mauldeth Road West, itself something of a urban oddity. Connecting Princess Road to Barlow Moor Road, it is a wide dual carriageway with a large central reservation completely at odds with the amount of traffic using it. Smaller, busier roads to the north and south render it obsolete, so why is it so wide? Well, back in the 1930's it was part of a failed plan for a road connecting with Old Hall Lane in Sale. The road and wide central reservation carrying a double track of electric trams was due to connect with Hardy lane and soar over the River Mersey – near Jackson's Boathouse Pub. Ironically, the Metrolink tram route to the airport soars over the River Mersey on the original planned route, only minus the roads on either side.

Running west on Mauldeth Road West, I pass the forlorn exterior of Hough End Hall. A grand redbrick Elizabethan mansion, built back in 1596 for Nicholas Mosley, this listed gem sat neglected and ignored for so long, it's worth unnoticed. So much so, by the time people thought to preserve it late in the 20th century, classrooms and canteens had replaced its ripped out interiors. It sits partially obscured by two 1960's-style office blocks as part of Chorlton High School South like a Granddad who'd turned up to a business meeting in his most ancient suit. Its elegant formal gardens where generations of the family would have perambulated after feasting and mused on their troubles were buried beneath tarmac car parks and further modern school buildings to the rear long ago. It remains an unappreciated, partially hidden treasure washed up on a beach of modernity.

Across the road on the corner of Mauldeth Road West and Nell Lane is an impressive stone and brick building curving elegantly around the corner. Now a restaurant and training centre, it used to be the Southern Hotel - a large pub with four bars built in the 1920's and popular with the historically large Irish population in Chorlton. Much more recently in the 1990's and early 2000's, the bar upstairs was home to the Buzz Comedy

Club. Famous names such as Jack Dee, Lee Evans, Caroline Aherne, Steve Coogan, Peter Kay and John Thomson all performed here.

Whirling around the 1920's council estate beside Southern Cemetery and the aforementioned estate I'd visited on my previous run, I came out onto Princess Road. This six-lane highway arrives from a major junction on the M60 and M56 motorways and arrows north right into the heart of the city. It's one of the major arteries into Manchester and claimed to be one of the busiest roads in Europe. With a smattering of houses, a petrol station, two churches and an adjacent primary school, it's also on a list of 81 of the most polluted roads in the UK, with pollution at the school measuring six times the safe limits. The teachers and pupils say they can often taste metal in the air, even though the windows remain constantly shut. The main weapon scientists have put forward in the fight to protect the children? A hedge. Albeit a special type of evergreen hedge they hope will filter out some of the noxious particulates from the road. That and a controversial clean air act set to come in fruition in 2022. More electric cars on the roads will help, but as a lot of the pollution are particles of rubber and brake dust as well as exhaust fumes; maybe we all need to hedge our bets on a green solution. Given how much running I do near roads – albeit at times of low or no traffic – it certainly gives me fumes for thought.

Crossing briefly into West Didsbury and catching a glimpse of the once meandering and now tightly marshalled River Mersey, I headed North up Princess Road past the eastern end of the Southern Cemetery. In a particular unsavoury moment in local history, this was where they found one of the victims of the Yorkshire Ripper in the late seventies when the serial killer terrorised the north of England. On a patch of waste ground by some allotments that were later absorbed into the Cemetery. Running over the bridge straddling the Metrolink line running east into Didsbury, I curve my way past Hough End. Had it been a Sunday morning, I might have spied a sea of figures running, shouting, kicking and the occasional moment of brilliance. Much like Hackney Marshes in London, Hough End with its twenty-odd football pitches is grass-roots amateur football at its purest. Rain or shine, they come, in all shapes, sizes, ages and colours to chase the ball and pay homage to the game they love. Further north past Hough End Leisure Centre is an area of playing fields sheltered from the rest by trees and the Red Lion Brook. Now used for Rugby, the council built cheap prefabricated housing on it during World War II, for those bombed out during air raids and for returning soldiers. Knocked down in the 1960's, some of the cinder-track roads, stout brick bridges crossing Chorlton Brook and some odd lumps and bumps under the grass are all that remain of the community here.

Back over the Fallowfield Loop cycle path, I felt good, despite all the running I'd been putting in over the last week or two. So much so, I persuaded my legs to provide a spurt of speed on the flat ground to test myself against a Strava Segment up towards Alexandra Park. From there and with the rain easing, I headed home with my 31 streets for a well-earned mug of tea and something dangerously calorific.

Monday 24th February 2020 – 13.92 Km – Out on the Range

The rapid development of Manchester as the centre of the new industrial revolution in the early 19th century meant an equally rapid search for ways to escape the chaos and pollution. The draining of boggy land south of the city led to the innovation of an estate away from the centre aimed at Gentlemen and their families. Built by Banker Samuel Brooks in 1836 as a home for himself and other wealthy businessmen. Rather than the ad-hoc chaos of areas developed and redeveloped over decades if not centuries, this was a considered and carefully planned area of large houses and tree-lined avenues. Whilst not strictly a gated community, it had a tollgate and private police force paid by residents. No doubt running these streets back in the 19th century would have seen more than a few shouts, penny whistles, waved truncheons and a fine array of disgruntled moustaches.

Heading north of Chorlton today on an errand to pick up a parcel left at a nearby Post Office, I decided, naturally, to head in the most indirect route possible. Thankful I'm not in Italy where they have introduced strict lockdown restrictions against the spreading pandemic, I ignore the drizzly rain and the large puddles underfoot. I'm determined to make the most of my freedom and get out for a run around what some claim as one of the world's first modern suburbs.

Alas, these once elegant mansions and spacious villas slowly fell into decline. As the industrious city grew, it swelled in money, power, influence and above all population. The city crept outwards and soon overtook this exclusive suburb, the houses set in spacious surrounds crowded in on all sides by workers' terraces. The clean air turned to smog and the rich moved yet further afield. The large houses they left behind were too large to sustain single families, landlords cutting them up into smaller bedsits and even smaller studio apartments. Sandwiched between the quirkiness of Chorlton and the earthiness of Moss Side, by the 1980's Whalley Range became a bohemian land of bedsits and a rather tawdry red-light district, as Morrissey sang famously in the lyrics of 'Miserable life' on his debut album in 1984. The area spawned many other artists and bands, including Mancunian stalwarts James back in 1982. There was no sitting down for me though as I headed up the tree-lined Withington Road, passing St Margaret's School where comedian Jason Manford was once a pupil, before heading west onto College Road.

Unsurprisingly the grandest building on this road is indeed an old College, albeit a magnificent building that wouldn't look out of place in Oxford or Cambridge. And for good reason, it was built between 1840-

1843 as Lancashire Independent College, a place for educating Non-Conformists (Protestants) who were banned from Oxbridge until 1871. A beautiful early gothic revival building in large grounds with a soaring tower at its centre, it never ceases to stop me for a couple of minutes and drink it in – my excuse and I'm sticking to it - whenever I've passed this way. Reflecting the ever-changing heritage of the area, it's now lovingly cared for as the British Muslim Heritage Centre.

Past the college and I'm back in semi-detached suburbia, but this wasn't always the case. As the suburb grew, Sam Mendel – the Merchant Prince of Manchester's textile trade – built his home here, a two storey, 50 room palace filled with handcrafted furniture and fine art; Manley Hall. Set in 80 acres of landscaped gardens with grand lakes, bridges and no less than forty-four greenhouses full of fruit and orchids. Alas, his business faltered in the 1870's and he was declared bankrupt. The grounds though had a brief renaissance as Pleasure Gardens. Looking like the Victorian Manchester equivalent of the Eden project in Cornwall, all manner of flora from around the world sat amongst waterfalls and stepping stones, delighting visitors with this vast collection of non-native plants. A tropical paradise of palms and ferns must have whisked the visitors a world away from the damp Manchester climate beyond the steamed-up glass.

The Pleasure Gardens also hosted Buffalo Bill's Wild West Show. This huge travelling show with its large cast of horse-riding showmen, led by the legendary Bill Cody traversed the world with their romanticised tales of cowboys and re-enactments of the gun battles on the American frontier. After the Wild West was 'won', Buffalo Bill toured the globe with real cowboys and Native Americans, rough riders, trick shooters, stagecoaches, wagon trains, and sometimes even a herd of buffaloes. One can only imagine how extraordinary and exciting this must have been to the Victorian families of Manchester, drawing crowds in from miles around for the shows. Nonetheless, the gardens eventually closed, the Hall was subsequently demolished in 1905 and the grounds turned over to housing, the hunger for land in Manchester always insatiable.

The only remaining piece of the gardens still accessible is Manley Park, a small community park, notable today only for its WWII air raid shelter. Built for five hundred people and with an entrance at the corner of Clarendon Road and York Avenue, it remains hidden a couple of metres beneath the park's grass. As I pass the park and head back up Cromwell Avenue, it becomes apparent just how much of a lifesaver this would have been at a time when destruction rained from the sky. The terraced housing here contains gaps filled in by modern architecture. I picture the families and neighbours huddled underground, silently terrified as the muffled thuds came through to them, the brick walls around them shaking and dust trickling from the ceiling. Many wondering not only if they would have a home still standing by morning, but if they would even make it through the night.

Further north, I traverse up and down the wide leafy streets and closes off Carlton Road, Dudley Road and Whalley Road; the big houses mostly converted to flats or replaced by apartments. Finally I emerge at Brooks Bar where The Whalley Pub once stood and head on down Upper Chorlton Road. This is border territory and because of it quite an unusual road. Despite its mundane appearance, the East side of the road is technically in Manchester and the West is in the borough of Old Trafford. Two different councils look after different sides of the same road, to the extent that if you look carefully enough you can see the difference in street furniture, bins and the like. At the bottom of the road, I dutifully stepped soggily into the warm interior of the Post Office, pulled my delivery card and I.D from a plastic bag and smiled as the steam climbed from my shoulders and water dripped onto the counter from my hat and the end of my nose. I got my parcel and a look that didn't need translating and headed home, the box tucked under my arm like a bandit run-slinger hotfooting it for the hills before the local sheriff can round up a posse from the saloon.

Yeehaw! 36 more streets added to the total, another footnote added to my outlaw reputation at the Pony Express Office.

Monday 2nd March 2020 – 20.55km – More?!

Searching for a Victorian place of last resort, where redemption was unlikely and escape impossible.

With Edinburgh Marathon only twelve weeks away, I'd begun in earnest that impossible extended juggle of work, life and long-distance training. More importantly, I'd begun the dedicated monotony of boring my friends and family at every opportunity with conversations about speed work, minor niggles, fartleks, stretching, long runs and how I now often prefer buildings without stairs. So much so, when I drop 'bagging streets' into a conversation, I often find people have to stand 'over there' because of non-specific reasons and distinct levels of urgency.

So on the first Monday morning of March, I find myself heading out for another parcel collection run, this time from an Amazon box at a petrol station on Princess Road. There and back it'd be around 6km, but like a homing pigeon with a cold, I headed off in the completely wrong direction.

Merrily heading past the rush-hour traffic queuing on Nell Lane and enjoying the sparkling frost lingering on the grass and headstones in the cemetery, I crossed the chaos of Princess Road and continued east along Nell Lane into the virgin territory of West Didsbury. After several modern apartment blocks on a gentle curve, I came across the extended frontage of a grand establishment. Two blocks of imposing authoritarian buildings in red brick dressed with sandstone edges and ornate uprights in an Italianate style flank black cast iron gates. Beyond, a chapel stands before an accommodation block stretching away on either side. Built in 1855, if you were passing through these gates, it was a fair assumption your life was about to get a whole lot worse. While it did indeed hold 1500 inmates, this wasn't a prison. This was Withington Workhouse.

Before benefits, care in the community and the National Health Service, society corralled the poor, infirm and sick in one building and where feasible put to work fixing stockings or sacks. Men, women and children lived in different parts of the building, all working to pay for their upkeep. Unlike many such establishments though, Withington rapidly expanded to become more of a hospital than a place for the destitute, with several airy, spacious pavilions - built to the north in 1864 - praised by none other than Florence Nightingale as an example for others to follow. While the grade II listed parts remain on Nell Lane - now converted into modern apartments - the hospital buildings and accommodation are gone, replaced with modern housing. Meanwhile next door, medical provision for the area continues with the thoroughly modern and welcoming Withington Community Hospital.

A short spurt along the busy pavements of Burton Road's shops and cafe-bars and I was back onto the relative calm of Cavendish Road. Just a short run along here and I'd be back on Princess Road; alas it would take me some time. Despite only being a smidge over 600m long, it had no less than nine cul-de-sacs on it, all but one on the same side of the road. Safe to say, I took a little longer than most people to get from one end to the other. Shaking away the dizziness, I headed north along Princess Road to key in my code at the Amazon box, which opened sesame to reveal my treasure, like a disappointingly modern and all too brief version of Indiana Jones.

Home with my 37 streets for food, glorious food.

Thursday 19th March 2020 – 21.04km – Keep calm and run on

Covid-19 has washed up on our shores and is spreading like the proverbial wildfire. Out on the streets there is uncertainty, distrust and unease marked in everyone's faces. The unknown has appeared, only it's invisible and is apparently killing people we know in a most horrible way. Suddenly, this distant disaster from China sweeping across the world, all felt very real. Boris Johnson has started giving daily briefings on the television, making it feel as if the nation was now on a war footing, announcing that schools would shut tomorrow on Friday 20th until further notice.

In the last fortnight, I'd been largely carrying on regardless bar washing hands and keeping my distance from people. I'd even run an actual Half-Marathon race in Liverpool with several thousand other runners. Everyone keeping separate until about thirty seconds from the start, yet it still seemed nothing to worry about. Since then every day has brought graver news and rising concerns that far from keeping the country free from the virus or even controlling its spread, it was already completely out of control. The world beyond my window appeared to be gradually turning itself upside down like a freshly calved iceberg. With this maelstrom of frightening news whirling through the city, I'd not had much thought for collecting streets or exploring local history. There seemed no need when living through it.

Running had always been my stress relief though, so with a little trepidation and a real sense that it might be my last run for a while before society closes up, I forced myself out for the reasonably close areas of West Didsbury and Withington, counting streets solely as a distraction.

With government advice for people to work from home if possible and avoid pubs and restaurants to help the NHS, it was little surprise to find the streets half-empty of traffic and the pavements devoid of all but the most stoic individuals. Throughout the run, I wasn't sure which side of the stoic/foolish line I was running, perhaps both sides at once. I certainly got a few uncertain looks and instinctively began giving everyone a wide-berth, even if it meant stepping out into the road.

Sticking to the backstreets and the centre of the roads wherever possible to keep out of people's way, I quietly went about my business up Burton Road, Palatine Road and all the closes and side roads in-between. On Lapwing Lane at the corner of Raleigh Close, I come across the former Withington Town Hall. Built in the 1880's it is of a modest size, but built in bands of buff stone adorned with red brick and terracotta tiles, it stands out from the surrounding houses and positively glows in civic pride. Topped with a turreted clock tower and weather vane, it looks in fine fettle and is now a solicitor's office.

Further along on the opposite side is an old cobbled street to nowhere. Sided by an original brick wall and ending at some garages and a pair of green wire gates, this was the approach to the Withington and Albert Railway Station, built as the Midland Line arrived in 1880. The steam trains are long gone, with the line now used by Metrolink Trams. Towards the end of Lapwing Lane at the corner with Burton Road we see the grand three storey brick and half-timbered Metropolitan Pub. A giant of West Didsbury's food and drink scene, the Midland Hotel arrived here at the same time as the railway in the 1880's. Famed for its live jazz and big band music in the 50's to 70's, it hit a rough patch of in the 80's and 90's, before a refurbishment back to its current glory. Opposite is the aptly named Railway Pub, a modest tidy pub created from a cottage, it's main claim to notoriety is that of a haunted cellar where an old customer is said to roll barrels around later at night. Perhaps they just need some thicker wooden wedges under the firkins. Blagg's hardware store across on Burton Road would surely be able to help. Something of a local institution, the Hardware store formed by the Blagg's Brothers has been here since 1871.

From there I struggled to concentrate and meandered on without a set plan, simply following my feet and staying wherever seemed quietest. That said, I stumbled across a couple of surprises; an armoured people carrier parked up outside someone's house and a robust army lorry hidden in a back street. Perhaps the good people of Didsbury are a little better prepared for all eventualities than the rest of us. It did remind me though of the last time Manchester hid indoors and hoped for the best, albeit then the threat wasn't on the streets, but came from above.

In August 1940, the Luftwaffe of the Nazi Germany war machine spread its destructive, morale-sapping raids from London to other cities around the British Isles. Manchester with its armaments and war factories in Trafford Park and neighbouring Stretford was a prime target for obliteration. The bombing went on for several months with the most intense coming during the 'Christmas Blitz' on the 22nd and 23rd December 1940. Nearly five-hundred tonnes of high explosives and over one thousand incendiaries fell on those two nights, killing 684, injuring over 2000 and traumatising a whole city.

Inevitably, many of the bombs missed their targets; so much so, even Didsbury and Withington were hit, some four or so miles away from the targets. Like many places across Manchester, hastily built air raid shelters appeared in public places, back gardens and at schools. At

Withington Girls School, the children continued their lessons in the shelters built in the playground, merrily cramming themselves in like sardines, with pictures of aeroplanes and motor cars pinned to the walls. The pupils busied themselves making knitted clothes for soldiers and sailors as well as blankets for the Red Cross. During total war, even children helped the country in any way they could.

As schools prepare to close in 2020, a passage from the Withington School archive seems rather apt:

"In 1939 conscription was introduced and the Second World War brought war to the home front, yet it appears that at a time of great strife, when so many families and communities were torn apart, our school offered a place of safety and normality which was undoubtedly invaluable to ensuring that pupils could carry on with their education throughout the war years."

Heading home with tired legs and 54 streets completed, I closed the door on the world and like so many others waited to see what our own time of great strife might look like.

Sunday 22nd March 2020 – 22.81km – Closed and no closer

Cafes, pubs, clubs, theatres, gyms, cinemas, libraries, churches, playgrounds and all non-essential shops are now closed. New restrictions are in force stating people must work from home unless a key worker, like myself. The government has urged the public to stay home apart from visits to the supermarket, for medical needs, to care for someone vulnerable or for one session of exercise. With the infections and deaths spiralling upwards, the Government is fighting a deadly enemy and threatening further restrictions if necessary.

In this climate of fear and with the depressing sight of people in Spain and Italy locked in their homes for weeks on end, I look out the window at the bright dawn skies and pull on my running shoes. I have no enthusiasm for it, but who knows how long it'll be until I can go running again.

Heading south out of Chorlton, I didn't even bother looking at my map. I had no enthusiasm for gathering streets or the challenge at hand, the country was in a crisis and everyone's mental health was at Defcon 2. Despite feeling permanently off-balance and scared at what it might mean for the ones I love and the most vulnerable of my friends, I knew I could and would naturally reset to this new normal in a couple of weeks or a month. But at the time of peak shock, the toxicity of worry mutes all logic or reason.

Even early on a Sunday morning, I certainly wasn't ready for the eeriness of the empty streets. Aside from the odd taxi, I barely saw ten vehicles in the time I was out. Even the dog walkers I normally share the pavements with were hiding away. Running along Barlow Moor Road towards Didsbury, I simply followed my feet and found myself cutting through Northenden and out of Manchester entirely. I turned east into Gatley and on through the ghost town of Cheadle centre. Headed north back towards Parrs Wood and on into Burnage, I saw no one but the odd passing car – essential workers headed to or from work. Being alone in this great city, gave me the creeps, like an enemy invasion was imminent, the tanks ready to roll in and the citizens in hiding or already fleeing out of the city. So much so, I began to feel out of place and that I was perhaps doing something if not illegal, but immoral. It felt like a police car would stop by any second and tell me I shouldn't be out.

It was only as I passed through Withington that I saw another runner and with an exchanged nod of the heads, came to my senses. The map came out and I found a few cul-de-sacs and side roads to bag on the last couple of miles home. Possibly the strangest run I've ever had through a seemingly post-apocalyptic city. One leaving me more uncertain and lost than when I set off.

Seeking 23 eerie, empty streets from a world in hiding.

Saturday 4th April 2020 – 16.48km – We are not, we're not really here

A curate's egg of a run that comes around only once in a blue moon...

Moss Side was named after the large boggy land stretching across much of South Manchester from Chorlton to Rusholme. This great moss was part of the Trafford estates and is described in Elizabeth Gaskell's novel Mary Barton as a rural idyll complete with a black and white timbered farmstead. With lush vegetation and clear ponds, it must have been a haven for wildlife; the skies full of insects and birdsong. Times change in a city, sometimes quicker than anyone can fathom.

Lockdown has arrived in Manchester and everyone has taken a step into the internal unknown. As the underlying emotion of the world's leaders walked the tightrope between reassurance and fear, the majority of the populous stayed trapped in their homes with partners and children, isolated from work, fun, family and friends. As a key worker, I found life equally unsettling in a large open plan building of nearly two hundred people, all of us looking at one another with wide eyes.

I had not run for two long weeks. Just when I needed the de-stress of a lung-bursting, leg aching run, I couldn't face it. I didn't want to. I simply went wearily to work, warily to the supermarket and hid from the world as it burned invisible flames beyond my window. I had never felt so uncertain of the route ahead and so aware of living through a chapter of a future history textbook. When the Prime Minister is making grave warnings on the television and then contracts the deadly disease himself, it is not a time for flippancy or fun. Yet as the nation unites to clap, shout and ring bells for the nurses and doctors at the sharp end of the pandemic, a glimmer of togetherness and hope gleams through. Like so many, I wasn't immune to the cold grip of fear and unease that permeated the land, the suspicious eyes and strained looks of strangers battling an unseen foe were hard to fend off. Not watching television fast became the best coping mechanism for me, the impulse to hide myself away strong while people panic-bought toilet rolls and called the police on neighbours daring to walk their dog twice in a day.

Amidst the cancellations of football, concerts and anyone leaving the house, inevitable news came through of the Edinburgh marathon postponement until September. I thought about carrying on and running it virtually nearby, but the motivation and concentration levels weren't there. I had tried to delay and contain my running challenge, now I must enter the third stage; research and planning. It gave me something, a precious something to cling to and mitigate the anxiety of living through such a strange time in such a strange world.

Firstly, I needed to be responsible. I studied the rules over and over, exercise outside was safe and encouraged as long as you stuck to your local area. Despite repeated mentions in the media of a one-hour time limit, Boris Johnson and the law allowed people to exercise outside, but this was not legally limited by frequency, length, distance or time. One prominent politician arbitrarily mentioned an hour for walking and thirty minutes for running, seemingly based on the fact he'd just finished a twenty-five minute run. Ambushed by a heavyweight television interviewer on his doorstep, he confidently declared that 30 minutes was enough for anyone. Presumably before declaring he could have gone further if he wanted, and faster, but it looked like rain and he had some washing on the line. Besides, his hamstring has been a bit tight recently. And he has a blister. None of which was reported in the newspapers. Instead, the 30 minutes got reported and somehow enshrined in people's mind.

Nonetheless, I agreed wholeheartedly with social distancing and making minimum impact on others and decided on my own stringent rules: I would only run early in the morning when the streets were empty and on the road not the pavements, I would clean my hands before and after, wear gloves and touch absolutely nothing.

As fear receded to routine and my mood lightened from apocalypse to nervous acceptance of the new strained version of normality, the urge to run grew too large to ignore. With it came the realisation that one trivial side-effect of this emergency was that the not so hospitable areas of Manchester, where I might face an inquisitive or worse still anti-social reception, would be temporarily empty. Ignoring the bigger picture, I now focused on bagging as many streets as I could in places I wouldn't normally go.

Six o'clock on a crisp Saturday morning, I stepped out the door once more and headed for the empty streets of east Moss Side. Bounding up Alexandra Road and across the top of the park with only an occasional minicab for company was both eerie and bliss. It was so good to be outside and drawing the unpolluted frigid air deep into my lungs and feeling its chilled embrace on my face. If this was to be my one run of the week, I was going to enjoy it.

Crossing Princess Road I pushed deeper into the terraced streets than the last run over here and watched the indifferent sun creep up and over the rooftops to start another beautiful clear day. I picked up the pace, heading down the middle of all the parked cars, the only sound my laboured breath and my feet kissing the black tarmac. These streets of

Moss Side were where pop and rock star Barry Adamson grew up. A member of the post-punk band Magazine in the late 1970's, he would later work with Visage, Depeche Mode and Nick Cave and the Bad Seeds. His first solo album, Moss Side Story, was an imaginary soundtrack to a non-existent film-noir set in the area.

Much earlier, back in 1852, this area gave birth to a most unusual man with a colourful life. George Garrett was born the son of a Church of England Curate, following in his father's theological footsteps, he too became a curate, but not before a minor diversion in his studies into science and chemistry. This strange mix of clergyman and curiosity somehow led him to invent and build the world's first steam-powered submarine in 1879. There's a sentence you never thought you'd ever read. Offered £60,000 by the Royal navy if it passed sea trials in Portsmouth, the Resurgam – nicknamed the Curate's Egg – sadly sank in bad weather on the journey there, the tether towing it snapping just off Rhyl. He would go on to trial another one-man sub with the Swedish, Greek and Turkish navies, before failing to make a success of farming in Florida. He eventually joined the U.S Army Engineer Corps until his early death in 1902. A full sized replica of his submarine sits on Birkenhead waterfront close to where it launched for Portsmouth on its fateful last journey.

The sense of trying, trying and somehow plucking defeat from the jaws of success probably resonates with older fans of another Moss Side institution. This highlight of my day was the new development on the site of Manchester City's old home: Maine Road. Amidst the 434 new homes and the wonderfully named Blue Moon Way is a circle of grass complete with metal centre-spot surrounded by a commemorative inscription. Delightfully, it sits exactly where the old centre circle used to be on the pitch that the club played upon for eighty years. Nearby there is one other connection to the club with a road named after an ex-player, surprising not just that there was only one, but also the choice. Trautmann Close was named after Bert Trautmann, the much-loved Manchester City goalkeeper most famous for breaking his neck and playing on in the 1956 cup final win. More interesting is the fact the German not only joined the club in 1949 – just four years after the second world war when relations were naturally strained – but after capture on the Eastern front, the nazi paratrooper was sent as a prisoner of war to a camp in Northern England, near Northwich in Cheshire. Whilst there, the prisoners helped build the ring roads and bridges in and around Manchester Airport.
52 completed streets today and for a little while nothing else mattered.

Sunday 12th April 2020 – 10.41km – Guns, Drugs and Women's Suffrage

Street names often form a fascinating glimpse into a city's history. While flowers, trees, animals and place-names are the norm, many others commemorate a famous person or industry from the area's past. While these street-names are seemingly eternal, there's often some intrigue in the roads that get renamed and erased from history for very different reasons.

Life was still a whirlwind of stern-faced experts and frightening statistics, but as day followed night and the birds still sang in the trees, I too had to carry on and find as smooth a path as possible through the ruffled anxieties of an uncertain world. While there was a lot I couldn't do, a lot of places I couldn't go and a lot of people I couldn't see, I could go out and run, so running was what I was going to do.

Early Sunday morning and beneath overcast skies, I once more ventured into the deserted streets of Moss Side, concentrating on the Alexandra estate north of the park with the same name. Starting at the western edge of the estate, I swiftly came across the Methodist Church on Sedgeborough Road. Back in 1858, when the road was Sloan Street, Emmeline Pankhurst was born at number 8 Alpha Terrace, a site somewhere beneath the Church's car park or the property to the south. She would grow up to be the leader of the British suffragette movement and rightfully regarded as one of the most important figures in modern British history.

Founding the Women's Social and Political Union in Manchester in 1903, she campaigned relentlessly for Women to have the vote and a fairer stake in society. While she travelled widely speaking at rallies, the WSPU also took up civil disobedience and militant action to raise awareness of their cause, many of her supporters ending up in prison on hunger strike and being brutally force-fed. Pankhurst was herself arrested seven times in her battle for the women's vote, famously stating in court in 1908, "We are here not because we are law-breakers; we are here in our efforts to become law-makers." Partial victory came with the 1918 Representation of the People Act, granting women over the age of thirty the vote. Just weeks after her death in June 1928, the vote was extended down to all women over twenty-one. It's a shame there is nothing on the street to mark the place of her birth, all trace of her childhood here wiped away when the slum clearances brought about this new estate, which may or may not have been a coincidence.

Three hundred metres and nearly seventy years later, it was violence and disobedience of a different nature that had the police and local authorities concerned. In the 1990's and 2000's, Manchester had so serious a gang problem with firearms, drugs and violent deaths, the national press labelled it 'Gunchester'. One of two such gangs in Moss Side hung out at an illegal shebeen on Gooch Close, the other gang congregated at the Pepperhill Pub on Doddington Street, barely four hundred metres to the east (both taking the names of their streets as their gang name). Both had a rivalry with the Cheetham Hill gang from the north of the city centre and all controlled the drugs trade across Manchester. Turf wars, feuds, slights and even petty disputes over girls and the ownership of a bike led to a spate of shootings; 170 incidents from 1996-98 leading to 90 injured and 12 dead. The next year, there were more shots fired in the city than ever before, the police finding 270 spent shell casings across South Manchester. Thankfully, these fearful days wouldn't last and multiple arrests of the Gooch Close and Cheetham Hill gangs broke the cycle of retribution and drug wars. The streets synonymous with the gangs were renamed Westerling Way and Brentwood Street; the Pepperhill Pub closed down and made into a community centre. There have been great efforts to protect and grow the community in Moss Side and while it still has problems, its residents no longer live in fear as they did in the late 90's.

Still, even with the ghosts of anger and violence long past, I couldn't help but speed up over these troubled streets, my early-morning footfalls a little lighter, my breathing a tad quieter than normal. Chancing across the grand old Big Western Hotel and Pub on Great Western Street – a relic of the time when all the surrounding streets were terraced – I couldn't help imagine all the stories this drinking hole had seen. From payday at the local rope and twine works to all the christenings, birthdays, weddings and wakes celebrated inside and the fights and arguments settled on the pavement outside. The pub now stands boarded up and quiet; full of echoed laughter and drunken ghosts.

37 streets added to the total including those in the road name equivalent of the Witness Protection program.

Monday 13th April – 19.47km – A tale of two parks, a red tower and a little ditch.

As Manchester grew in the late 19th century, Moss Side was always seen as an area of the working classes, one culturally rich with the influx of migrants. Initially popular with the Irish and Poles, the area later saw the Windrush generation arrive from the Caribbean. They brought with them a sunshine culture celebrated each year in the ever-popular annual carnival street party, now held in Alexandra Park and headed for its fiftieth year in 2022. Row upon row of terraced houses bred a strong community spirit amidst the hardships until the 1970's when slum clearances and a lack of jobs fragmented the networks of families, churches and friends and an anti-social rot of drugs and violence seeped onto the streets. With the success of the previous days run and a sleep-pattern broken by ever-earlier starts at work, I found myself stepping out for a run at 5.40am on a Monday morning. It was safe to say, I was alone.

Heading once more to Moss Side, I figured with a good plan and a steady rhythm I might finally see off this much-maligned suburb. Despite its poor reputation lingering on from its troubled past, it wasn't always that way.

Passing the Royal Moss Side Brewery, now owned by Heineken with its towering silos and billowing clouds of steam, I'm reminded that the UK's first lager was brewed on this site, back in 1927. Beer has been brewed here since 1875 when it was known as the Albert Brewery. Red Tower Lager became a premium drink in London's finest restaurants and hotels in the late 1920's. It was so successful, the brewery named itself Red Tower Brewery in 1933 and hasn't stopped making lager since. Changes of ownership and parent company has seen it make McEwan Younger and Harp lagers. Now it produces a truly ridiculous eighteen million pints of Kronenbourg 1664 and Fosters lager every single week. Every week! At the packing plant next door, they fill up a staggering ninety thousand cans each hour. And behind all the cladding, the red brick tower that started it all is still there at the heart of the brewery.

Weaving my way east up and down several empty roads, I eventually come to Whitworth Park. Built in 1890 at a time when there was much concern about the welfare of workers packed tightly into their streets amidst the coal smoke and pollution. A desire to provide them clean, green open spaces to walk, relax and - more importantly - keep them out of the drinking houses all weekend, saw many parks spring up towards the end of the 19th century. The plan and location of this park was the idea of the legatees of Sir Joseph Whitworth after his death in 1887,

32

who chose Potter's Field – a mansion and gardens on the corner of Moss Lane East and Oxford Road owned by Beatrix Potter's uncle. The park and the adjacent Art Gallery were seen as fitting memorials to commemorate the great engineer, who amongst many other achievements ironically made much of his fortune from the design and manufacture of the Whitworth rifled musket. It seems firearms and Moss Side cannot escape one another. On a lighter note, back in 1912, a huge crowd gathered around the bandstand for a demonstration of a new music sensation, the Auxeto Gramophone. Many listeners were reportedly less than impressed by the sound quality from the record player; even over a hundred years ago it took a lot to impress a Mancunian.

Skirting the back of the dormant Indian restaurants on Rusholme's Curry Mile, I meandered up and down, back and forth along street after street of terraces, seeing a few lights come on in bedrooms and kitchens as the clock ticked closer to 7am. Generally drifting south, I bump into the northern edge of Platt Fields and the boundary of Fallowfield. Another larger park than Whitworth, it was once a private residence (Platt Hall), but then converted into an urban park for sports and recreation back in 1908. Much has changed over the decades, at different times it had a 25m Lido swimming pool, a sunken amphitheatre, a boating lake with steamboat rides, a ride-on model railway and an annual flower festival. Until recently, Platt Hall held a Costume museum, but now it sits empty, awaiting a new purpose. Likewise, with the pandemic shutting down the city, its show fields sit empty awaiting the return of festivals like Eid and various concerts through the summer months.

What does remain in the park is also possibly the least impressive of scheduled monuments across the City, the Nico Ditch. Looking like any other overgrown drainage ditch at the edge of a field, this Anglo-Saxon ditch originally ran for 9.7km across South Manchester and dates from somewhere between the 5th and 11th centuries. Many believe it to be a defensive ditch against invading Vikings. Others think it is a boundary marker at the edge of the boggy moss land. Then again, some think it is just a drainage ditch. Frankly, the only thing agreed upon is that it's old and much of it is gone, buried under redevelopments across the city. Here in Platt Fields though, it remains, protected behind a fence, to keep the crowds back from marvelling at whatever it was and whatever it still is.

Not that crowds are much of a problem right now. Despite being out running for an hour and forty minutes in a big city – albeit mainly before 7am – I'd seen a grand total of six men, each dressed all in black, one old man with a beard, not dressed in black and exactly four cars on the move. If I'd rounded a corner and seen zombies ambling towards me, I wouldn't have been surprised. It was that eerie. Still, all the more room for me to bag a whopping 73 streets in a run of around 12 miles. Or the equivalent of running the length of the Nico Ditch and back, but with significantly drier feet.

Sunday 26ᵗʰ April – 17.17km – Out for the Atmosphere and some morning Eyre

Searching Chorlton-on Medlock for a dutiful daughter who scored one in the eye of the literary patriarchy.

Sunday morning and despite being tired from a busy working week keeping the country supplied with what they need, I resisted the sofa gravity and returned to the streets. This early morning jaunt beneath overcast skies was a longer venture north-east of Moss Side into Chorlton-on-Medlock, an area now more commonly known as 'Oxford Road' or 'the Universities'.

Heading north east of the Royal Moss Side Brewery, I headed into the Oxford Road Corridor Enterprise Zone, which appeared to be a rather protracted phrase for a series of roads around office blocks. On past some grand apartment buildings and I entered a small estate of newish social housing with two roads in particular catching the eye, Bronte Street and Eyre Street. The West Yorkshire literary sisters, why were they here in South Manchester? I wouldn't have long to find out.

Meandering back and forth - and sometimes venturing in several random-looking loops that to the untrained eye could look like someone a bit lost – I edged my way north and by degrees, entered University Land. I wasn't quite on the campus proper of Manchester Metropolitan University, but I was amongst the student halls and takeaways on the fringes. Amidst all the modern four and five storey accommodation blocks and apartments with their uniform rows of windows and drawn curtains, one building stood out.

On Boundary Street West stands The Salutation Inn. With cranes standing over it as the University builds a towering new building next door, this Victorian relic dates back to 1840 and is one of only two pubs in the city to retain its Victorian interior – the other being The Briton's Protection on Great Bridgewater Street. With its sandy brown tiles and red brick exterior it is a gorgeous building now owned by the University and known lovingly by the students as the 'Sally'. It's place in history alas goes much further, as back in 1846 – when it was still a boarding House – Patrick Bronte stayed here while seeing a specialist for an operation on his cataracts. Accompanying him was his daughter Charlotte Bronte. A keen writer like her sisters Anne and Emily, all three adopted pen names lest their work be dismissed outright because they were women. Whilst caring for her father here at the Inn, Charlotte put pen to paper and began writing the classic novel Jane Eyre, under the pseudonym, Currer Bell.

Leaving this deserted world of learning and drinking behind, I finished off a few more roads, before crossing the wide Princess Parkway and meandering south back through Moss Side towards home. However there was one little cultural treat left in store, as I crossed the Epping Walk Bridge. An ordinary paved footbridge with white railings, it owes its fame to one snowy photo from the 6th January 1979. Used as a promo photo for the iconic Manchester band Joy Division, it lives on as the cover of their 'Best of' album. The band often practiced in a rehearsal studio next to the bridge, also used for the promo video for 'Love Will Tear Us Apart', sadly long since demolished.

42 streets today, which is one more than the number of years since Joy Division released their debut album; Unknown Pleasures. So that's a win for me I think...

Thursday 30th April – 17.72km – Closer to Holmes

A reluctant run close to home in the footsteps of a real life thief-taker who inspired a literary giant and where the seeds of thousands of iconic cultural images were sown.

Thursday morning, early, my day off. Feeling tired, unenthusiastic and fatigued, I stare at the ceiling above my bed willing my body clock to switch off and let me sleep. The radio clicks on, the snooze button an annoying inch too far from my flapping fingers.

'...fortnight after completing his epic 100 lengths of his garden, Captain (Sir) Tom Moore celebrates his 100th birthday today. He's so far raised over £30 million for-'

With a sigh, I got up and pulled on my running kit, the world had spoken, laziness was not an option.

Through Moss Side and sleep-encrusted eyes, I initially only followed my feet, large parts of my brain still in denial that I was even out of bed. Heading north up Lloyd St (probably), I sleepily discovered three closes near to the Maine Road redevelopment named after ex-Manchester City players from 1920s, 30s and 40s; Horace Barnes, Fred Tilson and Sam Cowan. I'm sure someone's Great-Granddad could tell you more, but that's all I've got and to be fair, at this point I might have dreamt them.

Twenty minutes passed, that was enough, that'd do, right? Sadly, my legs were just warming up and with my achiness easing, my lazy brain was overruled and we headed east along Claremont Road towards Rusholme and Manchester's famous 'Curry Mile'. This main arterial route into the city centre had been popular with textile mill workers from the Indian sub-continent in the 1950's when they made the cafes here a place to meet friends and relax. From this seed, cafes and restaurants sprang up from a growing Pakistani community until Wilmslow Road became a centre for South Asian cuisine and earned its nickname in the 1980's. But nothing ever stands still and a new influx of immigrants from Kurdistan, Turkey, Syria, Afghanistan and other parts of the middle east have set up shop in this multi-cultural buffet of food heaven. The large curry restaurants remain with their unique atmosphere and bright lights, but these new usurpers dwell in the side streets offering authentic, wholesome food for their loyal customers at cheap prices without the frills and waistcoats of the main strip. Even running past early in the morning, I catch an occasional waft of fried onions, spices, sweet treats and the lure of strong coffee. I resist but breathe deeply, imagining it as fuel for the soul, if not the legs.

To the north, Wilmslow Road becomes Oxford Road and I pass Whitworth Park once more, before heading west to take in the roads around the strangely shaped Whitworth Park halls of residence. Triangular-prism shaped and looking more like something from an alpine ski resort, they are affectionately known by locals as the 'Toblerones'. One of them, Aberdeen House, bears a blue plaque marking where number six Thorncliffe Grove stood, the lodging place of social philosopher and writer Friedrich Engels while he stayed in the city in the 19th century.

Looping around to the west, I reach a street where a man didn't simply write about the city's ills, but actively sought the criminals lurking in the labyrinth of murky alleyways and seedy corners of smoggy streets. Cecil Street in Moss Side was the home of Jerome Caminada, who served as a detective with Manchester Police from 1868 for 31 years. Something of a maverick, he would often dress in disguise and meet members of his large network of informers in the last pew of the Hidden Gem church close to the Town Hall. He even had a nemesis from the slum of Angel Meadow by the name of Bob Horridge, a blacksmith by day who turned burglar at night. Helping to imprison well over 1200 criminals in his career including suspected terrorists of the Fenian dynamite campaign, a gang of thieves at the Grand National in Aintree and the famous Manchester Cab Murder in 1889, Caminada soon shot to national fame. His exploits and cases were well publicised in the papers just as a certain Arthur Conan Doyle was inventing another Victorian-era detective - who used disguises, a network of informants and had a shady nemesis - for his novel A Study In Scarlet. Caminada may not have worn a Deerstalker hat, but it's plain to see why he's been dubbed Manchester's Sherlock Holmes.

Back into University land, I decide on a whim to run the deserted streets in and around Manchester Metropolitan University. Made into a University in 1992, it can trace its history back through various collectives of schools, colleges and centres of excellence to the Manchester Mechanic's Institute in 1824 and the School of Design in 1838. The latter of which became the School of Art and had the artist L.S.Lowry as a student in the years after the First World War. Other notable alumni of the University include comedians John Bishop, Jenny Eclair and Steve Coogan, actors Richard Griffiths, Julie Walters, John Thomson and Debra Stephenson, presenters Vernon Kay, Peter Purves, Matthew Kelly and Gethin Jones and a whole falsehood of politicians – or whatever the collective noun is for MP's.

Onto Cavendish Street at the heart of the University, I find something of a glorious white elephant in Chorlton-on-Medlock Town Hall. Built in 1831 in a grand neoclassical style with pillars and an ornate pediment, it is every bit a sign of how important and proud this expanding township had become. So it must have come as something of a shock just seven years later in 1838 when the municipal borough of Manchester was formed rendering it obsolete. No doubt the Chorlton Aldermen took the news gracefully and didn't barricade themselves inside like municipal despots. Thankfully the police stepped in... with boxes of paperwork, a large tea urn and long wall rack of wooden truncheons...Probably...as they took over the grand building for their own offices. They didn't leave until the 20th century.

The old Town Hall also rather randomly hosted the fifth Pan-African Congress in October 1945, where decisions made by several future African presidents and premiers led to the independence of Nigeria, Malawi, Ghana and Kenya. The building was later absorbed into the wonderfully neo-gothic sandstone School of Art next door, with its large bright windows and almost ecclesiastical pinnacle turrets. It's seen many fine artists, photographers, designers and musicians study here. And of course, Mick Hucknall of Simply Red fame.

One person with a most colourful life who didn't take to the Art School was someone we all know the work of, but possibly don't know his name; Tom Chantrell. Born in 1916, he left school at 15, working locally before moving to London to work for the Allardyce and Palmer Advertising Agency. Somehow surviving six years with the Royal Engineers Bomb Disposal unit digging unexploded bombs out of Sussex beaches, he returned to the Advertising Agency after the Second World War and his career really took off. For the next thirty years, he would design and paint more than 7000 film posters from little more than a synopsis and a few photos, often before the film had even been made or commissioned. He would often have his wife and friends sit for him in costumes, their faces appearing in many of his pictures. Working at a phenomenal rate, on average he turned out three designs a week! From Star Wars to the Carry On films, One Million Years BC and Hammer Horror movies to musicals like South Pacific and The King & I, Chantrell was the go-to man for the images that drew millions into the cinemas.

With a gurgle in my stomach and a happy ache in my legs I turned for home, heading west along Stretford Road and over the iconic Hulme Arch bridge before one final historic titbit. Just beyond the Job Centre and opposite the Morrisons Daily is a small patch of grassland and trees, Hulme Park. It was on this spot that Henry Royce and Charles Rolls started to design and build their first motor car in 1904; the Silver Ghost. They also invented the Rolls-Royce V8 engine on this site the following year before moving production to a much bigger site in Derby.

With the V8 growl in my stomach growing by the minute, I changed gears and made for my kitchen before I ran out of fuel. Only 33 streets added today and at times a bit of a trudge, but as ever I never regret a run. I only hope I still manage to get outside and move around on my hundredth birthday.

Saturday 16ᵗʰ May 2020 - 14.21km - Waller's Wall and Old Moat's Moat

As the terrifying Covid figures fall away and optimism returns, the country surfaces from lockdown like a bear wakening from hibernation. On the first weekend of freedom after lockdown, everyone in the city has had the same idea about having a walk and enjoying the newfound liberty of meeting a friend from a different household. Yet, the two metre rule remains in place, so my commute to running in Rusholme along the Fallowfield Loop largely involves throwing myself into hedges and undergrowth to dodge the families, dogs, children, pushchairs, bikes, skateboards and scooters.

The F'loop, runs from Chorlton in the West to Fairfield in the East, almost across the full width of southern Manchester from Old Trafford to Tameside. Around eight miles in length, it claims to be the longest urban cycleway in the country. Formerly a railway branch line that ran from 1892 to 1988, it's had a few issues with anti-social behaviour, but has recently secured a £5m investment to improve access and security to make it a family-friendly route. As a mostly flat, traffic-free route, I've spent many a mile pounding up and down its length, building endurance and sprint training. In many ways, stepping off the familiar F'Loop and getting lost in unfamiliar territory on my way home probably sowed the seeds of this crazy challenge.

Today though, it was just too crowded. After a couple of miles of pinball from one side of the cycle-path to the other, I curtailed any plans of Rusholme and bailed out at Old Moat. Situated at the northern end of West Didsbury and Withington, Old Moat is an area that appears more on the map than in reality. Aside from Old Moat Park, many would probably not even notice they'd passed through it. Working my way down Yew Tree Road past the park and in and out of several back streets, I come to Davenport Avenue, once the site of a notorious wall.

Back in the early years of the 20ᵗʰ century, a Mr McInn ran a grocer's shop at the corner of Moorfield Street and Davenport Avenue serving the nearby community. At a time of less mobility and no supermarkets, he would have had a captive market in the surrounding terraced streets, known every face and heard all the gossip. In 1908, he somehow fell into something of a dispute with the wealthy and influential Egerton family of Tatton Hall, who owned much of the land nearby, including the eastern end of Davenport Avenue. So being the reasonable and understanding Mancunian that he was, Mr McInn hired a local Electrician (obviously) named Frank Waller to construct a brick wall right

41

across the road to prevent any carts travelling onto the Egerton land. About five feet in height and with spikes on top, it completely blocked the road to all traffic and pedestrians, becoming known locally as Waller's Wall. No doubt, upon hearing the news the Egerton family immediately sent an urgent telegram to their plumber, Frank Bulldozer...

Heading further west along Mauldeth Road and close to the busy Princess Road, I reach Eddisbury Avenue, under which lies the site of Hough Hall, the medieval seat of power in the manor of Withington. During the middle ages, the Lords of the manor, lorded over a considerable area of southern Manchester covering Didsbury, Chorlton, Moss Side, Burnage and further east through Levenshulme into Denton. I wonder what the Lord would have given for a convenient paved route like the F'Loop through his vast territory of boggy meadows and bubbling brooks.

The manor house was grand enough – and no doubt the Lords so confident in the affection of their farming tenants - to have a substantial moat built around it. In 1596, the Lord built a new grander manor house, Hough End Hall (See Feb 19th), the original seemingly kept as a spare until it was pulled down and replaced by Old Hall Farm in 1750. The old moat still half circled the farmstead and gave the area its name. Alas, growing cities have little sentiment for the past when there are workers needing housing and the farming fields of Withington were rapidly devoured in the inter-war years. A plaque at the site of the Old Manor Farm champions the completion of ten thousand houses built by the corporation of Manchester for the working classes in the ten years from 1919 to 1928.

Wandering amongst these houses on weary legs, I saw nothing much of interest, except for the odd unusual road sign to keep me amused. I chanced upon the improbable Mornington Crescent – which I said aloud and immediately won the nonsense game of the same name – and Colgate Crescent, which I imagine is the kind of residential street recommended by nine out of ten dentists.

With little distraction, I suspected I wasn't going to last long and although glad to be out, felt a little out of sorts. Seeing so many people walking dogs and chatting on the pavements was a little disconcerting after my apocalypse adventures of the past couple of months, but heading home with 23 streets, at least I didn't hit the wall.

Wednesday 20th May 2020 – 17.72km – Danger, Danger, Danger

Staying close to home, today I searched for the home of animated childhood memories and when the world exploded on the Scott Allotments.

The UK experts add loss of taste to its list of Covid-19 symptoms, but as I gaze into the mirror at my mismatched running clothes and cheap sunglasses, I'm reassured by the thought I probably had little to lose in the first place. Today is also World Bee day, which as the emblem for Manchester and its industrious workers, can only mean I need to step out on this sunny Wednesday morning and get busy gathering in the streets. Staying local today, I decide to pick up a few strays from previous runs and then focus on the area in Chorlton to the west of Manchester Road and north of Wilbraham Road. First though, I head back to my childhood.

On Albany Street, behind the Esso garage and just down from the Unicorn Co-operative is a block of modern apartments on the site of television history and treasured memories. For it was here in the early 1970's that Brian Cosgrove and Mark Hall formed their animation studios; Cosgrove Hall. An unassuming building produced the cornerstones of many a child's early cartoon favourites from Noddy, Chorlton and the Wheelies, Jamie and the Magic Torch and Danger Mouse to Wind in the Willows, Count Duckula and Bob the Builder. They also made several films and television specials including the feature-length BFG in 1989. Closed in 2009, it's sad such a cultural influence known by so many is now largely forgotten. Some years back there were a few murmurs about building a Danger Mouse statue to generate visitors to Chorlton, but sadly the campaign petered out almost before it began.

Bouncing down Manchester Road, I pass the Sedge Lynn – an attractive green and white public house in a semi-circular arched construction with a turret at one corner. Designed to attract visitors in from the often grey and drizzly streets – it's tempting even at half eight in the morning – it's an irony that this Wetherspoons pub originally opened as a Temperance Billiard Hall back in 1907 to steer locals away from the demon drink. Oh well, moving on...

Looping back to the north, I find my road. Not the road where I live, finding that is something of a daily habit, no I mean Scott Avenue. Situated just off Oswald Road, I like to think a future fan of this book time-travelled into the past to change the name to Scott Avenue as homage to this challenge. That might seem fanciful, but pleasingly there's no actual way of proving it didn't/won't happen. What is without doubt is that the neighbouring Scott Allotments took a direct hit from a huge bomb during the Christmas Blitz of December 1940. A parachuted German Land Mine over five feet in length and weighing five hundred kilograms was dropped from a German bomber in the skies over Manchester. Slung beneath its parachute, its sheer weight meant it still plummeted to earth at forty miles per hour. Smashing into the soft vegetable patches of Scott Allotments, the heavy thud must have shook the neighbourhood and widened eyes of those in backyard shelters. Not designed to explode on impact, hitting the ground would have started the internal timer even before the parachute settled over its muddy cover.

Twenty-five seconds later, the timer detonated the three hundred kilograms of high explosive with a deafening roar and changed Scott Avenue forever. The shockwaves, plume of debris and rush of air killed two, injured many more, demolished several houses and blew in doors and windows over a hundred and fifty metres away. The gap at the end of Scott Avenue where two houses once stood remains as a large garden for what became the end house.

Heading west towards Longford Park in the forbidden land of Old Trafford, I feel strong and put in a burst of pace, making short work of the long straight streets. Close to the neighbouring borough though, I discover something of a curious anomaly that stops me in my tracks. On Grange Road, the tarmac halts at an old brick wall, six foot high and blocking all progress to the road on the other side. Looking akin to something from post-war Berlin or the work of some Edwardian electrician, this is the border between Manchester and Old Trafford and it really rather looks like they don't get on. I half expected to see a patrolling guard and a spotlight pick me out, but I guess they and their Dobermans were on a break. In reality, this appears to be the original perimeter wall of Firs Farm to the north when this was all farmland. Manchester built Grange Road up to the wall first, Old Trafford built Edward Charlton Road second – named after the last Victoria Cross winner in Europe in WWII. For whatever reason, neither council ever got around to knocking the wall down uniting the roads and so, the Chorlton Wall remains to this day.

Talking of difficulty getting from one side to the other, running back up around to Oswald Road, I reach number six; the home of great aviator Arthur Brown. It was just over a hundred years ago that he and John Alcock etched their names in history as they made the first ever non-stop transatlantic flight from Newfoundland, Canada to Galway, Ireland in June 1919. Just sixteen years after the Wright Brothers flew thirty-seven metres, they were attempting to fly over three thousand kilometres. Understandably, it was far from an easy flight. A series of failures on board deprived them of first their radio, then their intercom and their heating. They hit a large bank of fog, twice losing orientation and nearly spiralling into the sea. Already cold in their open cockpit, night fell and the temperatures at altitude plunged. At 3am, they hit a large snowstorm that not only drenched them, but threatened to ice up the plane and render it unflyable. With the carburettors icing up, Brown had to climb out onto the wings to clear the engines lest they seize up and stop. After sixteen hours of hellish drama, they crash-landed in an Irish bog at 8.40am, completing the first leap over an ocean, averaging 115mph and claiming their £10,000 prize from the Daily Mail (worth £160,000 in 2021).

Whilst I couldn't claim such a grand prize for my ninety minute journey across Chorlton-Cum-Hardy, I gladly crash-landed back on my sofa with a further 37 streets in my hands and fond memories of childhood cartoons. Crumbs!

Sunday 31st May 2020 – 23.19km – The training has already left the station

Bored of collecting roads, I initiate my own house rules and monopolise a different set around Manchester City Centre.

Days after my cancelled Edinburgh Marathon date has come and gone, I go rogue. Faced with another suburban trawl across South Manchester, I realise I can't face another stop-start run up and down cul-de sacs. I can't deal with all the map-reading and brainwork required to solve the maze-like puzzle. Today isn't a day for maths and geometry, orienteering and problem-solving. This dazzling Sunday morning is going to be about freedom and the joy of having your head in the skies and your heart beating a rhythm that makes your soul dance.

So I ran.

I ran like a kid let out on his bike with his friends. Like a dog chasing a bouncing ball or a herd of cows released out to spring pasture for the first time of the year. I had no idea of the route or even the destination, I simply ran and took joy in familiar places I'd not been in months and new places I'd yet to explore. Heading east from Chorlton I followed the F'Loop out to Fallowfield, allowing myself to wake slowly without the need for vigilance amongst traffic. Stepping off onto Kingsway, I headed three miles north up Birchfields Road and Upper Brook Street to the city centre, finding myself at Sackville Gardens on the street with the same name.

Here, sandwiched between the Manchester University and the Gay Village, the memorial to Alan Turing is situated. After his revolutionary work at Bletchley Park in WWII, deciphering the Nazi's unbreakable Enigma code, Turing continued his great work on computers at the University before his tragic death in 1954. The plinth at his feet describes him as the: 'Father of computer science, mathematician, logician, wartime code breaker, victim of prejudice'.

Headed east past the functional elegance of Piccadilly Railway Station, I pass through under the tracks into a much grimier area of bricked-up arches and weeds growing from cracks in the walls. It feels like I've passed backstage in a grand theatre, where there's no longer any need for a lick of paint or more than a serviceable repair. On I go, turning left onto the ring road and round between the new shops and apartments in New Islington and Ancoats, the once drab vista now bristling with large blocks of gleaming brickwork, shiny glass and endless balconies. Past the Northern and Green Quarters I run, on around Manchester Victoria Station – seemingly I'm playing Monopoly and collecting the stations.

Without a care in the world, I cross the River Irwell on Trinity Way, cheating on Manchester with a dalliance into Salford. Passing Salford Central Railway Station – seriously didn't even know it was there – I head down New Bailey Street and cross Albert Bridge back over the river into Manchester. Beside the law courts, I stop to explain to Manchester that Salford meant nothing to me, that it won't happen again and that I do love the city and all its streets. Besides, I was drunk on the rush of accidentally collecting three railway stations in less than an hour. Thankfully, Manchester has given me one last chance, but any more funny business and I'll have to go live in Liverpool.

Moving swiftly on, I made for an empty China Town, the restaurants all closed and no visitors taking photos at the Chinese gardens and the ornate Imperial Arch straddling Faulkner Street. The memories of impressive meals and delightful buffets I'd devoured around here set a gurgle in my stomach and my first niggle of wanting to be elsewhere at another time. Around the corner, I hit Portland Street on what was once an unbroken parade of tall brick and terracotta warehouses full of cotton and textiles. Sadly, while some remain, most fell victim to the bombs and incendiaries that set this part of Manchester ablaze back in 1940. A few old weavers' cottages survive from a time before the industrial revolution as a run of shops opposite Abingdon Street.

Its here two pubs battle it out to be the smallest pub in Manchester. Harking back to a time when a Public House was simply someone's home opened to the public, these tiny one room pubs have barely space for a few tables and at a push, maybe forty people standing inside. The Grey Horse with its black timbered ceiling is perhaps the smaller of the two, but the Circus can also claim to be the smallest bar in Europe, by nature of its having the smallest bar top - being only about one metre wide.

Running is great and uplifting, but as the energy wanes and I start noticing pubs, I know the inner homing pigeon is kicking in and it is time to head home. Obviously south via Oxford Road Railway Station for a full set of stations, I'm not daft. Only 29 roads added today, but the smile on my face was worth every mile.

Wednesday 3rd June 2020 – 12.78km – Siege the Moment

Manchester has a fine reputation for many things, but amongst them is its rain. With most weather coming in from the south-west, it's almost inevitable that most clouds passing overhead shed a little weight as they hit the Pennine hills to the north and east of the city. This can be torrential, but more often than not consists of rain showers and a fine drizzle that most natives no longer even notice. Yet, at least once in the City's past, this propensity to being a rainy place has saved its inhabitants from those wishing to destroy it.

Setting off once more into the drizzle of a weekday morning, the rain and gusting breeze reminded me that despite the light mornings and mild temperatures, the summer had yet to get going in these parts. Fighting to warm myself, I picked up the pace along Upper Chorlton Road and Withington Road as I bounded north towards the city centre. Running swiftly in a straight line was a joy as I dodged the puddles in Hulme and fought my way across rush-hour traffic towards the shops of Deansgate.

Feeling a little out of place amongst the raincoats and umbrellas of those commuters who couldn't or wouldn't work from home, I bounced past the architectural mish-mash of Manchester's main thoroughfare. I'd always thought of that as one of the joys of getting lost in the centre, unlike some great planned architectural triumph like Paris or the regular blocks of Madrid or New York, Manchester has modern and old, red brick and glass, stone and steel all jumbled up together in an informal pattern. A city with civic pride in its buildings, but no overall plan means the contrasts only make the unusual stand out more. There are so many stories of the great and good along here, I'll only pick out a few stories that caught my eye.

The Grade-I listed John Ryland's Library on Deansgate is hardly a secret, but as my favourite building in the city, it's going to be celebrated here regardless. John Rylands was the Cotton King of Manchester, a wealthy businessman who died in 1888, leaving his fortune to his widow, Enriqueta. She endeavoured to build this late Victorian neo-gothic shrine to scholarly learning in her husband's name. Taking ten years to build in red sandstone and with the vast reading room inside laid out like a three-storey cathedral, it is truly one of the great libraries of the world. From a 2nd century fragment of a papyrus bible and rare medieval illuminated manuscripts to early books printed by Caxton and first editions of Classics, it's become an important place to study works within its vast collections. I never tire of climbing up the stone steps to the Reading

Room, raised high above the noisy street and basking in the silent glory of this treasure of knowledge.

Further north and much less known or noticed amongst the shops is the little visited gem, Barton Arcade. Situated towards the north end of Deansgate, the grade-II listed Victorian Shopping arcade is four storeys high complete with ornate cast-iron balustrades and a glass domed roof. It is easy to picture elegant ladies in long dresses and wide hats swishing across the black and white tiled floor and being fussed over inside the most exclusive boutiques and shops in the city. It's a survivor of another time, one of so few, with many such arcades, rows of shops and old pubs succumbing not just to progress but the bombs and fires of the Manchester Blitz.

Around the corner from Deansgate on St Mary's Gate used to be the beating heart of the city centre. Here where the large Mark's and Spencer's store is today, used to be the Market Place and the glorious medieval buildings of the Old Shambles where animals were butchered in the street and the gutters ran red with blood. Market stalls sold their wares and shops bustled with customers. (The medieval buildings survived the Manchester blitz and later moved to a place beside the cathedral.) To picture the hustle and bustle of this area amidst the market stalls, animals, noisy traders and shoppers, it is interesting to note there were no less than fourteen public houses within fifty metres of the market place and also numerous Coffee Houses and Tea Rooms. Elizabeth Cooper's Old Coffee House stood near the Market Place in the Georgian period and showed how times were changing. Serving Coffee or Chocolate for a penny, Cooper's even admitted ladies – fancy that – but only in the evening when they started to serve tea. None of that strong stuff for the delicate ladies, that'd be far too scandalous.

On the other side of the Market Place was the Cotton Exchange where lucrative trades and deals passed back and forth between the top hats, prim frock coats and bristling moustaches. The huge four-storey Royal Exchange that majestically stands there today is resplendent in the finest Portland stone, built in a Classical style in 1867. Badly damaged during the war, it survives in a simpler form without its fine original interior or tall clock tower. It is the third Exchange on this site, each larger than the last.

The first Exchange, built in 1729 had a macabre function of criminal deterrent that came to a head in 1745. Or rather, four heads. Back at a time when Bonnie Prince Charlie was inciting the Jacobite Rebellion and marching on London to claim the throne, he picked up many followers along the way. As he came through Manchester, four soldiers from the Manchester Regiment must have helped him, as the judiciary found them guilty of treason, executed them and put their heads on spikes outside the Exchange. On the 17th January, the city was in uproar, not because of the grisly sight of the four severed heads in a shopping area, but because the heads were gone, stolen during the night. They were never recovered.

Nearby at the top of Deansgate is the Cathedral and beside it the Chetham's School of Music. Both have a long colourful history, the school building built in 1421 on the site of Manchester Castle. Albeit more a fortified Manor House on a sandstone bluff than a true castle, three defensive ditches have been found around the site, although historians say the castle was of little political or military importance. Which sounds a little like the attitude of most leaders of England towards the North since the Norman Conquest. A church built next door to the manor house was on the site of an earlier Saxon church. The fortified manor house would later be used in the 15th century to house Collegiate priests before soldiers of the English Civil War ousted the priests as sympathisers to the king. The Parliamentarian Roundheads then used it as a prison and gunpowder factory. Chetham's School developed after the civil war in 1653, its beautiful library remains the oldest public library in the English-speaking world. The Cathedral has had extensive changes and repairs over the years. As the city grew and bombs from the Luftwaffe and I.R.A. damaged or destroyed the interiors, it has lost its stained glass windows and has many different styles. As such, the Grade-I listed building reflects the scars and damage of a City that has survived great change and shocking attacks and come out the other side.

Victoria Bridge, just west of Cathedral at the far north of Deansgate was finished in 1839 and named after the famously unamused monarch. Its opening drew large crowds to witness a procession of soldiers and marching band cross the bridge amidst bunting and large flags on surrounding buildings. Meanwhile workers in nearby forges along the river, created the sound of celebratory cannon fire by striking gunpowder on their anvils. The Queen naturally kept everyone by being fashionably late, arriving a full twelve years later, on her way to an art exhibition at White City in (the forbidden land of) Trafford. Before the Victoria Bridge, this crossing spot was occupied by a narrow three-arched stone bridge built in the mid-14th century and complete with a small chapel in the middle; Salford Bridge. It was here the first battle of the English Civil War was fought.

As the country headed towards conflict in the summer of 1642, both sides raided town magazines and stores for weapons and gunpowder.

An early visit from the Royalists in July led to a skirmish with the locals on Market Street in which linen weaver, Richard Perceval died from a single gunshot, becoming the first victim of the war. Manchester, siding with the Parliamentarians, bolstered its meagre defences and awaited its fate. After raiding several other Lancashire towns, Lord Strange returned with several thousand Royalists in September, laid siege to Manchester and demanded the surrender of their ten barrels of gunpowder. He was told he'd 'get nothing, not even a rusty dagger', showing the Mancunian stubborn attitude has little changed in five hundred years.

What followed was a week-long battle of repulsed charges by the Royalists across the medieval bridge towards the Parliamentarian defences surrounding the Cathedral, in a battle known as the Siege of Manchester. Cannon-fire came from the southern fields along Deansgate (Now the St John's area and the appropriately named Artillery Street) and further attacks came from that direction, but it was to no avail. Barns caught fire amid the chaos, but as the smoke cleared after another failed attack over the bridge on October 1st and with morale at a low, Lord Strange withdrew having lost over 200 men. The defenders (somewhat dubiously) claim only to have lost four men.

It rained heavily throughout the seven-day siege, the first dry day coming after Strange departed. The Parliamentarians wrote of their triumph, 'You came with fire, but God gave us water'.

Dampened, but unbowed, I took my 16 streets home and vowed to never complain about the rain again.

Thursday 11th June 2020 – 16.03km – Universally Challenged

There are no Nobel Prizes for Running, but if there were, I'm sure Manchester would do all it could to lead the pack and win the race to athletic achievement.

Returning to Chorlton-on-Medlock, I once more head for the Universities. Approaching along Oxford Road in the traffic free, bus-only zone, the sandstone glory of the neo-gothic Whitworth Hall looms into view. With its pinnacle towers, large stained glass windows and steeply pitched roof, the 1902 building looks more like a medieval cathedral than a place of learning. Forming the Southeast corner of an internal quadrangle, it is a suitably prestigious space still used by students for their graduation ceremonies. Continuing the gothic revival frontage next door is the treasure-filled Manchester Museum. Inside are all the traditional Victorian exhibits of dinosaur bones, Egyptian mummies, statues, medieval weaponry, old coins, fossils and stuffed animals, but presented in a modern way that discards much of the obsession with glass cases found in many museums of the same era.

Turning off Oxford Road, I start exploring the completely empty campus where roads look like footpaths and footpaths look like roads. The mish-mash of buildings and closed doors gives me an unsettling feeling. With the students sent home and using remote learning because of the pandemic, a place so usually full of life is devoid of its academic soul. I feel like a trespasser, constantly awaiting that annoyed shout from someone in a fluorescent jacket with a clipboard and a bristling moustache. Yet, amidst the blocked view of what goes on inside these classrooms, halls and lecture theatres, there are information boards and signs proclaiming just a fragment of the many achievements and the stunning history of this place of learning.

The University takes great pride in being linked with an amazing twenty-five Nobel prize winners, either as students, as former staff or currently working on campus. In comparison and cheating slightly, that's two less than the whole of Japan and five more than the whole of Italy since Nobel prizes began in 1901. Among the winners in Manchester is Niels Bohr, who investigated the structure of atoms in 1922, James Chadwick who discovered the Neutron at the heart of the atom in 1935 and Walter Haworth who perfected the synthesis of Vitamin C in 1937. Even as recently as 2010, Manchester was at the centre of scientific discovery once more with Andre Geim and Konstantin Novoselov who potentially revolutionised the world of electronics and composite materials with the discovery of graphene. The granddad of them all though is Ernest Rutherford. Working in the Physics department from 1907-19 in the building that now bears his name, Rutherford and a team of great minds discovered the nuclear atom, split the atom and initiated the field of nuclear physics. He won his Nobel Prize for Chemistry in 1908.

Running these roads, tracing the paths of these revered students and lecturers as they shuffled from class to class, their heads abuzz with new ideas and unproven solutions was a humbling experience. I loved reading all the information so much, I almost forgot why I was there. Two other pleasing firsts were William Arthur Lewis who became the country's first black professor in 1948 and 'Baby', the world's first digital computer, built in the same year by Freddie Williams and Tom Kilburn.

Heading for home with more knowledge than streets bagged, I accepted my haul of 12 roads completed as a lesson learned. Today was more a day for noble pride rather than Nobel prizes.

Sunday 14th June 2020 – 13.2km – Power and the Money, Money and the Power

Putting on my imaginary I heart Manchester baseball cap, I head for the city centre to join the 1.3 million overseas visitors who come to Manchester for a city break, for business or to visit family or friends each year. Like most of them, I want to stand in awe before the Victorian shrine to the power and wealth generated in those smoke-belching satanic mills.

Delighting in my new taste for ambling runs along the main roads into the city centre and back, I head for the tourist trail and the buildings that give Manchester its unique neo-gothic style. Crossing the Mancunian Way I run past the grand Bridgewater Hall; an international concert hall built in 1996 with a refined modern look that causes little offence and reserves all its grandeur for the beloved acoustics inside. I trot on past the magnificent Midland Hotel built beside the former railway station that is now a conference centre and exhibition space. Across the road, I skirt around the gorgeous circular Library building and enter Albert Square, where a building embodies the city in every Mancunian's heart.

Completed in 1877 at a time when the money from cotton, coal, steel and heavy industry was rolling in across the North-West, Manchester Town Hall is perhaps the grandest example of civic leaders attempting to outdo neighbouring towns. Designed in a neo-gothic style by Alfred Waterhouse, the architect who also designed the natural history Museum in London, this vast building of fourteen million bricks took nine years to build and cost £1m (£92m in 2020 prices). An impressive 85m high clock tower, complete with an eight tonne bell, known as Great Abel, tops the Town Hall. It remained the tallest building in the city until the CIS Tower office block, built in 1962. All of which shows how much confidence and wealth was being generated in the city at the time and just how much care and attention was put into the craftsmanship of this administrative giant.

In front of the Town Hall are various listed statues and a fountain erected for Queen Victoria's diamond jubilee. However, the most impressive of them is the Grade I listed memorial to her husband that gave the square its name, the Albert Memorial. The first of several built around the country, it bears a striking resemblance to the Albert Memorial built seven years later in Kensington Gardens in London. But obviously, that was a totally original design and different in every way, because London would never copy something from the dirty, uncultured north. Besides the London statue has an extra step and the stone sometimes looks a different colour, in certain lights. Anyway, look they're just different...and all similarities must have just been a huge coincidence.

Talking of north and south, I stride down Brazenose Street from Albert Square to Lincoln Square to find the unlikely home of a statue of U.S. President, Abraham Lincoln. The story behind it is one of the American Civil War in the 1860's and the abolition of the slave trade in America's confederate south. What do distant transatlantic squabbles have to do with Manchester? In a word, cotton. At a time when Manchester clothed much of the world, the mill-owner's decision to back Lincoln's embargo on cotton exports left mills idle and warehouses empty across the north-west. The statue was a gift to the people of Britain as a thank you for the self-imposed hardships they faced in standing united against the evils of slavery. Originally destined for Liverpool, it came to Manchester in what looks like a civic backslapping exercise. One wonders just how sympathetic the destitute mill workers were to some far-flung humanitarian cause they only read about in the penny broadsheets, when they themselves had no money for food, ale or fuel to keep their families warm.

Looping back around to King Street, I get the whiff of Victorian money and power once more. At the corner of Cross Street stood the first Town Hall, replaced in 1912 by the Edwardian baroque bank that until recently housed the Lloyds TSB bank. The City leaders at the time saved the original Town Hall's facade and moved it to Heaton Park. Throughout the 19th century and pre-war in the 20th century, King Street and Spring Gardens at the top of the slope were at the epicentre of the North-West banking empire. Monetary and trade deals were done here and further along Cross Street at the Royal Exchange and Corn Exchange. Several banks built premises along the street, to draw in the wealth of the rich industrialists in the city and nearby mill towns. At a time when banks were only as solvent as the trust put into them by their patrons, the banks invested heavily in heavyweight, classically styled buildings that looked as permanent a fixture as the Bank of England itself. Quite literally, as one of the most impressive banks on the street is the Grade-I listed branch of the Bank of England. With six fluted columns, heavy pediment and grand fanned arch windows, this bank built in 1846 wasn't just elegant but also built for defence with thick reinforced vaults that are still there in its basement. At the top of the hill is the king of King St, an unusual white-walled art-deco fortress designed by Edwin Lutyens for Midland Bank in 1928. Looking more akin to one of Liverpool's 'three graces' than the neo-gothic Mancunian style, the (HSBC) bank here closed in 2008, its banking hall next occupied by one of Jamie Oliver's restaurants. The boutique hotel occupying its upper floors since 2015, aptly market its unusual architectural style by calling themselves Hotel Gotham. There's a joke somewhere in there about Robin and banks, but I'm far too sophisticated to mention it. Pow!

Leaving King Street behind, I loop around to another giant of Manchester's civic buildings, its Art Gallery on Mosley Street. The main building was built in a Greek Ionic style between 1824 and 1835 and originally housed the Royal Manchester Institute - a society the wealthy set-up to push back at the accusations of Manchester being an uncultured hell. One can fair imagine the snobbery of the landed gentry at these merchants with their new wealth and the doors closed to them in societies further afield in London. Holding exhibitions, purchasing artworks and supporting artists, the Institute even had its own school of art funded by its patrons. After an act of parliament in 1882, it transferred to the Manchester Corporation and became Manchester Art Gallery. With a fine art collection of over 5000 oil paintings, watercolours and drawings, it is perhaps most renowned for its collection of Victorian art from the Pre-Raphaelite brotherhood, including the works by John William Waterhouse. Other artists displayed include Valette, Renoir, Cezanne, Degas, Constable, Stubbs, Turner and of course, J.S. Lowry.

Heading south, I pass some of the new additions to the Manchester skyline. After many years of the booming City being clad in scaffolding and towering cranes, some new skyscrapers to rival Beetham tower at the base of Deansgate are emerging. Already nearly fifteen years old and iconic of Manchester's growing confidence in the 21st century, Beetham Tower at 169m was the tallest building in Manchester. It's now been usurped by its new neighbour, Deansgate Square South Tower at 201m tall, one of four colossal towers built on the former site of Knott Mill Iron Works. Founded in 1790, W.J. Galloway and Sons were the company at the heart of making steam-powered boilers and engines to drive Manchester's industrial revolution. It somehow seems fitting that the city reaches new heights on the ground of a firm doing just the same over two hundred years before.

Invigorated and fully-stoked, I steam home with my 27 roads.

Tuesday June 16th 2020 – 8.8km - Tragedy

The wind of change brought a summer storm overnight, the warm air and humidity making me fear the tragedy of a night fever or worse. Stayin' alive as a pandemic rages is too much, heaven knows I don't need hypochondria too. You should be dancing over those streets, my brain gurgles as I stare at my dark bedroom ceiling. If I can't have you, sweet slumber, maybe I should get up and go bag some streets. Five a.m. I ask myself, just how deep is your love of running? Is now the time for some nights on Broadway...

...alas no, Broadway in Manchester is a dual carriageway running from New Moston up past Oldham and frankly I'd rather sing falsetto in a Working Men's Club than go there in the dark.

Up and out the door at twenty past five because I couldn't sleep was a new level of running weirdness, even for me, especially as I was headed to work for half seven. So, I kept it local and headed for some roads to the west of Chorlton Green and a few across Chorlton that I'd not yet ticked off. First on that list was Keppel Road and – for those capable of deciphering my jive talkin' above – home in the late 1950's of a certain Gibb family. At number 51, brothers Barry, Maurice and Robin lived with their parents for three years before the family emigrated to Australia. Long before they formed the world famous pop group The Bee Gees, they practiced their harmonies on the front steps for their first band; a skiffle group called the Rattlesnakes. One hundred metres away across the rooftops at the corner of Manchester Road and Nicolas Road is the old Gaumont Cinema building, now converted into a plain office building and under threat of demolition. For Bee Gee fans though this is sacrilege, as the Gaumont was the first venue that the brothers – as the Rattlesnakes - ever played in 1957. Their debut included a cover of the Everley Brothers hit; 'Wake Up Little Susie'.

The Bee Gees went on to sell over 120 million records worldwide, enter the rock and roll hall of fame and gain numerous Grammys and other music awards. Yet, despite the global success of the Saturday Night Fever film and the soundtrack they made for it, they never won an Oscar. That accolade would instead go to another Chorlton-born man...and he'd go on to win three Academy Awards!

Born in 1935, Anthony Powell was a successful Costume Designer for both stage and screen. He gained Oscars for: Travels With My Aunt (1972), Death On The Nile (1978) and Tess(1979). An often-overlooked art of portraying characters and meaning in film, Powell was a much sought-after master. Other notable films of his that conjure up such vivid imagery include: Papillon, Indiana Jones (Temple of Doom and Last Crusade), Frantic, Hook, 101 Dalmatians and Miss Potter. Sadly, he passed away at a care facility in London just this April, aged 85.

Someone who was definitely more than a woman was Madge Addy, a Mancunian woman who was a shining light in the darkest of times. Born in Chorlton Upon Medlock in 1904 and growing up just off Wilmslow Road in Rusholme, she has been claimed by Chorlton as one of their own. Commemorated at 34 Manchester Road (opposite the old Gaumont Cinema), this is where she lived and worked as a hairdresser from 1932-37 and no doubt where she made up her mind to leave everything behind. Also registered as a nurse, she left her husband, her home and all that she knew to head for a war-zone, working as a head nurse for the International Brigade fighting fascism in Spain.

Imprisoned at the end of the war in 1939, she came to the attention of the British secret service and when she was released months later, she settled with her new Norwegian husband as a Norwegian citizen in Marseille, France. She would go on to work as a spy; delivering and receiving messages sewn into the lining of her coat whilst travelling to and from Lisbon on German aircraft. She would go on to help form more than one of the escape lines that helped smuggle escaped P.O.W's and downed airmen out of enemy territory to neutral Spain. At the end of the war, her Norwegian marriage was annulled and she married a Danish Agent - her first MI5 contact in France - before returning to live out her days in London. Risking her life and with more close shaves than you can imagine, the brave, calm and stoic Madge Addy rightly deserves to be remembered.

Finishing my run around the streets off Kingshill and Ivygreen Roads, I head east along Beech Road, happy to see signs of the boutiques and independent shops along there coming back to life after being closed for so many months. Embodying much of the spirit of Chorlton, this area has a relaxed, bohemian style to it and when the sun shines, sitting outside the pubs and bars here and people watching, there's no better place to be.

Out onto Barlow Moor Road, I pass a queue already forming outside the McDonalds' Drive-Thru for breakfast, although the restaurant is still closed, it's another small step towards normality as things slowly open up again. Thinking more of my own breakfast with every stride, I cut through Chorlton Park and make a push for home to get ready for work. Only 16 streets added, but another corner of the map satisfyingly coloured-in and more importantly I've struck my first significant milestone. Nineteen runs into the challenge over three turbulent months and I'd moved my opening total of three hundred roads up to a thousand completed roads. To paraphrase Churchill on the challenge ahead, this is not the beginning of the end, but perhaps the end of the beginning.

Friday 19th June 2020 – 26.15km – Beginnings, Legends and Immeasurable Filth

Buoyed by my progress, I headed back to the beginning. From fledgling record labels and first gigs to the best of Edwardian entertainment and worst of the Victorian streets. And even further back through the misty centuries and cawing crows to Roman invaders and the stuff of Arthurian legends.

First stop on this warm day though was Hulme. Much maligned for the social disaster that was the Crescents estate in the 1970's, a compromise between tower blocks and tight communities, these hi-rise concrete streets in the sky became damp, mouldy, vermin-ridden hellholes flooded with crime and desperation. By the 80's the families left and the bohemians and punks moved in, including Nico, troubled singer of the cult 1960's band Velvet Underground who'd adopted Manchester as her home. She's quoted as saying the Crescents reminded her of her native upbringing in post-war Berlin. That'd be the same Berlin, the RAF and USAF had spent several years reducing to piles of smouldering rubble. The Crescents reminded her fondly of that. Ironically, during the Manchester Christmas blitz, the German Luftwaffe dropped a bomb on a wedding party at the Manley Arms on the corner of Clopton Street (now Ellis St) and Warde Street, killing fourteen. One of the City's deadliest bombings over the war, the site was later covered by the Crescents estate.

Hulme has happily recovered from being a black hole of dilapidated housing stock, crime and despair to an area as popular with young families and students as an affordable area close to the centre. For me, two cultural highlights remain, one only in collective memories, the other at great peril.

Long before the Madchester music scene in the late 1980s and the rise of bands such as New Order and the Happy Mondays, new bands were feeling their way into a new sound influenced by a country in turmoil. Way before those bands were releasing hit albums with Factory Records, the label's boss, Tony Wilson was organising a club night for post-punk bands like the Durutti Column and Joy Division. Calling it 'The Factory' in homage to the New York nightclub of the same name, the night began in May 1978 in a music venue in Hulme; The Russell Club. Situated at the N.E corner of the Crescents estate, it was demolished in 2001.

Half a kilometre run to the south is the Hippodrome; a listed Edwardian theatre built in 1901. Actually two theatres back-to-back in one building, the Playhouse has been saved and renovated by an Arts

60

Collective, it is the music hall side with its red velvet seats and its purple, green and gilded interiors that's most at risk. Not used as a theatre since the 60's its clung on at different times as a bingo hall, meeting hall and snooker club, surviving through squatters and an evangelical preacher, but the theatre still awaits the resurrection it so deserves. Laurel and Hardy, Nina Simone and the Beatles are among the long list of stars to tread the boards here.

Crossing the footbridge over the busy Mancunian Way, I rounded the new skyscrapers of Knott Mill, the sign on the front of Deansgate Station still bearing the area's name. Beside the station is the original route of Deansgate, curving down to a shallow ford over the River Medlock – now long since buried beneath the road and adjoining apartments – and the unlikely location of an Arthurian legend. It is here that a large, evil Saxon knight by the name of Sir Tarquin rode out from his nearby castle to fight Sir Lancelot beside a tree festooned with his victim's shields and weapons. In a duel lasting some four hours, Lancelot prevails and lops the giant villain's head from his shoulders, releasing no less than sixty-four captured knights from the castle. No doubt, Lancelot also won the favour of a smitten princess, all the while cheered by mud-wallowing peasants. This legend reaches us from down the centuries, preserved through the fireside telling and retelling of 'The Ancient Ballad of Tarquin'.

I cross through Castlefield basin, a small dock at the end of the Bridgewater Canal where 18th and 19th century narrowboats and barges loaded and unloaded their wares into the surrounding warehouses and onto waiting carts. Passing evocative names such as the Coal Wharves, Timber Yard and Potato Wharf, I loop round past the fabulous Science Museum and head on towards even more ancient history.

Mamucium, just off Duke Street is the original site and name of the Roman fort that founded Manchester back in AD79. The name of the City is thought to derive from a breast-shaped hill nearby, which just goes to show that soldiers a long way from home, still had the same bawdy sense of humour and loneliness as young lads nearly two millennia later. Later abandoned by the Romans when they left Britain, it became known as the castle in the field, giving the area its name and an opportunity for storytellers to give Sir Lancelot a scene for a legendary fight. The archaeological ruins were added to in the 1980's when a section of wall and gatehouse were mocked up on the site and while not earth-shattering, they have weathered and worn in the intervening years, so that with a squint and a bit of imagination, you get the faintest of glimpses deep into the city's origins.

Back in the narrow, quiet, sett-paved streets of old warehouses and modern apartments behind Deansgate Station, I find a cultural landmark in Manchester's music history. Here on Little Peter Street, I reach the former site of the Boardwalk nightclub. A popular music venue in the late 80's and early 90's, it and the nearby Hacienda saw early performances from many bands who would go on to international stardom. Bands such as James, The Charlatans and the Happy Mondays. Other influential bands such as Hole, Rage Against the Machine, Sonic Youth and the Verve also played here. Its most significant moment though came on the 14th August 1991, when an 18 year-old lad from Burnage played his first gig with his new band; Rain, who were bottom of the bill of the three bands playing that night. In the audience, watching the set of four songs was his song-writing brother who saw potential and subsequently joined the band as their guitar-playing leader. They would later change their name to Oasis, sign a record deal two years later and go on to sell an estimated 70 million records.

Further east, in the shadow of another railway station, I find a less glorious morning story. In Victorian Britain, society was rigidly class-based and in the social pecking order, shamefully the Catholic Irish were treated as the lowest of the low. Pouring into Manchester in search of work – especially at the time of the Irish Famine in the late 1840's – they could only get the most menial and low paid labour work. Throw them into a culture of heavy drinking, crowded streets and simmering resentment, and it's easy to see how dirty looks soon spilled into violent attacks and even deaths. It was little wonder then that these Irish immigrants stuck together for protection. The result was both shocking and inevitable. Shunned from everywhere else, these Irish immigrants settled in five terrible, over-crowded streets wedged in a tiny space between Oxford Road Station and the unbearable stench of a bend in the tar-black River Medlock. A notoriously crowded slum formed there in 1827 and soon became known as the worst place in the city; the slum of Little Ireland.

Friedrich Engels visited it in 1844 and described it in his critical work, 'The Conditions of the Working Class in England' the following year. He describes a sunken area inside a long curve of the River Medlock, surrounded on all sides by tall factories and belching chimneys that must have cast long shadows day and night. In this damp, dank hole, a couple of hundred homes built back to back with thin shared walls on three sides and windows only at the front. Even worse awaited those seeking refuge in the dank cellars. Yet, in these dirty, dilapidated homes on Wakefield, Anvil and Forge Streets, over four thousand souls eked out a sorry life, most of them from Ireland.

The streets were no better. Broken, muddy, rutted and strewn with rubbish, rotten food and pools of stagnant filth, they were the playgrounds of the dirty rag-wearing children. The grubby pigs grew fat on the rotting garbage heaps and the stink-laden puddles. The fetid smell hanging over this hellish place must have been constantly nauseating and full of all manner of heavy toxins and diseases. A place devoid of hope and humanity, the Irish inhabitants can be excused for drinking and outbursts of violence, cast into an urban oubliette of despair I'd drink myself to death too.

By 1847, after terrible floods and a particularly bad Cholera outbreak, the slum was cleared, but not fully demolished until 1877 when the railway expanded and industry replaced what was left of the dilapidated homes. Running every street in the city, I sometimes alight upon a familiar acrid smell in an alleyway or a patch of broken glass and grime. That's when I think of the unimaginable conditions in Little Ireland and remember never to complain.

With my mind full of history and soul full of wonder, I point the legs south and make for suburbia with 72 completed roads in my bag.

Sunday 28th June 2020 – 26.06km – Arrivals and Departures

Manchester is full of history and impressive industrial heritage, but it can also lay claim to technological revolutions that changed the country and with it the world. Behind all sudden transformations are the people seeking their place in the turmoil. In Manchester that led to a tragedy with such shocking repercussions, it's impact is still felt today.

After a mini-heatwave and a government panicking at the crowded beaches and parks across the country, all talk is now of the possibility of a second wave of the Covid virus and a plea for the public to use some common sense. Good luck with that one. Leaving the heavy news behind, I rebelliously meander through the forbidden streets of the neighbouring borough of Old Trafford to pick up a few Hulme streets close to a famous canal.

The Bridgewater Canal is the second purpose-built canal in England after the Sankey canal in Widnes, but the first to revolutionise a city. This canal opened in 1761 to transport coal from the third duke of Bridgewater's mines in Worsley to fuel the growing industry in Manchester. Without it, it is debateable that the city would have grown so large and so quickly. The marriage of abundant coal and water meant a new age of steam-power was set to revolutionise industry with Manchester at its heart. Its success ushered in a golden age of canal building that linked the towns and cities of Britain to each other and various ports, further allowing speedy and efficient transport of goods.

After a brief dalliance with the whirring cars and beeping pedestrian crossings of the ring-road – even on a Sunday morn - I divert on to Water Street. Passing beneath two rust-coloured bridges carrying the modern Metrolink trams overhead, I plunge back into the history of late Georgian Manchester and a revolutionary way to travel that put Bridgewater's canal into the shade.

On Liverpool Street, there is the World's first passenger railway station. Built in 1830, predominantly for shipping goods to and from the city to the port of Liverpool, the passenger side was almost an afterthought on the thirty-one mile line. Cutting the twelve-hour journey of a canal boat to just over an hour, it was a change that turbo-charged the industrial revolution and made many merchants very wealthy. Talking of which, it's interesting to see the difference in grandeur between the First and Second Class entrances serving two entirely separate booking halls. One can only imagine the excitement of passing through here to board this hissing monster, rattling you through the countryside faster than you'd ever travelled before. Many worried that travelling so fast might cause

64

damage to the human body, especially women, deemed as fragile as if made entirely from tissue paper and silk ribbons. Or rather, the men-folk of the time simply didn't want women to have the opportunity to travel. Today, the historic Grade I listed station is wonderfully preserved and forms part of the vast Science and Industry museum.

Moving on at a much more sedate pace, I meander around the St John's area of Deansgate, just north of the museum, enjoying the peaceful streets and admiring the sweeps of Georgian townhouses now occupied by the offices of solicitors, architects and accountants. Deansgate itself is an arrow-straight road forming part of the Roman road connecting Chester to York, it is Manchester's most ancient thoroughfare and has a long history of being the home of shops and alehouses.

On the eastern side, I head as far as Manchester's largest theatre, the Grand Old Lady of Oxford Street: Palace Theatre. It opened in 1891 with the ballet Cleopatra, struggling for a while before coming into its own in the early 20th century. Stars such as Judy Garland, Laurel and Hardy, Danny Kaye, Charles Laughton, Noel Coward and Gracie Fields all trod the boards here. Sadly, a direct hit from a Luftwaffe bomb during WWII destroyed its original interior and facade. Nearby is an underground public toilet converted into a bar called the Temple. It's said to be the hole in his neighbourhood Guy Garvey sang about in Elbow's 2008 hit 'Grounds For Divorce'. It was one of his favourite drinking holes during a time when he was in an unhappy relationship and wanted to leave Manchester. The band's album Seldom Seen Kid would go on to win a Mercury Prize in the same year.

Back down Peter Street and on to Windmill Street beside the Manchester Central Conference Centre, I stand on St Peter's Fields at a place of peaceful protest that rapidly turned into an atrocity that forever changed the political landscape. On 16th August 1819, a gathering of 60,000 people walked here from miles around for a meeting demanding parliamentary reform and greater representation amongst the working classes. With the usual subtlety of those in power and with their attempts to arrest the great orator, Henry Hunt failing, they read the riot act and summoned the 15th Hussars in to disperse the peaceful crowd. What followed was a cavalry charge with sabres drawn, into a panicking crowd that led to eighteen dead and 400-700 injured in what became known as the Peterloo Massacre. Reported far and wide across the country, this slaughter shocked people of all classes and made the demands for change – although resisted for many more years to come – an inevitable conclusion.

A revolution of another kind would happen further along Peter

Street at the now demolished Free Trade Hall. Witness to speeches by Benjamin Disraeli, Winston Churchill and Charles Dickens, it was as a music venue that it gets its cultural fame. It was here in 1966 that Bob Dylan performed an acoustic set of his hits. Returning for the second half, he blasted the audience with his electric guitar and accompanying band, garnering a famous heckle of "Judas" from the crowd for him supposedly turning his back on his folk roots. Dylan's response was apparently, only to play louder.

Leaving behind this blood-soaked ground of anger and outrage, I realise the common sense much needed during a pandemic, has always been in short supply. With 79 streets bagged and heavy legs to match my mood, I flee the area, grateful to at least live at a time when I don't have to worry about sabre-wielding Hussars at my heels.

Monday 6th July 2020 – 16.24km – A Final and Three Quarters

It's believed Jordan de Fallafeld, who owned some land across south Manchester in the 14th century gave Fallowfield its name. With words more spoken than written down, his descendants - and no doubt the area - bore names such as Fallofield, Fallafield, Fellowfield, Fellofield, but by 1530 it was recorded as Falowfelde. No doubt the fallow fields of this farming community still provided a bumper harvest of L's and I's at some point to nudge the name into its final arrangement. Although I quite like Fallafeld, it makes me think of a gritty Danish Detective series where it always rains and everyone sneers intensely at the camera.

Much like Chorlton Green, Fallowfield was a quiet village with agriculture at its heart. And like Didsbury and Withington, the clean air and pastoral views were soon coveted by the industrialists and merchants from the city – some things never change. Having built their factories and mills amidst the forest of smoke-belching chimneys, filth-strewn cobbled streets and the dark, stinking waters of the canals and rivers, they merrily waved goodbye to the filth they'd created and their struggling workforce. Building mansions away from the choking smog to gain more respectable neighbours, they moved to places like Fallowfield. These grand houses made Wilmslow Road an important route into the city and almost inevitably the population grew as the middle classes followed, slowly devouring the fields and village life that had been the original appeal.

Two days after pubs, restaurants, places of worship and barbers celebrated their own independence day, I headed out with a freshly trimmed bonce. It'd been a while, an embarrassingly long, long while since I looked so trim and tidy. As Lockdown started I had to decide to either let it grow or shave it all off. Knowing I couldn't possibly pull off the hard man, startled skinhead look, I instead headed back to the 1970s and a poorly executed homage to Fleetwood Mac or Pink Floyd, less Go Your Own Way and more Dark Side of the Mirror.

Suitably de-rock-starred if not de-fatigued, I forced myself out after work to grab a few streets in the afternoon sun. Headed slowly east along Wilbrahim Road, I crossed the busy Princess Road and plunged into Fallowfield.

I move through some of the social housing roads and multi-cultural terraces in the west to the streets around the two remaining hints of fallow fields; Birchfields Park and Platt Fields. Ignoring the glimpses of picnics, barbecues and children playing in the tranquil green spaces, I stick to the dark tarmac underfoot and plod on between the parked cars and wheelie-bins. Doubling back south along Wilmslow Road I head past the modernist Hollings Building – known locally as the toast rack for its unusual shape – and go to the centre of what Fallowfield is most known for: Students.

The Fallowfield Campus is the University of Manchester's main accommodation complex and the surrounding streets are packed with all the bars, shops and take-aways to cater for them. Even back in 1986, Fallowfield was the first place in the country to have a drive-thru McDonalds. The campus though has a fine hidden history of a more sporting nature.

Long before it was used as the Athletes Village for the 2002 Commonwealth Games, it was the site of the Fallowfield Stadium – an athletics track, pitch and velodrome that held 15,000 spectators. Just a year after it was opened, it hosted the 1893 F.A. Cup Final in front of phenomenal 45,000 people, with most unable to even see the pitch. Wolves beat Everton 1-0, according to some bloke at the front. On the 6th of June 1939, Sydney Wooderson – the Mighty Atom – set a world athletics record for the ¾ mile on the cinder track here at 2mins 59 seconds. I'm sure he was much congratulated by his friends Norman and Dee Day who probably reassured him nothing more important would happen that year or more momentous on any 6th of June ever again.

At a much more leisurely pace, I left Fallowfield with my 43 streets before any nearby students spilled out onto the streets hunting beer and pot noodles. Or whatever they have for breakfast these days at 3pm.

Sunday 19ᵗʰ July 2020 – 21.14km – Without or Withington

Withington derives from Anglo-Saxon origins, roughly meaning 'enclosed area of willow branches fit for bundling'. It was a village on the main route from Manchester to Wilmslow, its growth similar to that further north along Wilmslow Road in Fallowfield. The rich and middle classes desperately wanted to move upwind of the smoke and destitution that plagued the inner city areas. With horse drawn – and later electric – tramways reaching down Wilmslow and Palatine Roads and the Railway station opening in West Didsbury, the idea of a commuter belt was born. With this influx of wealth came the civic and religious grandeur of churches, schools, a public library and town hall, all designed and built with as much thought for local pride as functionality. Even the public houses were bold in scale and ornate in architecture, raising them above the dark drinking dens of the lower classes.

Nowadays, situated between the wealthier suburb of Didsbury and the student land of Fallowfield, it has become a mix of families, students and young professionals – themselves often ex-students. One of its most well known residents, apart from Money Saving expert Martin Lewis who was born here, was actor John Mahoney. Born in Blackpool after evacuation during WWII, his family returned and he grew up on these streets before moving to America in 1959. Leaving his teaching job in 1977 to act, encouraged by none other than John Malkovich, he went on to star in dozens of films and television roles. However, he was undoubtedly best known for his part as Martin Crane in the hit American television show, Frasier.

For me, an oxymoronic summer fatigue has struck. As work pressure eases a tiny amount, I find myself not with extra energy, but a sense of my body demanding that as the war was plainly over, I must now relax and recuperate. Yet the lazier I become, the less interest and energy I have for getting out onto the streets. The surrender to cake and mindless television is a delicious temptation, but I know it's an illusion. I know the more I run, the happier I'll be. The more I run, the easier it'll be. But despite the blue skies and sunshine outside, it's still a battle to get my trainers on and get out the door.

'This too shall pass' seems an apt philosophy to cling to right now and for more reasons than just a running fug. Winning over the inner chimp, I escape the house and slowly run the five kilometres south-east .

I run through what now feels like the centre of Withington village, the clock tower of the grand White Lion – now a Sainsbury's Local – standing tall over the crossroads where Wilmslow, Palatine and Burton

Roads meet. Pushing on east down Wilmslow Road, I come to the rather special Christie's Hospital; one of the largest cancer treatment centres in Europe. Opposite, on the corner of Cotton lane is the old centre of the village. The triangular patch of grass before the new striking Cancer Research Centre on that corner is an apt nod to Withington village green that stood on that spot when it was only a small farming community.

With little of this area visited at all so far, I decided to put my map away and simply run like I used to when I'd get lost down back streets and discover dead ends the hard way. East of Christies Hospital the roads are roughly in a grid pattern too, so I quickly fell into a pattern of to-ing and fro-ing, working out a map in my mind and a route through this maze of my making. The mental exercise and occasional mistake helped keep my mind off my legs and while I still struggled, the puzzle element gave me a sense of challenge and achievement. Knowing I could always add any missed roads to a later run helped too. Having planned only to do ten kilometres or so, I was pleasantly surprised to be closer to sixteen kilometres and still to make the journey home.

On the way I pass an Edwardian gem, Withington Baths. Built in 1911 and embellished with an ornate brick and stone frontage, stained glass windows and separate entrances for men and women. Rescued from closure in 2015 by a charitable trust formed by local residents, it remains the only working Edwardian pool in Manchester. Back in 1914, it became the centre of controversy and scandal amongst the chattering classes when it became the first Manchester baths to allow mixed male and female bathing. Albeit, only on a trial basis and to proceed 'with great caution' according to reports at the time. Heading past, I can almost hear echoes of the ear-piercing whistles and cries of an overworked attendant barking at any swimmer getting within six feet or two metres of one another.

Some things never change. I leave Withington 44 roads better off.

Thursday 23rd July 2020 – 30.09km – This Charming Run

Whether it is the uplifting news of the Oxford vaccine clinical trials showing it to be effective and safe or that fitness coach Joe Wicks has finally stopped torturing the unfit masses with his P.E lessons, I step forth on my day off from work, a new man and a new runner. With the fug of apathy passed, I headed south from home beneath cloudy but bright skies with a puffed out chest and pendulum arm swings. I have a new plan, a fresh innovative stratagem for gathering streets. A new way, a bold, unique plan of action I was exceedingly well placed to implement; determined stupidity. I was simply going to bound and prance far away from my home, running and running and running until my legs fell off. By guaranteeing myself failure, I had eliminated the worry of failing and with it, any sense of stress just evaporated away. As a stratagem, it was plainly nonsense and therefore made perfect sense to me.

Rounding Chorlton Water, I cross the River Mersey, sweep through Kenworthy Woods and head south of the M60 motorway into the northern clutches of Wythenshawe. Long after the middle and upper classes had escaped the cramped environs and fetid air of the inner city to the suburbs of southern Manchester, the City Corporation decided to help the workers too. As they cleared the slums after the First World War, they built Manchester's first overspill town on the agricultural fields of what was North Cheshire. By 1936, they constructed eight thousand houses, fifty-nine shops and two factories in a new, spacious, garden city far from the dank slums of the centre. And that was a problem. The new residents, split from their friends and communities found everything was now a long way from home, if there at all. Queues formed at shops, the few pubs were crowded and work was a long bus ride into the city. This was a new town without a centre, without a sense of belonging and with little money on hand to fix the issues after the Second World War, it would drift into a place of poverty and crime. Lessons learned over the years have seen investment in business parks around the airport and in transport links, improving the prospects of the area no end.

I meander around the council estates of Northern Moor on the former deer-hunting grounds of the Tatton family. Down Rackhouse Road I pass the location of the UK's first municipal airfield; Manchester Aerodrome. This all sounds rather grand, until you discover that a barn was used as a hangar and a farmhouse as the admin building. It opened in a rush to become the first municipal aerodrome in the country, lasting just over a year before closing in 1930, when the purpose-built aerodrome at Barton-upon-Irwell was ready.

Nearby is the Northenden campus of Manchester College - set to close in 2022 – that produced not one but two stellar guitarists. Billy Duffy is the guitarist of The Cult; a 1980's band famed for songs such as Rain, Fire Woman and She Sell's Sanctuary. Despite numerous line-up changes, Dufy still tours with the band. The other famous musician is John Martin Maher – better known as Johnny Marr of The Smiths, The Pretenders, The The, Electronic, Modest Mouse and the Cribs or solo as Johnny Marr. Both men grew up in Wythenshawe and were friends whilst studying at the college. Both are legends of the Mancunian music scene. Yew Tree High School had stood on the same site before the college and was attended by Syd Little of 70s and 80s comedic duo Little and Large. Still, two out of three isn't bad...

On I went to a long series of closes, dead-ends and cul-de-sacs just south of Altrincham Road in Baguley. Looking much less on a map, I clocked up a fair distance before heading north, back across the road into the large park containing Wythenshawe Hall – a glorious 16th century black and white timber-framed manor house and home of the aforementioned Tattons. Now owned by the council, its sadly only open to the public once a month and for special events. Facing the Hall is a large statue of Oliver Cromwell, moved from its original site at the Cathedral opposite Victoria Bridge to commemorate the victory at the Siege of Manchester in 1642. Much like an away leg in football, the Parliamentarians would hold the Royalists in their own siege here, a year later in the winter of 1643-44. During the prolonged stand-off, a servant at the hall – Mary Webb - saw her betrothed killed. Legend has it she took revenge by taking up a musket and shooting dead a Colonel Adams who sat on a nearby wall. The siege only ended in February 1644, when the Roundheads brought two cannons down from their stronghold in Manchester and took the hall by force.

Enjoying the novelty of running through a pleasant green space, I ignore the heaviness in my legs and my empty water bottle and dive back into bagging more streets in Northern Moor. My pace slows and enthusiasm wanes as I edge nearer to the perpetual drone of the motorway. Bounding up the steps onto a footbridge and across Wythenshawe Sports ground to Fairy Lane, I realise I'm going to have to 'Jeff' the last three or four kilometres home. Taking these walking breaks between running, I get home thoroughly exhausted with a bag of 64 roads in my hand and a broad grin on my face.

Sunday 26th July 2020 – 26.76km – Better or Worse? How About Now?

Longsight is an area in southeast Manchester with a romantic link to Bonnie Prince Charlie. The pretender to the throne rested briefly at the Waggon and Horses Inn on Stockport Road with his Scottish rebels during his rebellious walking holiday down to Derbyshire in 1745. Whilst there he reputedly declared Manchester a 'Long Sight' away, no doubt to the eager amusement of the keenest of his soldiers. He was indeed incredibly long-sighted as the name appears on several maps before this date, but why let a legend go to waste. Besides, it was an improvement on its previous depressing name of Grindlow Marsh.

This week the lottery of rule changes that currently shape our lives came up with compulsory face masks in shops, Spanish holidays abandoned and Gyms and Swimming Pools reopening – presumably 'proceeding with great caution'. And the bonus ball was holidaymakers returning from St Vincent and the Grenadines no longer have to quarantine themselves. Tears up ticket, maybe next week. It is strange though, trying to work through the weekly roulette of rule changes that currently shape our lives, everyone seemingly unsure how things are simultaneously getting better and worse at the same time. Still, while obesity and lack of fitness gets the thumbs down from the medical science boffins, thankfully the freedom to run remains off that wheel of fortune.

So, on this bright, yet overcast Sunday morning, I pointed the toes of my running shoes east and worked my way through Moss Side to an area just north of Dickenson Road in Longsight. Rounding the corner with Plymouth Grove where the Waggon and Horses pub once stood, I head down Stockport Road to the junction with Slade Lane to the former site of a tollbooth. Being two of the main arteries connecting Manchester to Stockport, Buxton, Cheadle and Wilmslow these roads became increasingly busy and required much maintenance. The tollgates across both roads were set up to levy a charge on the road's users. No doubt, their operators were hugely popular and respected, just like traffic wardens today.

In the 19th century, with the coming of the main line railway and the roads bisecting it ever busier, a community of middle and working classes made Longsight their home. Without the canals of other areas, it avoided the wealthy industrialists and their dirty factories and mills, instead becoming a centre of leisure and fun. Theatres, Picture Houses, Ballrooms, Roller-Skating rinks, Taverns and Billiard Halls proliferated in the area. Besides employment in these centres of joy and frivolity, locals could also make a living at the Co-Operative Printing works or amongst the aromatic delights of Sarson's vinegar factory. Nowadays, this suburb is far more sedate and changed to an increasingly multicultural area where immigrants from across Asia and the Middle East have made it their home.

Zigzagging down a tightly-packed grid of terraced streets east of the railway line and north of Crowcroft Park, I can sense how tight the community must have been; vigilance and gossip the currency of friendship, judgement instant, secrets impossible. Now if anything it feels even more cramped and claustrophobic with crowds of wheelie bins and fleets of parked cars blocking all the pavements and thoroughfares. Heading down dead-end after dead-end, I'm suddenly self-conscious of my pounding feet echoing off the terraced walls on either side of me, bedroom windows open to my thunderous progress. I grimace guiltily and pad gently up onto my toes like a cartoon cat past a snoozing dog.

Rapidly despatching the last four streets on this side of Stockport Road, I head south and into the neighbouring ward of Levenshulme to grab all the streets in a small estate between Crowcroft Park and Nutsford Vale. Here at 112 Hemmons Road in a small red-brick terraced house, a certain Arthur Lowe spent much of his childhood in the 1910s and 20s. Fifty years later, millions would know and love the actor as the pompous and uptight Captain Mainwaring in nine series of the television sitcom Dad's Army. Feeling every part a 'Stupid Boy', I head back up across the main road to explore the Slade Lane side of Longsight.

Crossing under the railway line opposite Crowcroft Park, I turn left and chance across the unmistakeable black and white chequered timbers of an Elizabethan manor house, peeking out between the trees and tall hedge of a verdant garden. This half-hidden 16th century gem is Slade Hall. Looking both well preserved and equally ignored, it almost looks like an over the top version of the faux black and white houses in the close beside it. Built and owned by the Siddall family, they lived there for over 300 years. As recently as the 1990s a housing association used it for offices, but it now appears to be a shared residence with fourteen rooms and communal areas. An online advert for an empty room within reads, 'House is an eclectic mix of artists, musicians, DJs, students, hippies, and general laid back people who enjoy everything from reggae to football.' Seems wholesome and if it keeps a house built during Shakespeare's lifetime in good repair? Well, I guess all's well that ends well.

On which point, I sense my legs growing heavier and shoulders tightening and begin the long 4 km trek home. With a staggering haul of 92 completed streets from such a small area, it has been worth it.

74

Tuesday 28th July 2020 – 29.02km – Help Me Ziggy Stardust, You're My Only Hope!

In Eastern Europe, there is a Slavic goddess of rain by the name of Dodola. Slavs believed that when this warlike mistress of the rainclouds milked her herd, it rained steadily below. Looking out at the forbidding skies and breezy showers this warm weekday morning, I can only surmise she's visiting on some kind of extended Weather Deity Exchange Program. And in return we've presumably sent one of our weather gods to the Balkans. We've probably just told Michael Fish it's a free holiday.

With my shower proof jacket on making me feel like some sandwiches wrapped in wax paper, I head stickily along the F'Loop, dodging the bikes as they zip past at speed and shower me with their spray. After nearly thirty minutes of running due east and being a decent distance from home, something of the size of the task-at-hand starts to dawn on me. I'd travelled over six kilometres and only just reached the edge of today's area of exploration. Nudging up to the border with North Reddish and the forbidden lands of Tameside, I was close to unknown kingdoms full of dragons and mythical beasts...possibly. Flowing off the F'Loop opposite Highfield Country Park, I squelch into Levenshulme.

Much like the neighbouring Longsight up the road, Levenshulme was once a suburb of the wealthy and middle classes that subsequently fell on hard times. It retains a gritty atmosphere of decline and a brighter past but one now embellished with the first hints of gentrification and a sense of it turning a corner.

Working my way in and out of all the terraced streets between the F'Loop and Greenbank Playing Fields, I take joy in the small front gardens and the trees lining the roads, the green contrasting brightly against the red brick walls, even in the drizzle. It makes a fine difference to the stark terraces I saw at the weekend. My mood only soars higher at the uplifting Trafford Parsons mural on the gable end of Molyneux Street. The beautiful black and white painting of Princess Leia's face comes complete with a David Bowie-esque red and blue lightning bolt over one eye in possibly the most seventies crossover I've ever seen.

Up onto Barlow road, I head east to the edge of Manchester and am not disappointed. Where the houses abruptly stop by Marquis Street, the road kinks right and heads between the large hedge of some allotments on one side and the high green corrugated fence and barbed wire of a breakers yard on the other. Add in barriers, watchtowers and armed guards with large barking dogs and you could be anywhere behind the Iron

Curtain. Possibly sweating as you queue in your Trabant to get over the border back to the west, hoping they don't find your suitcase of cash in the boot. Or an equally nervous Michael Fish beside it.

Talking of nervous, a little way back along Barlow Road, I discover my first scrapyard of this challenge. My pace slows as I head down a side road, the main road disappearing behind me, the fly-tipped fridge and pile of used tyres at the roadside drawing me to a stop. Ahead of me there are some open gates, but my map insists the road runs for another two hundred metres. It appears the scrapyard has eaten my road. I like to think I'm a sensible intelligent soul and in the grand scheme of things it won't matter if I miss part of a road that looks like private property. I'm not one of those total idiots who just follows their satnav into river, off a cliff or into a scrapyard. So obviously, I turn around and go on my way, leaving this grubby place well alone. Don't I? Don't...I?

I push on through the gates at a slow jog. It's ten past eight on a weekday morning and although I can hear vehicles and machinery working, they seem far off. I glide on between an old windowless building and a high painted fence with a high pile of twisted metal behind it. My head telling me any second I'd round a corner and see something involving gangsters, drugs, money, guns and a pitiful bloke on the floor pleading for his life. Thanks brain, useful.

On I go, tiptoeing over the potholed and cracked tarmac, waiting for a shout or a canine snarl. Rounding the end of the building I see yet more old, crumbling workshops and backstreet garages popular only with the likes of the A-Team. Still I nudge on a few metres more, trying to see on my phone where the road ends. Looking up, I almost run into a mechanic in overalls as he pushed open a gate in the fence and stepped away from me. Freezing like a terrible spy in a spotlight, I wring the last drip from my courage, tiptoe back a few paces into a deep puddle and bolt for freedom just as he turned around. I didn't look back.

Resting out of sight behind a postbox, after a spontaneous bit of sprint training, I kept the heart rate high as I headed west. I worked through the streets close to Stockport Road, including the fine St Peter's Church; which was once touched by the flamboyant interior designer Laurence Llewelyn-Bowen in one of his TV specials. Both church and congregation have since recovered. Across the main road, where above the gaudy signs and bright lights you can still catch glimpses of the Edwardian splendour and pride once imbued in this parade of shops, I find the childhood home of a true genius of design. Aptly tucked away behind a builders merchants and the new library is number four Crescent Grove where architect and designer Norman Foster (Baron Foster of Thames

76

Bank, no less) grew up. His astounding list of achievements includes; the Gherkin, Millennium Bridge, Wembley Stadium and the City Hall in London, the Reichstag dome in Berlin, SSE Hydro arena in Glasgow and Apple Park in California. Perhaps his most staggering design is the Millau Viaduct in France: the tallest bridge in the world at a mind-melting 336m tall.

More by accident than design, I finish my planned haul by The Gherkin restaurant on my old friend, Slade Lane. It's then, as the rain falls once more and I pause to find my way that the fatigue catches up and I'm reminded just how far I've still to run to get home. With a deep sigh, I put one foot in front of the other and shovel another load into the box marked 'Character Building'. On route, I distract myself with thoughts of the mural from before and wonder if Princess Leia Stardust and the Slavic rain goddess Dodola would have liked our city, I speculate neither of them would have fled a scrapyard.

81 roads completed today. I sweated inside my jacket, I got soaked outside. My legs grew heavy and stiff, my head grew light and loose. Home is slow to appear, but appear it does and I stumble gratefully inside.

I've still not heard from Michael Fish...

Friday 31st July 2020 – 20.05km – Feeling hot, hot, hot.

      Summer has arrived in Manchester and this year I'm determined to make the most of both days. With temperatures expected to be so high the newspapers will report them in Fahrenheit, I look out at a dazzling bright sunny morning. At midnight, Manchester had been plunged into tighter restrictions on meeting indoors as punishment for not adhering to social distancing rules. At 7am, it was already 20C, so the likelihood of anyone wanting to be indoors was probably not that high anyway. It felt like the kind of day where smiles are a little broader, even if people are sweating like a crocodile in a handbag factory. I wasn't immune, pulling on my trainers with a grin on my face, for the quiet roads and empty streets were my running playground.

      Much like one of those disappointing mid-season episodes in an American sitcom or drama, this run was going to be a cheap revisit to all the best bits of the last few runs. Seeking gaps on the map, I'll be filling in streets I'd missed across Withington, Fallowfield, Rusholme and Longsight. It's a kind of filler run that leaves you wondering if anything new is in fact going to happen, or if it's all going to be knowing nods, winks and long rambling sections like this, that are full of words in coherent sentences with more than adequate punctuation, yet somehow full of little or no meaning. Well, I promise not to do too much of that, nor will I be doing whatever the writing equivalent is of a wavy dream sequence propelling us back into a memory. No, I wouldn't do that again, not since that moment a long, long time...ago...

      Returning through north Withington, I turn and commence up Wilmslow Road, weaving my way in and out of the roads on the western side, already sweating profusely like Zebedee in a minefield. Pausing to mop my brow just north of the junction with Mauldeth Road, I find Rutherford Lodge at number 407, named after the renowned nuclear scientist who lived there while working at Manchester University from 1907-19. That hazy lesson you had at school about atoms, protons, electrons, alpha and beta particles was down to all the revolutionary discoveries by Rutherford and his erstwhile team, including a certain Hans Geiger – a man you could truly count on. After Rutherford's death in 1937, he was buried in Westminster Abbey close to Sir Isaac Newton. Sixty years after his death, the science community commemorated his achievements by naming an element after him: Rutherfordium. He's one of only fourteen people to have such an honour bestowed upon them including Mendeleev, Einstein and Marie and Pierre Curie.

      Heading on up Wilmslow Road past the old Fallowfield Railway

Station building – now absorbed into an upmarket supermarket. On past the closed bars and kebab shops, I venture in and out more back streets, past the toast rack and Platt Chapel in the grounds of Platt Fields and leaping over the buried line of the Nico ditch.

My next road was marked Private Property - residents only. I guess the sweat must have blurred my vision. Besides, this was Appleby Lodge, described by Historic England as 'an urban oasis' and selected as one of the city's best-looking streets by the Manchester Evening News. Intrigued and a little starstruck, I passed between the two tall Leyland Cypress trees at the entrance and entered a cul-de-sac lined with long three-storey brick buildings on either side, complete with white balconies and rounded ends. There were manicured lawns and everything looked slick in the Moderne style of the 1930s art deco movement, but I was rather underwhelmed. I can only imagine the insides of the grade II listed buildings are what enthralled the likes of Sir John Barbirolli, conductor of the Halle Orchestra, who lived here for twenty years from 1943.

Up into Rusholme, I turn onto Dickenson Road to a lost shrine of music history. Here at 6.36pm on the 1st January 1964, in an old Wesleyan Chapel – opposite the wonderfully named Moon Grove – the Rolling Stones mimed their hit 'I Wanna Be Your Man' on the first ever episode of BBC's Top of the Pops. Sadly, the host was a certain DJ least known for his cigar-chomping, chains and tacky gold tracksuits, someone whose name won't be typed by me. Other acts on that first night included The Dave Clark Five, Dusty Springfield and The Swinging Blue Jeans. An immediate success, the show stayed at the Dickenson Road studios until 1967 when it moved to larger studios in London. Dickenson Road was also the temporary home of a certain pair of musical students who would make six UK number one albums, two UK number one singles and sell millions of records worldwide, but more about that later.*

On I went around the back streets I'd missed around here and further east into Longsight, the sun growing higher and more powerful by the minute, leaving me sweating like an avocado in the Northern Quarter. Although only grabbing a meagre 30 roads, I decide I've had enough. I'm not sure it was even that hot, just the humidity and sudden climb in temperatures had me coming over all English – pale, sticky and suffering. Dreaming of ice cream for breakfast, I head home for a clandestine meeting with the fridge-freezer in my kitchen. Don't tell anyone.

*(see 27th April 2021 Run if the mystery is killing you and you absolutely must know right this minute).

Saturday 1ˢᵗ August 2020 – 21.44km - Un petit pas pour l'homme...

Ladybarn is a small area west of Burnage with a name of unknown origin. Some speculate it may be a corruption of Layday; an important date in the farming year that we now call the Spring Equinox. The driest, monotone sensible types point out it was probably simply named after the largest building in the area at the time; Lady Barn House. While other racier types would fancifully have you believe it was named after a 17ᵗʰ century wench escort service. You pays your money, you takes your choice. Moving swiftly on...

As a small hamlet of rural cottages and houses, the city has long since devoured Ladybarn's fields and turned the clay underfoot into streets filled with red brick houses. Yet a handful of the quaint farm-workers homes remain, almost hidden in plain sight amongst the semis and terraced houses.

At the village's heart is St Chad's, a brick built church from 1907 perhaps best known locally for its own 'Royal' wedding in 1993. On April 24ᵗʰ, beneath beautiful sunny skies, Alison Wardley - a former royal nanny to Princesses Beatrice and Eugenie - married royal bodyguard Ben Dady. Both princesses attended with their mother Sarah Ferguson and several smartly dressed security personnel secreted discreetly amongst the congregation.

After a period of calm and optimism, Coronavirus infections are rising once more across the country and in certain places alarmingly so. Boris Johnson has ordered officials to draw up plans for a second lockdown, while experts ponder the stark choice between closing pubs or schools. Once more, I have to stop and take a hard look at what I'm doing and ask myself if I'm not part of the problem. But, the advice remains the same about being outside and if groups of six can meet in the park, I can surely run alone on a tarmac road or ten.

Around the corner from St Chad's is the site of the Ladybarn Pub and a Manchester City link to the tragic Munich air disaster that killed 23 – including eight of Manchester United's 'Busby Babes'. Frank Swift played 376 games as a goalkeeper for the Blues and 19 for England between 1933-49, making him a firm favourite amongst fans, before retiring as that rarity in football, a one-club man. Staying in the area, he ran the pub – then known as the Talbot - before later turning his hand to journalism. He was a sports columnist for the News of the World travelling with the Manchester United team on that fateful night in 1958. Initially surviving the crash, he was still alive when pulled from the wreckage, but sadly died on the way to the hospital, aged only 44 years old. A small block of flats has now replaced the pub.

Looping back past Ladybarn Park, I pass Withington's Hedgehog hospital as I complete many of the roads at the rear of the church. Working my way repetitively up and down some long, parallel roads, I emerge back out on Parrs Wood Road and cross over into a new area; Burnage. Working my way southwards I weave and dart in and out of several closes, avenues and crescents of the Kingsway Housing Scheme. Built by the council in the 1930's, it provided 1200 homes on the fields beside the recently finished Kingsway – a dual carriageway complete with tramway in the central reservation - and named after George V. Like a lot of social housing, it's a mix of much loved homes and the odd house looking like the aftermath of a kid's birthday party. It's a bit drab in places, but there's no broken glass or graffiti. In fact, unlike some of the free books and toys people have put outside their houses for others during lockdown, here there were small food parcels in shopping bags for anyone struggling to make ends meet. Humbling and real, this is plainly a community looking after one another.

Finishing my exploring close to the fabulously Dickensian sounding Fog Lane Park, which disappointedly appears to be named after a grass – still found throughout the park – called Yorkshire Fog. It was probably on similar turf that this area's most famous visitor took a giant leap for monsieur-kind...

In 1906, just 3 years after the Wright brothers had famously defied gravity for 12 seconds, the Daily Mail offered a prize to the first person to fly from London to Manchester (a distance of 314 kilometres), within 24 hours journey time and with a maximum of two stops. They may as well have made it a journey to the moon and back. Nonetheless, by April 1910, flying fever and numerous brave aviators had propelled the technology skyward at a frenetic rate and two flyers, one Englishman and a Frenchman were racing to take on the challenge. Claude Grahame-White and Louis Paulhan raced neck and neck, both pilots using the lights of railway stations below to guide their biplanes north through the darkness, but at 5.30am on the 28th April, Louis Paulhan landed at Barcicroft Fields, claiming the prize for France and becoming the first ever flight into the city from outside. Only 12 hours after setting off and including a stop for repairs and refuelling in Lichfield, he'd spent an amazing 4 hours and 12 minutes in the air.

Such was the acclaim and hysteria surrounding the air race, two crowded chartered trains transported passengers to the - as yet - unopened Burnage Station to welcome the flyers. The same trains whisked Paulhan away to Manchester Town Hall for a sparkling civic reception with the

81

Lord Mayor. Two days later, he was back in London at a luncheon at the Savoy Hotel, there he would receive his prize from the Daily Mail of £10,000 (The equivalent today of £1.2M).
My prize of 40 roads came with much less fanfare but accounting for inflation since, it's now worth an equally staggering 40 roads. Oh well, worth a try...

Saturday 8th August 2020 – 28.03km – Dinner Party for One

Six months have passed since I began this challenge, six months quite like no other. This week we hear that even in the deep, dark cold of the planet's underbelly, there is no place to hide, with the British Antarctic Survey scaling back its operations due to Covid. In England's capital, the running festival of charity sponsorship, garish name vests and overambitious fancy dress that is the London Marathon has been cancelled. Instead, there will be a small lapped race for the elite instead.

I too am not immune to change. So far, my runs have centred on the southern suburbs of Manchester, mostly within easy reach of my home. Yet with each run, I've been venturing further and further on a 'commute' to and from my chosen area for street bagging. This has left me increasingly fatigued and demotivated. So I check and re-check the government rules and decide to use my car to take me down into Wythenshawe. Even though we're no longer in any kind of Lockdown, meaning the debated furore about using a car for 'local' exercise no longer applies, it still feels a little mischievous, a little taboo.

Parking up at half six in the morning on a street corner opposite a park, a colossal four miles from my home, I quietly close my car door as if I've just arrived in Barnard Castle to look at the river. Feeling ridiculous, but also exhilarated by the abundance of un-run streets surrounding me on all sides, I set off into the unknown. I'm in Woodhouse Park; the estate at the far south of the City, sandwiched between the airport and shops of Wythenshawe Town Centre. Made up mostly of the original cottage-style semis of the 1930's, with a smattering of new build houses and flats, it retains the leafy trees and open spaces of the original plan. The main road – Portway – snakes through it all in a large 'S' shape. The roads on either side twist and curl around one another like the folds of a brain, leaving me constantly disorientated and problem solving a best route. It's also on these side streets where I begin my hate/hate affair with the concrete roads of Wythenshawe. Unlike the forgiving tarmac elsewhere, these hard roads have absolutely no give in them whatsoever, sending all those jarring, ruinous vibrations directly up to the knees and hips. I may as well be pounding the roads barefooted. With the muggy, humid air turning it into a sweat fest, it's fast becoming a hard place for hard running.

On I go, hearing the M56 Motorway through the shady woodlands at the estate's edge long before I glimpse flashes of high-speed metal and glass through the trees. The dual-carriageway Princess Parkway connecting Wythenshawe to the city centre via Princess Road was originally a tree-lined boulevard. A neat, pretty design inspired by the more motorised America aimed to whisk the workers swiftly up into Manchester and prevent any new developments ruining the layout of the new estate. It would later morph into the hustle and bustle of the M56 Motorway; certainly swifter but no longer graceful.

Rounding Painswick park, I head south down Bailey Lane, the houses retreating, the horizon opening up to the roads, car parks and hotels around the airport. It's a welcome change to the monotonous, dizzying housing estate and feels like coming up for a breath of fresh air. At the far end is a large Georgian house stranded from a past when it dominated the surrounding fields; Moss House. Built in 1780 for a local schoolteacher called Mr Moss, it's a three-storey elegant country house of fine proportions. Dressed and mannered as a country gentleman, Mr Moss was said to be much admired, but also noted for certain eccentricities after his wife died, not least his dining every night with several fashionably-attired wax dummies, including one he called Mrs Moss. After his dinner, he'd sit the dummies in the windows and take great delight at any passer-by doffing their cap at his deceptive gallery of 'friends'. This only goes to remind me that if you are poor you're mad, but if you're rich you're harmlessly eccentric.

With my joints aching and a satisfying 86 completed roads in the bag, I return to my car, doffing my cap to the three static friends waiting for me in the back seat. Together we celebrate a rather significant milestone in my running adventure. I've completed over 25% of the city, with *only* 4642 roads left to run. Alright, let's call it harmlessly mad.

Monday 10th August 2020 – 26.86km – The other Chorlton

How do you make a place disappear?

Until the 1990's, Chorlton was largely still known by its Sunday name, the name it bore when in trouble with its mother; Chorlton-cum-Hardy. Yet when the tram network stretched its rails out to this corner of south-west Manchester, they confidently named the station Chorlton. There was no longer any need for the full name. Like Didsbury, the area gained national recognition of a healthy, bohemian, appealing place to live. But this brevity of name was aided by its sister across town being progressively erased from the map.

I meander my way once more up through Moss Side and Greenheys, picking up a few missed roads, hidden cul-de-sacs and roads that look like alleyways along the way. Passing Whitworth Park, I enter what the council now labels, in the way only councils can label things; 'The Knowledge Corridor.' Chorlton-on-Medlock sits close to the city centre, wedged between Hulme and Ardwick and hemmed in by the Mancunian Way. It's this section of elevated ring-road and the Universities at its core that hint at why this area faded from the Manchester maps.

Its 19th century development creep from the centre was one of large townhouses for the wealthy and middle classes along the grandly titled Oxford, Cambridge and Grosvenor streets. Later the masses moved into the area, but it retained a mixture of housing stock and grand buildings. The success of the University schools and the growing need to expand the hospital led to a steady devouring of the surrounding streets; knocking down houses and fracturing the community. By the 1950's though, the houses were becoming tired and old-fashioned. The council had the choice between renovating and adding innovations like central heating and indoor toilets to the housing stock or going power-crazy, wearing their pants on their heads and raving about freeways in the sky and no less than three concentric ring-roads in the city centre. Alright, maybe I exaggerate about the pants, but if you need an example of their vision for Manchester being more style over the needs of the residents, let's talk about the monorail.

Yes, the monorail.

In the post-war years when they thought anything was possible, if not practical, they drew up serious plans for an elevated Monorail running parallel to Oxford Road all the way from the airport in the south to Middleton in the North. A Manchester Monorail, A Manc-orail! Just imagine those shiny silver carriages whooshing overhead while Doreen and Elsie wait in their plastic rain bonnets at a drizzly bus stop below. This sort of Jetsons-fuelled council daydreaming in the 60's and 70's led to further plans for rooftop heli-pads, subterranean moving pavements and an underground railway connecting Piccadilly to Victoria Station, the latter of which even commenced construction and is now a void deep beneath Topshop in the Arndale centre. Thankfully or regretfully, this and the miles of elevated motorways carving through the city didn't come to fruition, but the urge to erase large areas and start again didn't. Levelling whole communities and replacing them with areas of housing like the New Brunswick estate only further distorted the area. Brunswick has largely superseded Chorlton-on-Medlock from this part of the map, with the fringes often labelled Hulme, Ardwick, Longsight or Rusholme. It's as if the demolition of the community streets simply broke the heart of the suburb and its name withered away.

Crossing Plymouth Grove – another main artery out of the city centre – I head into another new estate more synonymous with its boundary road name than its suburb: Grove Village. Full of new build boxes, trees, bollards and open spaces, it looks neat, tidy and instantly forgettable. I cover several kilometres systematically working my way along the roads and shuffling back and forth around block after block.

Working my way back up Plymouth Grove, I spot an elaborate three-storey clock tower built at the side of what must have been a grand Pub and Hotel. Amidst all the bland and inoffensive suburban architecture, it looks like an ornate glacial stone dropped in place from another era. One can only imagine the thirsty and road-weary travellers seeing this grand welcoming sight and eagerly alighting for a tankard or five before heading on into the smoggy city centre. The Plymouth Grove Hotel is a gem and thankfully lives on today as a Chinese Restaurant.

I find more survivors around here with famous suffragette Emmeline Pankhurst's later life home at 62 Nelson Street. Preserved in the grounds of Manchester Royal Infirmary, it's now the Pankhurst Centre – a museum of women's battle to get the vote and HQ of Manchester's Women's Aid. It's telling that this slice of history saved from a demolition order in 1978 for the nation and restored entirely by female labourers is nearly surrounded on all sides by the ever-expanding hospital complex. Almost nothing will stop the corridor of knowledge from growing ever larger. It was an unsettling feeling running near hospital, knowing how much of it lay empty and how much of it was full of people struggling for their lives. Sometimes my imagination is not my friend. It feels like a localised disaster in motion, but with none of the media scrum or wailing relatives at the doors, just quiet roads and the odd passer-by. Although doing nothing wrong, I felt almost guilty in my presence and hurried away as quickly as my legs would carry me.

Further south on Hathersage Road and on a lighter note, is a more famed survivor of the threatened wrecking ball; Victoria Baths. Opening in 1906 and built from the finest materials with stained glass, ceramic tiles and mosaic floors, described as 'a water palace of which every Mancunian citizen can be proud.' With its large swimming pool and Turkish bath suite of showers, steam rooms and rest areas, it must have been a revelation to the masses more used to the grime and grit of everyday life. Closed in 1993 and steadily declining despite fundraising attempts, its plight finally came to the nation's attention on the television show, Restoration. Winning a public vote from a short-list of ten other buildings in similar peril, it gained a grant of £3.4m from the Heritage Lottery Fund. Saved! For now at least...In Chorlton-on-Medlock, you never know when something might disappear.

A great run today with a grand 92 roads added to the total. Now, if only I could take the Monorail home...

Tuesday 18th August 2020 – 18.10km – You Only Learn Once

   Summer in Fallowfield is an odd, quiet time, like an out of season beach resort, only in reverse. For the residents in these parts, it must be a blissful time of brighter days, emptier streets and quieter nights. This year though, the student lifeblood of the area hasn't been away for a couple of months, but ever since the lockdown in March. After such a hiatus from the drunken drama, the locals might see it as payback for the times things got so out of hand, the area made the national news.

   Heading east along Wilbrahim Road on a rainy Tuesday morning, I find myself in that awful running conundrum of being both too cold and too warm all at once, the mild temperatures sucked away by the occasional gust of wind. I'm not one for sweating in a running jacket, so I speed up and hope the rain ebbs into drizzle. Nearing the Fallowfield campus, I enter the slumbering world of bars, take-away chicken shops and discount supermarkets.

   The freedom of living away from home for the first time, young, unsupervised and with infinite supplies of cheap alcohol and other distractions nearby, it's little wonder that students go a little wild. Turning off Wilmslow Road opposite Owens Park halls of residence, I head down Landcross Road, a street that would propel Fallowfield from local suburb onto the front pages of national newspapers in May 2008. When students discovered that five separate houses on the street had organised house parties on the same night, they turned it into an impromptu street party instead with loud music and much drunken revelry amongst the hundreds dancing in the street. Police allowed it to go on until an 11.30pm deadline, but at midnight with the party still in full swing they had to use police dogs to clear the area. The usual conservative news outlets leapt into their deep wells of shock and outrage and condemned the enjoyment of being young as binge Britain. The responsible middle classes across the country must have been so exasperated as to spill their nightly glass of wine, but I digress. Trawling for other localised stories of excess, they made much of the Tower drinking game, where students reportedly attempted a shot of spirits on each floor of the 21-storey Owens Park Tower not far from Landcross Street. Such was the furore, it was even discussed in the House of Commons.

   Heading south down Wilmslow Road, I reach Amherst Road, where another student house party in June 2014 would make the news. At 1am and with around a hundred party-goers in an old house, the lounge floor collapsed into the basement. Thankfully, it only fell a couple of feet and the injuries were minor, but it also generated the best quote I've read for a while, from a student at the party: 'I lost part of my watch and also a large chunk of my knee.' Perfectly summarising the priorities of a penniless student.

These incidents, tougher University rules, rising tuition fees and a new focus on health and fitness amongst the young have led to a decline of this sort of drunken hedonism around the area, or at least made it less prominent. Still, I don't doubt that alcohol had a hand in an incident in 2018 when Fallowfield once more barged its way into the newspapers. This time, several residents of a terraced street woke to find penises crudely spray-painted onto their front doors in white paint during the night. Perfectly summing up the area, the majority were student houses who thought it hilarious, while one or two older residents were rightfully upset and annoyed. Making my way down Ladybarn Avenue, I'm bemused to see that despite the council clean-up and the subsequent years of wind and rain, you can still faintly make out one or two of the crude phalluses daubed by this budget Banksy. Or as some locals nicknamed them...well, you can work that out for yourself.

I'm sure it's merely coincidence that the ballsy character Capt. Sir John Alcock also once lived in this area. Famed mostly for his heroic non-stop flight across the Atlantic with Chorlton-based Arthur Brown (see 20th May 2020) , he was also a distinguished military pilot, based in Greece during the first world war and downing several enemy in his Sopwith Camel. Tragically in 1919, just six months after his record-breaking flight, he flew into trouble in thick fog over Rouen in France. Struggling to see on the way to an Expo in Paris, he crashed his prototype Vickers plane and died instantly. He was only 27 years old. Passing the blue plaque on his house at number 6 Kingswood Road and thinking of his long journey into the unknown, I can't help but give him an appreciative nod of the head.

41 completed roads taking me to a grand total of 1766.

Sunday 23rd August 2020 – 20.76km - All Intense and Porpoises

In 2000, the ward of Benchill in Wythenshawe won first place in
the rather snappily titled Index of Multiple Deprivation. This national
study of social and economic study across the whole of England placed
Benchill at the very top - or should that be bottom – of the pile. Years if
not decades of ignoring the area's problems had left it rotten and its
residents with little hope for the future. They were half right, as three
years later the ward was dissolved and split amongst its neighbouring
wards; Sharston, Woodhouse Park and Northenden. Because a problem
trisected is a problem solved, said no-one ever.

Unsure of what to expect of this area notorious for anti-social
behaviour, ankle tags, muggings, robberies and drug problems, I headed in
at 7am on a Sunday morning when hopefully the bad apples are still
knocking out the Z's in bed and the only people around are the normal
residents out walking their dogs. I knew it'd be fine, but nonetheless I
treated this as a covert run, as if I was a spy tiptoeing around Moscow,
running as a subterfuge before collecting a top secret microfilm from
beneath a park bench. So as a rather budget secret agent, I parked my car
in the neighbouring ward of Sharston, next to Hollyhedge Park and
worked from there.

Starting round some pleasant new estates on the border of
Manchester and Gatley, I settle into a good rhythm and relax into the run.
Heading north, I leave the slumbering houses behind and make for the
whirring murmur of rushing modernity. Even on a quiet Sunday morning,
cars, vans and lorries bustle through the Sharston motorway link between
the M60 and M56. This four-lane tarmac trench was carved through the
area in 1973. Crossing the bridge, I head briefly into a small industrial
estate with its soulless roads. Slumbering workplaces at the weekend
always creep me out a little, having something of the apocalypse about
them, a place of industry and profit abruptly empty and silent. Returning
over the motorway, I visit a small estate south-east of the Sharston
Interchange roundabout where the Sharston baths once stood.

Built in 1959, it was a near Olympic-sized pool beneath an arched
concrete roof, with 800 spectator seats and large glass walls at either end.
A haven for the local kids to fool around and throw themselves off the
four metre high concrete diving boards much to the chagrin of the
lifeguards, it closed in 1991 and was later demolished. Bizarrely, in 1971
the pool was visited by 'Flipper' – the crime fighting dolphin from the U.S
television show of the same name. What sounds like a weird dream,
actually happened, albeit other performing porpoises – Flipper never left

America – were brought to the pool to perform tricks for a paying audience of giddy kids and their parents. In some kind of strange warm-up act for the star act, a waddle of penguins also performed in the pool, smiling and waving, no doubt. Probably best not to ask if they changed the water afterwards.

Further southwest and I'm into the semi-detached cottages of Benchill's original social housing estate. With no-one around it looks as leafy, quiet and as friendly as any other place, reminding me of a quote from a local resident stating a pleasurable, fulfilling life can be had in Wythenshawe but if you want trouble it can be found very quickly. Bad things happen here, but it has none of the detritus of inner city decay; the broken glass, crude graffiti, boarded up houses and burnt-out cars. I dare say I wouldn't feel the same out running when the sun was falling from the sky at night. I'm reminded of this on Hollyhedge Road where I pass the newsagents, the only shop open in a row of twelve. It was here on a balmy August evening almost ten years ago to the day, that a couple of hoodies burst in, demanding cash. Faced with a large kitchen knife and a hammer, the 58-y-o shop-owner did what anyone else might do...threw her cup of tea at them and the young punks fled empty-handed. They breed them hard in Benchill.

Talking of hoodies, this is also the estate famously visited by David Cameron when he was leader of the opposition back in 2007. He visited the community centre to see how local youth workers are trying to make a difference and improve the prospects of those on the estate. Fair play to him for actually visiting within a labour stronghold, if only for a photo opportunity. Inevitably though, it was the photograph of a local hoodie making a gun sign with his fingers behind the future leader of the country that hit the front pages of the national newspapers. I'm not sure this particular hoodie was up for a hug. Or even a socially distanced fist bump.

As I round the corner, I realise I'm tired and might be a bit lost. Supping hard on my orange energy drink, I realise I'm coincidentally on Woodhouse Lane, where Jason Orange from hugely successful boy band, Take That used to live. The singer, dancer and actor is still sometimes seen in the area visiting friends and relatives.

Realising a few more cars are appearing on the roads, travelling not at the reluctantly headed to work pace, but the look at me/what you looking at pace of the hungover boy racer. I've seen no other runners, walkers or cyclists on my travels, only those catching buses to work and walking their dogs. With a final dart down Hollyhedge Road to the border with Gatley and back, I decide now would be a good time to make my exit. I return to my car feeling triumphant with my clandestine visit to a less than glamorous area and my top-secret collection of 59 roads smuggled out of the area.

Sunday 30th August 2020 – 22.79km – Spilled Milk

In 2018, Michael Portillo came to Wythenshawe as part of a Channel Five documentary on the country's housing crisis. He visited a charity shop and spoke to residents about gangs, guns, benefits and joblessness. Pretty much pandering to all the stereotypes they could muster, with a local activist quoted as saying, 'To be beaten to death on the way to buy a pint of milk from the shops would be quite common place.'

This is plainly ridiculous...if the risk of death was so high from a simple journey to the shops, you'd want to get yourself a four-pinter at least. I jest, but the good residents were equally derisory and upset. They acknowledge the area has issues but this stereotyping and tarnishing of a whole community does rather highlight Wythenshawe's problem; all anyone wants to talk about are the bad news stories. So as I leave the terrible area of Chorlton - where also in 2018 a paranoid schizophrenic ran amok threatening passers-by and pursuing police officers with a samurai sword - and head for the safer streets of Wythenshawe.

Driving into Sharston again at around 7.30am, I park up just off Brownley Road, close to Manchester College. Heading north, I quickly hit Hollyhedge Road and that ping of deja vu as I recognise the outer fringes of my last run in this area. The sun is up and dazzlingly low, but there's still a chill in the air, enough to make me want to push on a little and get warmed up. Leaving the busier roads behind I begin a long winding path through the deepest parts of an area called Peel Hall.

Here I again meet what is fast becoming my bete noire; concrete roads. Maybe it's just a few roads this time, I lie to myself, knowing although this estate is a later, post-war addition to the garden city, my legs and aching joints aren't so blessed. An eon ebbs past. The empty streets twist and turn, the unmarked junctions come and go and the cul-de-sacs entice me in, then spit me back out again. The never-ending montage of box-like houses, trees, verges and shiny cars pass by on either side as I run and run and run.

Soon, I hit Lomond Road and head east on a straight, slightly undulating road. I stir from my running slumber, confused by the end of the houses and two fields on either side. Actual fields, green open spaces with hedges and gates and small copses of trees. This feels like I've found the exit from a maze, the path to redemption and salvation. I reach the main road at the end and see the first moving cars for over half an hour. I check my map and see it's Styal Rd...in Heald Green...in the neighbouring borough of Stockport. Turning around with a sigh, I run back into my concrete labyrinth.

Over the next hour, I continue my mind-bending tour of suburbia like an amnesiac trying to find his home. Needing respite and having seemingly passed it at least three times, I step into Peel Hall park and find a fragment of the area's rural past. The original 14th century Peel Hall is no more, nor is its replacement farm, but its location is still marked in the centre of a small park by the old moat that used to surround the manor house. Owned by the Tattons who lived nearby at Wythenshawe Hall and owned all the land in this area, they used Peel Hall as a manorial court.

It would be here that the Lord of the manor would act as judge and jury over his tenants misdemeanours on his land; dishing out fines and punishments for petty crimes such as property damage, fighting and late payment of tithes. Later it would become a dower house; a home for a widow on the estate – the medieval equivalent of a granny flat. The farmhouse survived into the 1970's but vandalism and arson after it was empty meant demolition was the only option. The only medieval remnant, but no less impressive is a small three-arch bridge spanning the murky moat. I say no less impressive...after ninety minutes of neighbourhood monotony, I could probably be beguiled by a shiny milk-bottle top. They're actually quite common around here...they sit next to all the chalk outlines on the pavements.

62 roads completed today. Or perhaps one road repeated 62 times, at times it's a little hard to tell.

Sunday 6th September 2020 – 24.03km – All the Papal, so many People.

Change is inevitable, change is good, change is no longer sanitary and we must all pay contactless instead. Alas, the sad pile of metal barter-tokens on my bedside table, which I believe some shops might still accept as a form of currency – the coins, not the table - aren't really relevant to today's run. Alterations to my plans were inevitable after the last non-adventure in Wythenshawe. With such a big challenge ahead, I couldn't afford to get bored, so I knew I'd need the new. I was making great progress in the South of Manchester, connecting roads and areas from the eastern border to the west. I'd dabbled into the centre and around the inner-city fringes, but the east of the city and the north were complete strangers. In typical fashion, I chose the furthest point away from home and headed right to the top of the city.

Plotting a route to Higher Blackley, I could either drive the 26 kilometres around the M60 Motorway or go the more direct 13 kilometres straight up through the centre. I chose the latter, in order to 'look my enemy in the eye.' I looked and it looked back with a steely gaze that nearly broke me. Up from the city centre, up through Strangeways and Cheetham Hill, on up between Crumpsall and Harpurhey I saw nothing but houses, roads and side streets. And beyond them, more rows of houses, roads and side streets. All of them are in Manchester, all of them needing running. As the miles and minutes slowly ticked by and I found myself still travelling north inside the city, I could feel my eyes widening and my sense of adventure ebbing away. I felt like Michaelangelo triumphantly completing the magnificent Last Judgement in the Sistine Chapel and suddenly realising there's three more walls and a ceiling still to do.

Parking up on Victoria Avenue, I head north into an estate hemmed in by the River Irk and the northern edge of the M60, not far from Simister Island – which sounds like a foreboding misprint, not where three motorways meet. I'm soon puffing and panting as the road rises and falls in a regular pattern, a few locals giving me the eye as I pass. They live here, climbing these hills every day, but running them is still a novelty. I love a good hill, enjoy the tightening muscles, the fight for breath, the battle of wills and rush you get when you reach the peak and the mind curses you and asks you serious questions. Southern Manchester is notoriously flat though, so it still comes as a bit of a shock to go long on such a wearying terrain. And go long I was determined to do. In what would become a regular problem, I knew when I travelled so far across the city, I really needed to grab as much territory as I could. Go big and go home. Or rather go big, stagger back to the car, curse my obdurate idiocy and try not to cramp up on the journey home.

Higher Blackley - and specifically the area I was running - retains a semi-rural air to it. There's a sense of space and big skies, a fringe attitude more akin to Lancashire than the Metropolitan pizzazz of the city centre. Most notable is the abundant greenery; the area is awash with street trees and gardens, verges and parks. Reaching the peak of Boothroyden Road, I catch an impressive view across open fields and treetops, past lines of pylons to the smudge of hills in the distance. Heading down the slope, I enter the tiny hamlet of Boothroyden, a relic of the River Irk's past. Here I find some of the old three-storey townhouses built for the middle managers of the nearby mills still standing tall and proud amongst the mundane boxy new builds. Reaching the bottom of the hill, the road abruptly stops in a hedge. The reason noisily rushes past in the cutting beyond, the motorway that took 46 years to build from start to finish and neatly severing this country road from its other half on the other side of the Irk valley; the M60. Turning around and staring back up the steep hill, I take a moment to enjoy reaching the most northerly road in Manchester .

Looping around what used to be a convent and catholic boarding school, I reach Rochdale Road and begin my long undulating journey back west along Victoria Road. Enjoying more downhill than up, I longingly glance at the car before continuing onto the busy Middleton Road, a dual-carriageway running along the edge of the 247 hectares of rolling parkland that is Heaton Park, one of the largest municipal parks in Europe.

I'd imagine nearly everyone in Manchester has visited the park at some point in their lives; for a stroll in the fresh air or playtime with family, to admire the views, play golf, go fishing, or to visit the Grade I listed Heaton Hall, its gardens or the animals on its farm. The vast area has hosted outdoor theatre performances, open-air concerts by the likes of Oasis, The Courteeners and The Stone Roses. Even Pope John Paul II came here in 1982 to hold an open air Mass for 250,000 people. Arriving by helicopter, he stayed around long enough afterwards at a nearby convent for a northern lunch of black pudding, roast beef and apple tart for pudding. Hallelujah!

My own running memories of the park apart are mainly based around a tough Half Marathon that takes you up the same steep hill four times, fun but psychologically tough. Races in the park though are nothing new. Back in the 1820's and 30's, the public flocked to hugely popular horse races around the park, then in 1839, the races moved to Aintree in Liverpool, giving birth to the Grand National. The place is absolutely well worth a visit, but none of this catches my attention like the hidden stories just under the surface. For instance, when the railway wanted to cross his land in the south of the park in the 1870's, Lord Wilton insisted it would have to go underground so as not to blight his view. The railway dutifully dug a railway tunnel said to be the shallowest in the UK – in some places only sixty centimetres beneath the grassy surface.

During times of war, the council naturally wasn't so fussy. In the First World War, the army trained and prepared the Pals Battalions of the Manchester Regiment in the parklands. Thinking of friends amiably digging trenches, bayoneting straw sacks and marching to and fro in this verdant slice of countryside with little idea of the boggy hell they were headed into brings with it a tang of sadness. More so, when I read the hall itself was used as a Military Hospital, for those lucky to come home. In the Second World War, it was the turn of the Royal Air Force to move in, training over a hundred thousand members of aircrew for combat. Even the cold war looms over the park in the form of the 72-metre-tall Heaton Park BT Tower. Built in the 1960's, some say the concrete communications tower was designed to survive a nuclear attack on the city as part of a network known as Backbone – a network denied under the Official Secrets Act. In the event of a crisis, the government and councils around the country in their secret bunkers could have used it to chat to one another about old times, move small blocks around on map-tables and report on the migratory movements of the hordes of poor mutants above ground. They could also probably audit stationery supplies, prepare a new radiation suit tax and exchange tinned-food recipes with one another. All while the rest of us crispy plebs fight in the streets over toilet rolls. It's always about the toilet rolls.

77 completed roads today, legs absolutely hating me by the end. I made sure to only look straight ahead on the drive home.

Friday 11th September 2020 – 24.63km – The Black Brook and the Orange Book

It's sometimes said writers are only second to teenage boys when worried about the contents of their internet search history. It's not that you want to search these things, but often plot-lines lead you astray. Sometimes you simply need to know how a specific poison affects the human body and how best to hide it in food. Or maybe for accuracy sake, you'd like the floor-plan for the gold vault beneath the Bank of England in London. Not to mention what happens when a colleague sees you scrolling through a baby names website for a key character in your book...and takes your flustered denials with a knowing wink and whispered congratulations, before silently zipping their lips.

After my venture to the north of the city and the dawning of the true size of this urban island I must conquer, I realise what I'd plainly been ignoring all along. Not everywhere I run is going to be nice, enjoyable or potentially safe. So, I decide to rip the plaster off in one go and head to as worse a place as I can find in Manchester, to get it out the way. But how would I decide where that is? I didn't want hearsay, tittle-tattle or biased news, I wanted facts. Fast forward to my forensic search through the anti-social and violent crime maps of the Manchester Police. I got what I needed to know and possibly a lot more that I didn't want to know. Along with some nightmare fodder, I had a list of three or four areas that fitted the bill. Then I chanced on a Government-backed study conducted in 2007 by researchers at Oxford University. Their 'Indices of Deprivation' report compared the quality of life of residents in 32,482 neighbourhoods across England, covering amongst other things; health, disability, income, jobs, education, training, crime, homes and surroundings. The winner – or maybe loser - across the whole nation was Harpurhey, Manchester.

Okay then, the dart has hit the dartboard.

I am generally a positive person, but I would be lying if I didn't have a knot of apprehension when I drove north through the centre on the way to this run. Parking up on Silchester Drive, by some new build flats just off the ring-road, I locked up my car and ventured into the unknown. I wasn't necessarily worried, but I was hyper-vigilant and alive to all that was going on around me. Initially all went well, the new estate lulling me into a sense I was being too sensitive or over-dramatic. Then I headed along Lathbury Road and my heart sank. Broken glass, litter, abandoned mattresses, overturned shopping trolleys, shiny Nitrous Oxide canisters all lay strewn across the road and pavements. Even a shocked Director of an apocalyptic film might go up to his over-eager set designer and pull a face. Forewarned but undeterred, I pushed past this welcome and headed onto Carisbrook Street.

Carisbrook is a strange street. It's lined with council houses, but none of them are addressed on it. They are all facing the other way, their back gardens and five-foot fences backing onto the tarmac road. It is an odd feeling being ignored by a whole street. Opposite is Moston Vale, once a wild, neglected heath littered with fly-tipping and burnt out cars. Almost £2million was spent turning it into a much-tidied parkland, only for the same sense of neglect that taints this area to return over the next two decades. The largely culverted Moston Brook, used to meander through the vale and was known locally as the 'Black Brook' because of a nearby dye-works and the industrial pollution from upstream. In 2013, a report found it was still one of the most polluted waterways in Manchester, if not the whole of the North West. Causes included sewer overflows during storms, leaching from the rubbish tip and – a phrase no one wants to hear - leakage from St Josephs's Cemetery. Suddenly, I'm not so thirsty. A well-funded recovery plan is underway to improve the watercourse and make this blot on the area, a clean haven for nature, but well...see above.

Until 1993, Moston Vale was also the site of a hospital. Originally opening by the banks of the brook as Monsall Fever Hospital in 1871 it mainly treated smallpox patients, later becoming a hospital for infectious diseases with room for 350 beds. The scenes during the 1918 Influenza Pandemic are now less unimaginable than they were just a year ago. History repeats and repeats and repeats.

Around a left turn on Carisbrook Street, I find a small uninviting outdoor market surrounded by tall breeze block walls topped with rusted barbed wire. With weeds growing outside and the white-washed walls cracked and daubed with faded graffiti, it looks more akin to something seen on the sun-baked streets of Kabul or Basra rather than a city in northern England. Further along there is the uninspiring, functional Harpurhey Park and two rays of community sunshine; the local Church and a community centre. Beneath grey skies, it's a depressing vista and the first time I've really rather wanted to be elsewhere.

Yet before the council houses and open ground, this land was crammed full with row upon row of smoke-stained terraced houses, a hive of worker bees for the city's mills. Back on the 25th February 1917, amidst this sea of blackened brickwork and hard living, at 91 Carisbrook Street – about where the community centre is today – Manchester's 'Greatest ever writer' came into the world. Born John Wilson, just a year after his arrival, the terrible influenza Pandemic would tragically claim the lives of both his mother and sister. He would later take his confirmation name and his mother's maiden name to become Anthony Burgess, author of dystopian novel; A Clockwork Orange.

Heading north, I found more streets with broken glass underfoot and a handful of flat-roofed estate pubs that had seen better days. Built cheaply and designed to be modern like the houses around them, they now have all the charisma and charm of a library reading area. Yet, as times change, these pubs are in danger of disappearing altogether, something future historians might not look back on so favourably. Every treasured building goes through a phase when they're neither impressively new or reassuringly traditional, but just old and a little tired. The long past is historical, the near past an embarrassment. The money to refresh them appears a waste, so they simply get bulldozed and replaced by the next big thing. It seems implausible now, but soon we may be protecting fine examples of obsolete technology like phone boxes, cash machines, post offices, petrol stations, photo booths, camera shops, cinemas, newsagents, maybe even whole office blocks.

I emerged briefly onto Rochdale Road almost opposite 'Comedian' Bernard Manning's Embassy Club, still there after he and his dated jokes are long gone. As the locals roused themselves and kids flooded the streets heading to school, I realised it was about time I got the heck out of here. A thought only underlined by a young woman smoking in the doorway of her house on a long dead-end street. She glared at me all the way to the brick wall at the end and all the way back again. It was less why is he running down here, more why is anyone running here...are they mad?

The way she looked at me only amped up the unsettling feelings I'd carried all the way around with me. This heavy burden of trepidation and need for awareness sapped all the remaining energy from my tired legs, the carefree escapism I normally associated with running tainted with tension. On that trek back to the car, it abruptly dawned on me that for me this state of hyper-vigilance is an unusual oddity, yet for many women, this must be a necessity when out running alone no matter the area. I came for 85 roads in an area deprived of funding, jobs and hope and left with sadness and even more respect for all the kick-ass women I see out pounding the pavements. Keep safe, keep running.

Saturday 19th September 2020 – 22.59km – Uh-oh...

Wary, but undeterred by my nervy adventure in Harpurhey, I headed for its North Manchester neighbour; Moston and nearly got myself into a whole heap of trouble.

Derived from the Old English for mossy marshland and a settlement, Moston literally means village by the peat bog. This already throws up questions of what kind of people eschew the rich, fertile soil of the Cheshire plains, the sheep-grazing idylls of the Lancashire hills or the lure of the bountiful sea and settle by a bog? More importantly, does the dark unforgiving landscape retain its power over the people still living here?

For many centuries, this area was made up of a few agricultural settlements eking out a living from the land, surrounded by a wild, untamed wilderness of moorland and steep sided-valleys, known locally as cloughs. It was these valleys, with their bubbling streams and babbling brooks that would bring the linen washing and bleaching industry to the area in the 16th century. Themselves a precursor to the dye works that sprung up here during Manchester's industrial revolution. Dean Brook still trickles through Broadhurst Clough – a park, playing fields and nature reserve full of serene woodland and ponds alive with frogs, toads and dragonflies – and where Moston Hall farmhouse once stood. It's rich industrialist owner – one Edward Tootal Broadhurst – donated the land to the people of Manchester as a thank you immediately after the First World War.

Parking up close to the southern tip of Broadhurst Clough on Joyce Road, I fought to stay positive about the run ahead, knowing that this early on a weekend morning, I could hopefully be in and out of the area before anyone really knew I was there. Not that I thought anything would happen, but with newspapers often mentioning stabbings, gangs, guns, drugs and neighbourhood feuds in Moston, I knew amongst all the good, good people of the area, the bad ones would soon be waking up, possibly grumpy from the previous night's excesses. And without knowing it, I was guaranteed to be running past their house.

With that in mind, I set off at a brisk pace, ticking off a few roads of semi-detached houses before plunging into row upon row of traditional terraced houses. There's something about these streets, with their front doorsteps actually on the pavement and the canyon-like brick walls on either side that make them very claustrophobic and eerie in the early morning light. I'd imagine it's the sort of place where simultaneously everyone knows your business and also looks the other way. I pass the house on Langworthy Road where six were arrested for torture and murder back in 1993, surprised to see it is not only still there, but occupied. Moving ever so swiftly on, I make short work of the grid like pattern of streets, the lack of gardens meaning I rapidly clocked up lots of streets for very little distance. Heading west along Joan street – which I like to imagine is filled entirely with old women called Joan – I turn left onto Lightbowne Road and head for a newer estate. It wasn't the only thing to rapidly go south.

Amidst some curving streets and cul-de-sacs, this small seventies estate was built on some old railway sidings and is more open with grassland on three sides. After the oppressive terraces, I began to relax and noticing some badly drawn graffiti at the end of a small dead-end. With houses on one side and open grass on the other, I decided to stop and take a picture. Hearing a growling hatchback rapidly charging along the end street, I looked up from my phone and watched transfixed across the grass as it thundered along the road. As it disappeared out of sight past the end house, I heard the tyres screech to a halt and I felt the ground fall out from beneath me. With a clunk, the idling car changed into the distinctive whine of reverse gear. I tensed and squirmed at the absolute cartoon-like cliché of what was happening. As the dark car reversed into view, I immediately dropped my eyes to my phone and resisted the two options of hiding behind a car like a child or running away across the grass like a slightly fitter child. Instead, rightly or wrongly, I went for my usual defence of bold, distracted indifference. Tapping on my phone and looking about as if orientating myself, I walked a few paces towards the car and started a slow run. The booming music in the car turned down, telling me someone was looking and concentrating, judging and assessing... Presumably all at me.

If I was being checked out and assessed for value, status and intentions, I had little defence or protection, except my wits and my chat. Still I looked everywhere but at the car, if I couldn't see them, maybe the eyes behind the tinted glass wouldn't see me as a threat. Then I was past and away, not looking back as I casually ran on down the street. Behind me, the booming music returned and the car roared off. They might have simply been picking someone up or dropping a little something off, maybe they thought I was up to no good, maybe they couldn't care less, all I knew was I was the stranger in their area and I needed to get away from there as quick as I could.

Obviously not before I ran the last three roads and cul-de-sacs on the estate first. I might be spooked, wired and desperate to flee, but more importantly I didn't want to ever have to come back!

102

Chastened but annoyed, I piled my energy into bagging as many streets around here as I could before the rest of Moston awoke or my legs dropped off. Onto Kenyon Lane and more terraced back streets to the west of Moston Cemetery. I make short work of these, criss-crossing the grid of streets and ending up on the main road, Moston Lane. Its row of shops hit national headlines for the wrong reasons in 2010 when dubbed 'alcohol alley' for its twenty-two licensed premises including five off-licenses all within 350 metres of one another. Thankfully the council, police and residents united to turn around the area by stopping this instant access to cheap booze and with a slow drip of funding, improvements are coming.

As I head wearily back to the car, I check my map and decide, on a whim, to do an out and back up Lightbowne Road. It takes me away from the houses and back up through the playing fields at the northern end of Broadhurst Park. Here on the left, during the second world war, there was a battery of four anti-aircraft guns, radar and barrage balloons, all manned by Polish soldiers as part of the territorial army. The concrete bases remain as well as some apple trees planted by the Poles as a thank you to the people of Manchester after the war. On the other side is the new football ground for FC United of Manchester, a thriving non-league club built and supported by disillusioned Manchester United fans back in 2015. After adding two of the longest ever miles to my day's eventful journey, I make it back to my car with my haul of 74 hard-earned streets and get the hell out of Dodge.

Only as the dust settled did I realise I'd crossed another line, that of the 33% roads completed, leaving me 4152 roads still to run, thankfully not all as taxing as today.

Tuesday 22nd September 2020 – 29.19km – Feud and Farm Between

One of the oldest fireside stories known to man is the next village over the hill is our sworn enemy. Embellished by all manner of outlandish claims about baby-eating, laziness or immoral behaviour, nothing unites a group into hard work and endured hardship like a common foe. It's a story repeated endlessly through history and still exploited by world leaders, politicians, unions, bosses, newspapers and anyone with an agenda. Yet sometimes, the rivalries don't stop at stories...

After the last two eventful runs, this time I head for North Manchester even earlier and arrive before dawn just off Nuthurst Road in New Moston. I hit the dual-carriageway of Broadway around six o'clock and immediately plunge into an estate of social housing. If running in daylight in insalubrious surrounds is nerve-wracking, heading off into the unknown beneath the soft glow of intermittent street-lighting is surreal. Bouncing quietly down the centre of the roads from one pool of light to the next has a strange rhythm to it, a sense of being so alone and unseen as to be invisible. Details muted and vision limited, the world shrinks in on you and it becomes all about what's going on inside your head rather than what's lurking in the shadows.

Back across Nuthurst Road and I run another couple of side roads, including Oakwood Ave. It's beneath the end of this cul-de-sac and the houses of Greenways to the west that Little Nuthurst Hall once stood. With nearby Great Nuthurst Hall, these manorial halls were the seats of power of the Manor of Nuthurst and home to a feud that would simmer throughout the Tudor period from the end of the 15th century to late in the 16th. To the east over Theale Moor ('The Hale Moor') was the manor of Chadderton, tenant farmers on both sides using the open moorland as grazing land for their animals. Alas, Edmund Chadderton of Little Nuthurst Hall wasn't for sharing and in 1526 he decided that Theale Moor was now his farmers' property alone and the farmers from over the hill could frankly 'do one'. Unsurprisingly this land grab wasn't well received from them there folk from over the hill and no doubt after a bit of verbal to and fro, Edmund sent Nuthurst bailiffs out to chase Chadderton manor's livestock off the moor. The manor of Chadderton retaliated by rounding up over 200 armed farmers and labourers and marching across Theale Moor towards Nuthurst. They were met on the moor by a similar group of Nuthurst men and bailiffs. Exchanges of words became heated and the quarrel fast descended into a scuffle, a brawl and then a miniature battle. No doubt both sides claiming the other lot threw the first pitchfork. The

104

feud and accompanying violence continued, passed down from one generation to the next and the next until the placing of a line of boundary stones across the moorland at the very end of the 16th century. One can only imagine the Lord of Nuthurst at the time telling his gathered farmers, "I will build a great wall, and nobody builds walls better than me, believe me, and I'll build it totally inexpensively. I will build a great wall on our border and I'll have Chadderton pay for that wall..."

Leaving historic feuds behind, I cross back over the railway tracks and head into another small estate of sixties bungalows and terraces complete with grey pebble dash that abruptly morphs into a muddle of new-build townhouses and apartments in warm red brick. The sun rises apologetically and in the half-light, I marvel at a pair of bright scarlet gates emblazoned with 'Please No Parking', the last five letters so squished, they immediately reminded me of several backseat car journeys to the swimming baths with four friends I endured as a child.

Running down St Mary's Road I turn into a darker part of Manchester's underground past. Until the 1950's this was a coal-mining community with Moston Colliery at its heart. On the grassland surrounded by Woodstock road, two of the four shafts along this valley plunged into the rich coal seams 550 metres below ground. The railway alongside surrounded the colliery with numerous sidings ready to whisk the heavy loads away. Working underground was perilous work and death was a constant threat. Sadly a disaster occurred claiming five lives in 1940 when the brakes on a carriage travelling down a slope into the mine began to fail. As it gathered speed, many miners leapt off it but many couldn't and it derailed. Ten years later and it would be one of many closed down by the National Coal Board. Thinking of living so close to a warren of shafts and tunnels, with so much death and grief poured into the land always makes me shudder a little.

Bouncing down the hill, all my troubles of the last couple of runs fade away and I realise just how arbitrary an area can be. From one place to another, even one road to the next, the atmosphere in a supposedly terrible neighbourhood can change from grim pessimism to hope and pride, from rundown houses and overgrown gardens to new-builds, extensions and expressions of individualism. Good neighbours are the building blocks of community.

Such is my optimism, I simply keep running. Instead of heading back up Fairway to my car, I go off-piste into Failsworth before making my way back up Broadway to where I began. Clocking up around 18 miles and 87 streets, I drive home happy.

Tuesday 29th September 2020 – 29.19km – Fog, Fear and Folklore

'Twas a dark, autumnal morn and the fog hung over Moston like an ominous blanket of doom. What ominous creature of the night doth stalk these dank streets, moving hither and thither whilst the masses slumber between their sheets? What crazed maniac glides sinisterly beneath the muted orbs of light, shadows dancing over the tarmac to the rhythmical beat of the night?'

Well, of course, that would be me. So accustomed to the delights of certain parts of North Manchester, I decided to up the ante and go whilst it was auditioning for a Hammer horror movie. Reluctantly stepping out of my car at quarter to six in the morning, I looked up and down the street, the wispy mist drifting and swirling around the street-lights like hands trying to dim their intrusive glow. I had the distinct feeling the world wanted me to pull up my collar against the wind and head up the long winding driveway of that creepy mansion to ask the butler for use of his master's phone.

Pulling myself together, I leave the sanctuary of Shackcliffe Road and head across Lightbowne Road to mop up a few streets I'd missed on my last run, immediately bumping into a man walking his dog, both of us eyeing one another with much trepidation. I resist advising him to stay on the road and keep clear of the moors, he seemingly restraining himself from saying we'll cover more ground if we split up. Moving swiftly back onto Moston Lane, I head downhill, the dazzling headlights of lost couples from 1930's Dracula movies climbing steadily up through the hazy gloom. Completing a few side streets, I round a corner and come across an eerie woodland guarding the rows of stones and crosses of Moston Cemetery.

Of course I do.

Unable to take my eyes off it for more than a few seconds, I peer at the inky shadows disappearing into the blackness, the electric light stubbornly refusing to venture too far over the hedge. I hear the unmistakeable cry of a tawny owl.

Of course I do.

Consecrated in 1875, the cemetery is dedicated to the patriarch St Joseph under his guise as 'Patron of a Happy Death.' I speed up and choose to stay miserable.

Heading west, I leave Moston behind and head into neighbouring Harpurhey as the first deep, dark blues of civil twilight appear overhead. I pound the streets north of Moston Lane in a surprisingly ordinary part of suburbia. There are large semi-detached houses, new builds and many much-loved homes. My apprehension wanes as the kilometres pass and I

106

settle into a rhythm. Like threading oneself through a maze, I loop round and round, head up and down roads and double back on myself several times, my eyes more on the map than my surrounds. I make sure not to miss any roads, my painted lines slowly drifting me west. The estate is roughly a mile long and about five hundred metres wide at its widest point, yet I clock up nearly twenty kilometres running all of its streets. As ever, the true horror is in the details.

Coming to the end of Moston Lane, a road referenced by grime artist and local lad Aitch - real name Harrison Armstrong – in his song 'Moston', I chance upon an Asda as part of Harpurhey Shopping Centre. This reminds me of a more vintage part of the Mancunian music with 80's alternative rock band; King of the Slums. Formed in Hulme, they had a song titled Bombs Away on Harpurhey with inspiring lyrics about how hope for the future falls away to shoplifting in Tesco and that the title was the only solution.

There's still no Tesco in Harpurhey.

The workers of Manchester had awakened and hit the commute as I wearily head north out of Harpurhey on Rochdale Road, enjoying the downhill but with the nagging knowledge that since starting more than two hours ago, I'd done a lot of downhill running. Thankful for the daylight and receding mists, I reach the former site of Blackley Hall; a fine half-timbered Hall built in the Tudor times of the 16th century. By 1636, it was being sublet, with one tenant, Mrs Shay said to have suffered an untimely death in the Hall so brutal, she never left. Whether the haunting of Blackley Hall was real or not, its spooky reputation meant by 1815, no-one wanted to live there. Bought for a pittance, the new owners demolished the haunted hall to make way for a print works. When the new business failed to prosper, superstitious locals whispered of the curse of Old Shay's wife. I would soon be proclaiming curses of my own as I headed the long way back to my car around Boggart Hole Clough; the home of a real monstrous legend.

With its eerie ancient woodland, boggy streams and dense undergrowth, this parkland of steep ravines and winding paths is steeped in folklore, magic, rituals and legends. There is the ghost of a White Lady in the woods, a bench reputedly set aside for the devil and a giant's tooth petrified into stone. The latter is said to mark the spot where a human fought the mythical creature most associated with these woods.

A Boggart is a mischievous hobgoblin-like creature stemming from Lancashire and Yorkshire folklore as a bad spirit with poltergeist tendencies. It's said they like to play tricks, turn milk sour, terrify dogs and screech a cackling laugh in the middle of the night. They also have a creepy attraction towards young children, with several disappearing in the park since the 18th century. The 'bogeyman' we all grew up dreading derives from a corruption of Boggart. This particular one was said to haunt a farmhouse in the clough – the overgrown ruins of which may still be hidden in the woods – before the family fled in terror. The Boggart then reputedly moved to hide - like a troll - under the footbridge before the famous ninety-nine steps climbing out of the ravine.

Believe what you want, but sadly I couldn't go check the veracity of these claims in the creepy wood. I totally would have gone too, I'd absolutely have gone...alone...to look for monsters in the haunted place, but unfortunately...I was...fatigued, yes that's it, I was just a little too fatigued to go seek the Boggart. Darn, what bad luck, maybe next time, etc, etc.

Back outside the woods, I turn right onto Charlestown Road and find my hill. Climbing steeply at six percent for half a kilometre and grinding on up for another full kilometre, I find some new curse words to motivate my leaden legs. A killer hill so late in a run, what kind of mischievous trickery is this? I glance across at the thick woodland on my right, unsure if the faint cackling laughter is all in my imagination.

With the trick behind me, I discovered my treat for such exertions was a cool 100 roads for the run. A century not out around Boggart Hole Clough and some say if you listen carefully and the wind conditions are just right, you can still hear me effing and jeffing my way up that big hill.

Wednesday 7th October 2020 – 30.05km – Among the Ancients

Running the roads of Manchester, it's often not what remains that spikes my interest but the historical glory of what once was. Yet sometimes, amongst the modern city, I find an unchanging ancient treasure overlooked and taken for granted by all but a few.

I continue my forays into north Manchester with another run in Blackley, starting once more beneath a dark, starless sky. It was damp underfoot and although not overly cold, the light rain reminded me that like a jilted teenager, summer was gone and was not coming back. Starting just north of foreboding Boggart Hole Clough, I make short work of a couple of estates south of Charlestown Road, several dead-ends backing onto the ominous woods. Often running past the last lamppost, I find myself heading towards a small patch of open grass, the only thing between me and the great, dark void of trees silhouetted against the distant orange glow of the city. It's like a sentient foe from a horror movie, the inky blackness full of knowing and threat. For the record, I like to think of this section of the run as one of structured sprint intervals and not just me wide-eyed and bristly hackled.

Rapidly distancing myself from any home for Boggarts, I head further north into Charlestown and get down to the steady accumulation of suburban streets. Unlike most areas on the fringes of Manchester, Blackley wasn't a suburb built solely on farmland, it's history goes way further back. Preserved against developments as a medieval deer park, the ancient woodlands was a fenced off playground for the local nobility to go hunting. Aside from some pastureland for a couple of hundred cows, the area with a seven-mile circumference was rich with wildlife like eagles, heron, wild boar and hawks. It included Heaton Park in the west and Broadhurst Park in the east, Alkrington Woods in the north and Boggart Hole Clough in the south.

By the early 1600's, the manor's fortunes had changed and the deer park was slowly broken up and sold off. Several wealthy families converted much of the woods to tenant farmland and built impressive Halls on their new estates, including Humphrey Booth – a successful fustian merchant. The heavy hard-wearing cloth made from cotton was often also used for padding, hence the Shakespearean use of fustian for meaningless words in speeches and pompous writings. Yet, even as Booth Hall was built opposite Boggart Hole Clough, a small crescent of ancient woodland remained at its rear; Bailey's Wood.

This thin ribbon of trees in a ravine carved by a babbling brook over thousands of years is an unchanged reminder of the natural history

109

often taken for granted. The insects buzzed and flitted, the birds sang and the trees dripped in the rain here five thousand years ago. People and animals have endlessly wandered through, fashions and hairstyles have changed, industry and cars have filled the air with noise and pollution, planes have soared overhead and even taken man higher to the moon and back. And still the insects buzz and flit, the birds sing and the trees drip in the Mancunian rain. Booth Hall passed through numerous hands before demolition and replacement in 1908 by a Children's Hospital, the woodland a tranquil backdrop to the nurses' hostel. A key part of Blackley life for over a century, the hospital was also demolished in 2014 and replaced by a Taylor-Wimpey building estate. Bailey's Wood was often unloved and the victim of fly-tipping and neglect, until some local residents got together to cherish this ancient survivor of a perpetually changing city, so others may appreciate the insects buzzing, birds singing and the smell of the trees dripping in the rain.

As I work my way around all the roads surrounding this slither of woodland, I leave the flat ground behind and find myself darting up and down the hills just west of Rochdale Road. The Dam Head estate was built in the 1970's on the land of a demolished farmstead of the same name; the last true connection to the area's agricultural past. Passing the sites of an old Bleach works and Lion Brow cotton mill – both built further down the brook that cut through Bailey's Wood – I reach St Peter's Church. A rather stout gothic revival church built in the middle of the 19th century, it is extremely unusual in that all the pews, boxes and galleries on all three sides are entirely original.

Heading for home, I once more find I've loaded a huge hill at the end of a long run. I should know better as it's only a energy gel's throw from the killer climb I did on my last run. Only this time its shorter, yay! Therefore much, much steeper...oh.

I didn't buzz or flit, nor could I have sung, but I did drip in the Mancunian rain. Two short of another century, I finish exhausted on 98 more roads for the total.

Thursday 15ᵗʰ October 2020 – 25.74km – Be Not Afeared

Despite those who would tell you otherwise, the United Kingdom has a long history of being a tolerant, welcoming society. Multiculturalism is not a modern phenomenon and despite the well-documented evils of empire and colonialism, over the centuries, many immigrants have fled to Britain to escape famines, wars and religious persecution. Often arriving into the least desirable areas, they make them their own and bring a little bit of home to their new world. Irish tenant farmers fleeing the 19ᵗʰ century potato famine, Jewish families fleeing growing Russian and European anti-Semitism up to the world wars. Indian and Caribbean immigrants answering Britain's call for post-war workers and later 20ᵗʰ century newcomers from the Far East, Africa and Eastern Europe; all have made new homes across Manchester, but there's an area north of the centre that's one of the most diverse in the whole country. With over 150 different languages spoken by its residents, that area is Cheetham Hill.

It was another early, pre-dawn run to an area with a not so great reputation of social depravation and estates dogged by petty crime. It's a sad fact that newcomers often find themselves housed where locals no longer wish to live, where anti-social behaviour is rife and communities struggling. A friend upon hearing my planned visit stared silently and simply raised one eyebrow. It wasn't the most rousing of endorsements. Most already think I need an intervention, running the dark streets of a place they're scared to drive through in the daylight. Hopefully, that says more about them than me. Still, it the growing knot of apprehension in my stomach was not entirely helped when I climbed silently out the car and stared across at the ruined shell of St Luke's church tower. A grade II listed building with bushes growing from the top and seemingly held together by prayers and scaffolding, it loomed ominously over me in the gloom, the dark voids in its belfry like judgemental eyes and a mouth silently screaming into the night.

Swallowing hard, I forcibly lowered my soaring eyebrows, unclenched my teeth and rapidly charged up Cheetham Hill Road. I soon passed a mosque and entered a commercial area of multicultural shops and restaurants. Some relics of the past live on, their Edwardian architecture hiding behind new use. Next to the red brick Trinity United Church are two ethnic superstores that used to be a small picture house and a billiard hall. These buildings hint at what was once a main thoroughfare climbing out of the centre and on up through a sea of terraced streets.

Back in 1911, these smoky, crowded urban streets gave birth to someone who fought for a right we now all take for granted. Benny

111

Rothman loved two things growing up in Cheetham Hill, reading activist books such as Robert Tressell's 'Ragged-Trousered Philanthropists' and the great outdoors. He was an avid cyclist and walker at a time when the countryside was almost entirely held in private hands and off-limits to city folk like Rothman. These two passions entwined and in 1932 he led the mass trespass of Kinder Scout in the peak district, where 400 people defied 20 gamekeepers to walk on private land. Rothman would be one of six men to be arrested and sent to prison for four months for the trespass, but it started a civil disobedience movement that would lead directly to the formation of National Parks in 1949, long distance footpaths such as the Pennine Way and the right to roam.

Heading in and out of some rather dodgy-looking alleyways amongst the shops, I drift south into an estate with a somewhat chequered past. This was gangland Manchester. The Cheetham Hill Gang and their drug trade rivalry with the gangs of Moss Side and Salford in the 1980's and 90's was the reason the city got the notorious 'Gunchester' tag. As the sun squints reluctantly up over the horizon, I find myself treading a little faster and quieter on my feet through these streets. At the corner of Levenhurst Street and Winterford Road, I find the former site of the Penny Black pub. Here in 1991, rival gangs ambushed and executed Cheetham Hill gang boss Anthony 'White-Tony' Johnson in the pub car park, as if from a scene in a Hollywood movie. The pub is now used as a mosque, the car park just as it was. Stood in the half-light, I curse my writer's imagination as I hear those gunshots echoing off the nearby houses, lights going out in homes overlooking the pub, pale faces appearing briefly at the windows. I hear the sirens and see the flashing blue lights, the fluttering police tape and media circus. Then I imagine the destructive ripples across the community and city as people feared going outside, to the shops or sending their kids to school. The traumatised people in the community who had escaped guns and violence in their home country only to have it wash up on their doorstep once more. Anxiety and worry hanging over the area like an oppressive storm.

Now travelling at the speed of spooked and noticing bats in the lightening skies, I swiftly make my way in and out of the estates on either side of Waterloo Road. I was running as quickly as a professional footballer, such as ex-Wimbledon and Nigerian international star Efan Ekoku, who was born and raised in Cheetham Hill. Yet, as the kilometres pass and the daylight comes, I find the scary monster of my mind is just the same series of brick boxes on almost every other estate I've visited. Even where I've spied a likely-looking character in an open doorway, sucking on a glowing tube of distinctly aromatic herbage, I'm gone like a bounding ghost out of sight before they can even say, 'heyyy!'

That said, I didn't feel totally relaxed until the area was fast receding in my rear-view mirror, my change of clothes and post-run shake still in my bag. 94 completed roads and a vow to never ask for an opinion from my friend's eyebrow ever again.

Friday 23rd October 2020 – 28.4km – The Manchester Mummy

It'd been over a week since my last run and I'd had a moment of questioning whether what I was doing was such a good idea. I wasn't hitting any Zen-like state or getting a runner's high, I wasn't escaping into deep thought or breathing the sweet fresh air, I was running around places with bad reputations as quickly as possible to get them ticked off my list. The news of Covid deaths rising once more across the country and particularly in the north put my fears in perspective. Life is short and full of risk, so best to get on with it while you can, for one day the double-decker bus of destiny may catch us in its headlights.

Stoically refusing the soft option of a local bounce around Didsbury, I head back through the dark streets to Cheetham Hill. Parking opposite my screaming church friend once more, I silently scream back at St Luke's and commence on the eastern side of Cheetham Hill Road. Bounding around these murky pre-dawn streets, I delight in the lights and displays in the windows to celebrate the Islamic festival Milad-un-Nabi – "the birth of the prophet." It means little to me, but running through a light drizzle on damp streets bathed in pools of green light was an ethereal experience I simply wasn't expecting. I later learnt the colour symbolises a happy occasion, which seemed apt as I had a broad smile on my face.

Further north I hit a grid of terraced houses, remnants of when the whole area, if not most of the city was row upon row of 'two-up two downs' with no gardens and an outside privy in a tiny backyard. These kinds of streets had a corner shop at one end, a pub at the other and were where everybody knows everyone business. Which seems rather fitting as this is where Jack Rosenthal was born. A screenwriter and playwright of over fifty series, films and plays, he's perhaps most famous for his work on Coronation Street through most of the sixties and the fire brigade drama London's Burning. He was married to Maureen Lipman and has had a new street named after him next to a performing arts theatre in the city centre...adding another road to the list I'll have to run, thanks Jack.

Often on these runs, I like to ask questions. Just for fun. Just my way of playing with fate, tempting some kind of grand design to show itself to me with a coincidental answer. Oh deity of the drizzle show me a sign! So I muse, ponder and decide on, 'Where should I run after I've finished all my Manchester runs?' I immediately round the corner off Cheetham Hill Road and come across a large supermarket with WORLDWIDE glowing on the side in metre-tall letters.

There may have been some swearing and an immediate end to the asking questions game.

Heading down Woodlands Road as it gets light, I head under the railway bridge and enter the wonderfully named area of Smedley. Now a green wooded valley either side of the River Irk, until the 1970's it was an industrial wasteland of bare earth and polluted water. The wire works, paper mill and ropewalks of the past only adding to the waste already coming from upstream. Back to a more pastural time in the early 19th century, this was also a place of peaceful radicalism.

On Smedley Lane – roughly where the Oasis Academy Primary School is – amidst the fields behind St Luke's church was Smedley Cottage. It was here in August 1819 where the great orator, Henry Hunt stayed with Joseph Johnson, the organiser of a peaceful demonstration for civil rights, fair taxation and the vote, at St Peter's Field in Manchester. The infamous day of peaceful protest would end with great bloodshed and Hunt's arrest. The shocked newspaper men who witnessed it likening it to the carnage of the Waterloo battlefield some four years earlier and named it the Peterloo Massacre.

On up Hazelbottom Road and over a grinding, lung-bursting hill into Harpurhey, I negotiate several deserted house-less roads that look like prime spots for me to stumble across my first dead body. Moments later, I come across several thousand.

One of the most interesting burials at Manchester General Cemetery is that of Hannah Beswick, known as the Manchester Mummy. Before her death in 1758, she told her physician Dr Charles White of her great fear of being buried alive and asked him to keep her above ground and every now and then check on her for signs of life. Dr White did just this, before embalming her and decidedly going off script by storing her in a grandfather clock and occasionally showing her off to visitors. Which rather one-ups anyone who's showing off their new kitchen. I also imagine Mrs White in the Conservatory with the Lead Piping in case her strange husband decides to start a new collection. After the Doctor's own death, the mummy passed firstly to the local Natural History Society and later the forerunner of Manchester University; Owen's College. By 1867, they appear to have had a clear out and decided that 109 years after she first showed acute symptoms of being dead, that that diagnosis had not changed in the intervening century. She was finally buried in July the following year.

Tired and with the undulations taking a toll on my legs, I loop back around, past the Irish World Heritage Centre and the Transport Museum. Manchester incidentally was the first place in the UK to have a regular horse-drawn bus service, travelling from Pendleton in Salford to Market Street in the city centre. Just next to the historic bus and tram depot is the wonderful Temple Square. A small peaceful estate of red brick houses, built just after the First World War for returning soldiers as part of a homes for heroes campaign. The mayor cut the first sod of earth, with the spade now on display in Manchester Town Hall. Which probably makes it the Ace of spades. This is either the height or depth of bad puns, I'll let you decide if we're deeming aces high or low.

Glad to have once more avoided the perils of double-tiered omnibuses, both on the roads and stationary in museums, I head back to the car with a weary smile on my face and 89 more roads in my legs.

Saturday 31st October 2020 – 20.78km – Trick or Threat

'Darkness falls across the land, the rising sun is in demand,
Critters ooze and slink like toads, terrorising those empty roads,
And whomsoever shall be they, without the pace for running away
Must stand and face the hounds of hell, but stop their Strava first,
if they look unwell.'

Harpurhey in the dark early hours of all hallow's eve, what could possibly go wrong?
I have temporarily stopped researching the areas before I run, as it has shades of looking up that nagging pain/cough/headache on the internet. What I didn't know, couldn't hurt me was the naive philosophy I was sticking to. That and to paraphrase what a Nazi soldier said of S.A.S. Commando raids in the Greek islands, 'They come like cats and leave like ghosts.' So, with no lights and dark kit, I set off from my car doing my best Halloween impression of a witch's cat.
Starting just over the boundary in Moston, no sooner had I left Lily Lane behind and entered a new estate, that I fell into step with someone else dressed in dark clothes. Moving from one pool of orange light to the next, he blended with the shadows, his careful gait propelling him silently over the pavement. Stocky and potentially bad news I ran past him on the other pavement, an exchanged glance and careful assessment and we both went our separate ways at the next junction. One cul-de-sac later and I'm back on his heels, like a monster from a low-rent horror movie! I hesitate and decide trailing him is worse than a second pass. I feel another furtive glance across, but I this time I don't reciprocate. I'm doing my bold, distracted act of indifference. Which, I admit, might have carried more power if I wasn't looking at my running pace on my watch-less wrist. Darting down another side street, I breathe a sigh of relief and follow it round and into another cul-de-sac. Only as I keep running do I realise the road is not just running parallel to the first but also slowly curling back to the original road. I continue as if on rails, like I'm having an out-of-body running experience. And sure enough as I get to the end of the road, who should be crossing in front of me on the other pavement but Mr Shadow. I'm not sure if he looks at me or not, I'm far too busy in my awkward happy place, focused on the dark sky over the rooftops. Feeling creepy and cold, my brain tells me to run on the spot in the middle of the road – like a runner might - until he's gone, because that's not a terrifying sight for him at all. Some crazed runner in dark clothes bouncing up and down on the side streets of Harpurhey like an escapee from an Olympic

117

hospital or Hannibal Lecter welcoming Clarice to the side room of a gym.

After a few minutes of awkward self-contemplation of what my life has become and how I was now a weird story probably being told to family and work colleagues, I move on. Bagging more streets away from the new estate, I enter some social housing and terraces that obviously need some love. Paint peels, litter accumulates and it sadly scores high on the Abandoned Mattress Index with two in three streets. At least no-one had set them alight, yet. Whilst I wasn't scared by these houses – more depressed – I did notice that given the date, there was a distinct lack of any Halloween decorations. The more this thought occurred, the more I looked for flash banners, plastic spiders, bed sheet ghosts or carved pumpkins on the doorsteps and the more it seemed incongruous by its absence. As the bruised overcast twilight replaced the darkness, I headed up and down several terraced streets, all devoid of spooky paraphernalia. Then, as I come down Waverley Road, I hear the most blood-curdling scream and cry from the next street over – the street I'd just run up. I slow my pace, gawping like a paranoid owl, ears set to panic, body fizzing with adrenaline.

'Maybe I should go check on them?' One neuron in my head asks.

And my brain, skeleton, muscles and other cowardly organs all nervously laugh and laugh and laugh.

'Warp speed, number one. Engage!' Says my Captain Picard brain, my Enterprise legs propelling me out of scream-shot in five nanoparsecs.

Rushing up and down Nigel Street – where all the Nigels live presumably – and hurtling down Ravine Avenue – which sounds more perilous than reality – I make my way north-west up the streets on either side of Church Lane. After several short ins and outs, I head down Moss Brook Lane and drop down towards Moston Vale. At the end is a Grade II listed Crofter's House, a beautifully proportioned Georgian House from the early 19th century, with semi-circular bow windows and elegant pilasters. It now forms part of the Manchester and Cheshire Dog's Home; a refuge for canine strays since 1897. Operating for over a hundred and twenty years, it's said they have cared for and rehoused over a million dogs since opening their doors.

Rounding up a couple of missed roads from previous runs over on Moston Road and near Harpurhey shopping centre, I chance upon a house with some skeletons in the front window and some gravestones on the front lawn. At last some Halloween decorations...

At least, I hope they're Halloween decorations...

With 72 roads in my spectral pockets, I leave Harpurhey like a ghost.

Monday 9th November 2020 – 28km – The Grey Lady

Lockdown II is here; the sequel nobody wanted. With the colder weather and people staying indoors more, the deadly virus is once more infecting and killing the vulnerable with impunity. Whereas before it was spring and despite the worry and fears, there was an element of novelty for the masses stuck at home, baking banana bread and spending time with their families. This time though, with the autumnal rain and short days, everyone is going into it with eyes wide open. People are tired, jaded and losing hope of ever seeing normality again.

Fighting the depressive fug hanging over the country, I seek solace in the mindlessness of my running. After several forays into the North of the city, I decide to stay closer to home and return to the indifferent embrace of Wythenshawe. Parking up just off Brownley Road in the semi-darkness at the start of another working week, the temperature is somewhere close to the goldilocks zone. It's not too warm, not too cold, not too breezy, not too porridgy. I also hoped no-one would break into my car, sleep on the back seat and eat my post-run breakfast either.

Setting off on the empty back streets, I rapidly settled into a decent rhythm and meandered my way south and east, crossing the tram tracks opposite the fire station before plunging back into the side streets. Seeing plenty of modern homes and leafy streets, I soon realised I was making good time, ticking off roads and plotting a good route, but I was also a bit bored. Now I know Wythenshawe is no paradise, but after some of my recent runs, I no longer felt any trepidation and with street after street having no notable history or heritage, I just thought it's something of a terribly dull place to run.

Of course, two-times Heavyweight Boxing Champion of the World, Tyson Fury might disagree having been born in Wythenshawe in August 1988. And I would disagree too as I abruptly find a new joy in running around here. It's a lovely place to visit, Mr Fury. I'm really enjoying myself, Mr Fury, sir.

The fabulous, lovely boxer is not the only famous person from around these parts. There's singer and songwriter Paul Young, not to be confused with Paul Young, the other singer and songwriter with the same name. The other Paul Young is from Luton and famously sang about the strategic placement of his headwear indicating the locale of his current abode. While this Paul Young sang Every Day Hurts and All I Need Is Miracle, both songs obviously no reflection on his idyllic birth and joyful upbringing in Benchill, Wythenshawe. Singing first with the band Sad

Cafe in the late 70's and 80's, he joined Paul Carrack as lead vocalists for Mike and the Mechanics in 1986, scoring three top forty hits and two top ten's in the U.S.

Caroline Aherne also grew up in Wythenshawe, the comedienne, actress and writer appeared on the comedy sketch show; The Fast Show and as the old lady interviewer on The Mrs Merton Show. She'll perhaps be most remembered though for the show she created, co-wrote and starred in; The Royle Family; a show for which she won Baftas for Best Sitcom and Best Comedy Performance.

Meanwhile, you're wondering where I am in my run around the lovely streets of Wythenshawe, well, I'm not totally sure either as I'm doing so many ins, outs, ups and downs, I've lost all track of where I am. All the roads and houses look the same and appear to be set out in a street-plan born from a bowl of spaghetti thrown at a kitchen wall. Obviously, in a good way, should any six foot nine pugilists ask? Every now and then, I emerge from the meandering pasta to a main road and get a sense of deja vu as I recognise a street opposite I've emerged from on a different run. Strangely I recall the same feelings of vibrant energy or deep exhaustion depending how far into the run I was at the time. Then I plunge back into the unknown, searching everywhere for nothing.

Then I find the Grey Lady of Wythenshawe.

At the corner of Broadoak Road and Honford Road, there is a patch of land encircled by roads and houses that was once described as 'one of the prettiest bits of countryside in Cheshire'. A copse of trees by a pond, it was a popular picnic spot for the Victorians and Edwardians before the huge estate arrived and the pond was first fenced off, then subject to the esoteric whims of modern sculpture, as locals threw in several shopping trolleys and old bicycles. However, this watering hole had long had a legend attached, that of a ghost treading the banks, her silken dress rustling in the breeze. Some claimed it was a mad woman who'd escaped a nearby castle, but drowned in the pond whilst fleeing. Others say it was a Victorian girl. More still a young maid who'd died when a horse and cart bolted into the water. It seems more likely the Grey Lady was another Boggart-like bogeyman to scare kids into not going in the water and/or come home before darkness descends, lest the Grey Lady gets them. More recently in 2019, long after the pond was filled in, the green was used without permission as a campaigning place for real-life bogeyman Tommy Robinson's unsuccessful dalliance into politics. As I pass, four new bungalows are going up on the site. One can only hope the Grey Lady has moved on to somewhere much less interesting rather than return in a fury beside someone's bathtub.

With 60 roads run and barely a single memory of any of them, I check the back seat of my car for spectral or slumbering passengers and head for the place I keep my hats.

Thursday 12th November 2020 – 24.09Km – Gorton's Alive!

After so much Northing and Southing, I decide to throw myself a curveball, and just as the Pet Shop Boys never sang, I go east.

With just six weeks to Christmas and work busier than ever, I only have to look around at my battle-weary colleagues to realise my running folly. While Santa may visit every road in one night – show off – I know if I do too much, I'll soon be doing nothing at all. So, with my sensible cap firmly on, I head out for what will probably be my last run of the year.

Heading away from the city centre, along the straight Hyde Road – believed to be on the route of an old Roman Road -, I aim for the Gore Brook area in Gorton. This area in Manchester was populated by people long before the Romans arrived, a Neolithic stone axe found during an excavation here dates back to somewhere between 3500-2000BC. With fresh water and fertile soil, this was obviously land worth fighting for and the Nico Ditch – last seen in Platt Fields – continues through Gorton Cemetery here. Whatever its use by the Saxons, Ryder Brow here – otherwise known as Winning Hill – is said to be the site of a decisive battle against the invading Danes.

Setting off from the car, I circle the pretty Sunny Brow park, enjoying the large Edwardian houses overlooking its steep sides to the tree-lined Gore Brook below. At one end is Old Hall Drive, which is now lined by houses but was literally the site of a driveway of a grand old hall; Gorton Hall. Built in the 17th century, its most famous resident was the wealthy Railway Industrialist, Richard Peacock who arrived in 1865. His family would remain until the last Peacock died and the Hall was demolished to make way for new housing and the park in 1906. Besides the street name, all that remains now is the Lodge that would have guarded the Hall's main gate, still sited at the base of the road, like a loyal dog sat awaiting his master's return.

I cross Maiden's bridge over the brook, the original said to have been built to stop ladies the indignity of hitching up their skirts to cross the stepping-stones here. Further along Far Lane, I step out of the city and onto an 18th century village lane. Here, curving around a bend, there's a higgledy-piggledy mix of brick and rendered cottages with different heights, styles and all with a pleasing weathered appearance. A recessed plaque on the one at the centre proudly proclaims the year of construction as 1792. Before the construction of the main road in the mid nineteenth century, this unassuming lane was the main route into Manchester from 'afar', giving the road its name.

122

Returning to reality on Hyde Road, I emerge into the rush hour traffic. Lockdown or no lockdown, the masses are still required to keep Manchester from grinding to a juddering stop. Edging east along the back streets around the cemetery, the sound of traffic is never far away, the air thick with that heaviness and imperceptible taint you can't place but know deep down isn't doing you any good. The fight to get people out of their cars and onto public transport is not a new one. Before the Fallowfield loop was decommissioned and long before it was converted into a cycle path, here just north of Hyde Road, the freight track was put to a different use. In 1987, a train set for the new Docklands Light Railway in east London, briefly gave public demonstrations and a mile long journey north and back to raise awareness of what a tram or light railway could do for Manchester. After the few weeks were up, the same train carried the Queen and Prince Phillip at the opening of the DLR in London. Later sold to Germany, the same train still runs on the Essen Stadtbahn.

I keep pushing on, but it's a very stop-start experience as I have to do more map-reading than running. At this far eastern edge of Manchester, I am not only nudging up against the forbidden land of Denton in Tameside, but also Reddish Bridge. I reach the road-sign for Tameside and look across to the Manchester one on the other side of the road. It is a strange feeling being here, at the edge of the map. For all those passing unheeded in either direction in their cars, they probably don't even notice the signs, for they have little meaning. Yet for me, they are as significant as country borders, another world I am forbidden to run. Turning back from the edge, I loop around a small estate just south of Debdale Park and Gorton Reservoirs. Unspectacularly, at the end of a pleasant road of semi-detached houses I come across some tall bushes between me and a field of allotments beyond. This unassuming spot is Kingsdale Road – the most easterly paved-road in Manchester. I cannot help but think I'm incredibly fortunate to have the place to myself, as I'm sure the coach loads of tourists will be here any minute. No sign of a gift shop or visitor's centre either. Shame, I would have loved a mug with some tall bushes on it.

Heading back towards Sunny Brow, I hit a throwback to industrial Manchester with a grid of back-to-back terraced streets close to a couple of old factories. Running up and down and criss-crossing my path in a pleasing pattern, I find the red brick overwhelming. With no gardens or views of anything natural at all, I find it a little depressing, even for this short space of time. I can only imagine what it must have been like when the swirling smoke from the works and chimneys coated everything with a layer of soot. Emerging to the verdant vista of the park and despite my

123

weariness, I feel myself soothed. I realise then how treasured this oasis of life, colour and hope must have been to the residents during those times, a chance to escape their homes or workplace. And now, during Lockdown, well over a century after it first lifted spirits, it gives locals a chance to do just the same and breathe deeply, if only for a short while.

Leaving with 81 streets, I wondered when I would next get chance to escape my home or workplace for a run through the streets.

Friday 25th December 2020 – 8.07km – It'ssss Chrrrrrrrrrissstmmmasss!

Obviously, the solution upon waking ridiculously early on a dark, cold Christmas morning – thanks, stupid body clock – should be to pull the duvet over my head and snuggle deeper into that warm cocoon of slumbering oblivion.

'So cold!' I said turning on a light and rising zombie-like to the edge of the bed.

'Who'd even think about...' I said standing, fighting a tingling shudder across my shoulders.

'It's -3C (feels -8C) outside...' I said, putting on more running clothes.

'It'll be too icy...' I said as I laced up my shoes and rubbed the goosebumps on my bare legs.

'You've got to be stupid and crazy.' I said pulling on my Santa hat.

The Christmas rush has been like nothing I've ever experienced before, the relentless waves of brown boxes washing in on a Yule-tide of seasonal lockdown. The four weeks of November restrictions failed to bring the R-number down and for most people Christmas is now either a single brief visit to family inside their bubble or cancelled entirely. With elderly parents living across the country, I reluctantly stay home in Manchester for the first time in forever. Six weeks since my last run and I am in a world beyond tired and broken.

Yet, I do love a Christmas morning run. There's something in the air, something magic about being out while everyone else is inside. It's akin to being Raymond Brigg's voyeuristic Snowman, touring the city and seeing the houses and gardens decorated for this festival of good cheer and good will. Every bedroom light gleaming in the darkness hints at the excited cries inside of children telling their sleepy parents, 'He's been! Santa's been!' and ruining any plans for a lie-in. It's a time of day when anything is possible on a day when the normal rules of life don't apply. Almost everyone is hoping for a day off from their normal stressful lives, a pause to repeat the traditions of the past and make future memories for those around them.

Setting off with little planned except keeping on my feet on the treacherous icy pavements and getting warm in the bitterly cold air, I head through the quiet centre of Chorlton and am reminded that not every Christmas in Manchester was a peaceful one. The single-storey modern Post Office and the charity shop next door sit in a gap between much older buildings, looking somewhat out of place. Yet, this is no cultural

125

vandalism but rather a site of explosive destruction and tragedy. Back in December 1940, the German Luftwaffe turned its sights onto Manchester as a place of war industry and bombed it on the nights of the 22nd and 23rd in the Christmas Blitz. Five people died here from one bomb, the raids over two nights taking a further 679 lives and injuring over 2000.

Manchester has its place in Christmas culture for Mancunians. For many, it's memories of a huge inflatable Santa scaling the tower of the town hall to a festive Winter Wonderland in Piccadilly Gardens, or the present appetite for the wonderful continental huts of handcrafted gifts and traditional food at the Christmas markets. Yet nationally and internationally, the city has played a part in adding joy to such a joyous day.

In 1939, 12 year-old child Eric Bartholomew from Lancashire came to the Odeon Cinema on Oxford Street for an audition for impresario Jack Hylton. In the audience was one of Hylton's child star acts, 13-year-old Ernest Wiseman. Manchester was the first meeting place of what would become possibly Britain's greatest comic double act; Morecambe and Wise. Apparently it was dislike at first sight, Morecambe thinking his rival 'too cocky' and Ernie proclaiming the young upstart as 'looking ridiculous'. Only after separating for war service, did they come back together and form their double act. Slowly climbing to fame, they reached a peak in their 1977 Christmas TV Show, watched by a staggering 20 million people.

In October 1843, frequent visitor to Manchester Charles Dickens, came to give a speech for the philanthropic organisation; the Manchester Athenaeum. Sharing a stage with renowned politicians of the time Richard Cobden and Benjamin Disraeli, this was a fundraiser for the working poor of the city. Inspired by the hardships suffered in the industrial districts, six weeks after his speech, he'd completed his seasonal classic; A Christmas Carol. Many even claiming he based the character Tiny Tim on the invalid son of a friend he often stayed with who lived and owned a cotton mill in Ardwick.

The 25th of December is a time for family and putting rivalries aside in a bid for peace, love and harmony. So, it comes as a surprise to many that until 1957 it was deemed perfectly normal to have a full set of football fixtures on Christmas Day afternoon. If that wasn't deemed crazy enough to our modern thoughts, back at the turn of the 19th century, it was even deemed sane and logical to make it derby day. Between 1896 and 1902, Manchester City and Manchester United (twice as Newton Heath) played each other three times, with one match gaining a boisterous crowd of 18,000 right up to the touchline at the Bank Street ground in Clayton. For the record, United won twice and the other game was a draw.

As I run through St Werburgh's to snag some roads and on aimlessly through Chorlton centre, glimpses of Christmas movies play in my mind and I'm reminded that Damon Gough hails from Chorlton. Otherwise known as Badly Drawn Boy, he wrote and performed the soundtrack of one of my favourite non-Christmas-Christmas-movies; About a Boy starring Hugh Grant. The title of which seems rather apt as I pause in a back street as two excitable children in pyjamas come into the living room of a grand house, the room only lit by the lights on a glistening tree. Dad comes in, ushering them away from the tree and no doubt the bounty of gifts and toys at its base. They leap and bounce around his legs as he leads them away out of sight. A picture book of my own childhood memories and giants no longer here cascade through my mind.

I smile, blow into my gloved hands and move on. The trail of coloured lights leading me home. 18 frosty roads added to my tally.

Thursday 18ᵗʰ February 2021 – 17.88km – The Jewel in Didsbury's Crown.

Heading on the wintry trail of a secret garden born out of heartbreak.

The trouble with stopping is starting again. Aside from the seasonal stomp on Christmas morning, I'd not run for about three months. It's not unusual for me to take a break in January to recover mind, body and soul from the excessive workload of November and December. Yet this year, I've really struggled to get restarted. The temporary lockdown to save Christmas has mutated into a full-blown crisis that has even eclipsed the terrifying first wave. The daily figures of infections and deaths have made staggeringly grave reading and Covid has been releasing newer variants quicker than we can invent and approve new vaccines. All in all its left me – like so many others – numbed to the point of inaction. I have still been working daily, but the thought of heading out for a run has been trampled by an instinct to hunker down and hide from the outside world. And eat and eat and eat.

Yet, as the lockdown and the amazing roll out of the vaccines take effect on the daily figures, I know it's time. Laying out my kit the night before, I ambush myself with a terrifyingly early start that sees me out running on the streets before the strong inner rebel wakes up. It's 4.50A.M. and unsurprisingly, I have the dark streets all to myself.

Headed south and east, I head for Didsbury and a park born out of tragedy. On the way there, I soon find myself running along Nell Lane. I plod past the houses and the school and despite feeling heavy and decidedly breathy, I am warming up nicely. Then I pass the last house, run around a kink in the road and recall that the next half mile heads between the two halves of Southern Cemetery.

'No big deal.' I say to myself, looking idly forward and back at the strip of empty tarmac disappearing off into the distance. The white street-lights bathe the damp road with a shimmering brightness that only makes the sky above and graveyards beyond the trees on either side even inkier in their blackness.

'No problem.' I mutter, the lack of colour bar the muted grey-green of the grass beyond the fences gives the scene a monochrome aesthetic that instantly reminds me of a poster for The Exorcist. Thank you brain, but that's not particularly helpful. I stop to take a picture and a selfie, to prove to others I wasn't being a wimp and I realised the longer I looked around, the less scared I was. There was nothing to worry about, it's just a road, it was all in my min-

<CRACK>

A noise like a foot stepping on a dead branch comes from the graveyard and I resume my training with a valiant attempt to break the speed of fear all the way into West Didsbury.

Panting somewhat indecently, I cross Barlow Moor Road close to Palatine Road and start ticking off roads between the main road and the meandering River Mersey. This is a place of wealth, where the rich Victorian industrialists chose to live in their large mansions on the edge of the city, the crisp clean air a long way from the smoggy purgatory of their worker's slums. Not that there's much to see even in the daylight, the large houses hide behind high hedges and foreboding gateways. But for an occasional chimney, gable-end or replacement block of apartments you might not know anyone lived here at all.

The latter introduces me to an exciting new game of awkwardness and peril. According to my map, Larke Rise is a road. According to reality, Larke Rise is a gated community.
The gate is open, permanently or temporarily I cannot discern. I pause and check my map again. I look inside and realise I have to bag the road. Stepping over the threshold, I see there is no push button for an exit on either the road gates or the pedestrian gate. I stand suspiciously waiting for the gates to close, sure they're on a timer, but they don't. So starts a recurring problem across many runs I've since dubbed the Gate Game. It requires a grown adult to act like a nine-year-old and double-dare oneself to run into the forbidden land and back again before the gates have a change of mind and close, locking in said child. Giggling mischievously is entirely optional. Rushing back from the far end like a tragically low-budget urban remake of Indiana Jones, I clutch onto my hat and make it out just in time for the gates to be exactly where they were when I entered. Phew!

Close by are Marie Louise Gardens, the hidden park fuelled by sorrow. Back in the 19th century, Johann Silkenstadt came to Manchester from Bremen, Germany and made a fortune as a cotton merchant. Marrying Josephine Genthe, they settled in West Didsbury and had a single child; Marie Louise in 1865. Marie Louise married and moved into a purpose-built mansion next door to her parents on Palatine Road. Sadly just three years after being married, Marie Louise died of Peritonitis in October 1891, aged 26. Her father, Johann also died around a year later. Tragedy continued in 1901 when Josephine's son-in-law who was serving in the Boer War, disappeared at sea off the coast of Madagascar, while recovering from a wound. In just ten years, Josephine, had lost her partner, daughter and son-in-law, leaving her alone and with no immediate family. Carrying her pain with dignity, she put her heart, soul and wealth into creating a park for the public to enjoy that would forever keep her daughter's memory alive. The gardens opened in 1903 and they remain a precious arboreal haven of tranquillity. Situated beside a busy road and raised above the eye line and traffic, many passers-by remain oblivious to the serene sanctuary just beyond the shrubbery. With seventy-two different types of mature trees from all around the world growing here, it's a place for a quiet contemplation and watching the incredibly tame and portly squirrels. Hidden in plain view, it feels like a clandestine place, unspoilt by the masses, visitors nodding to one another as if part of a secret club. Everyone's welcome, just don't tell anyone else.

Feeling as unfit and lethargic as one of Marie Louise's nut-nibbling greys, I cut my run short. Satisfied with my modest haul of 31 streets, I begin the long, plodding kilometres back through the darkness to my front door. No, I didn't run past the cemetery.

Friday 26th February 2021 – 19.63km – Northern Dawn in Northernden

Doves frontman Jimi Goodwin wrote a song about the suburb where he and guitarist Jez Williams used to live. Berating other nearby Mancunian suburbs and Stockport, he hails post-lunch band life in Northenden. I obviously can only concur slightly with the sentiment of the most underrated Mancunian indie band in a generation, in that I equally have little interest in the roads of Stockport...

Lockdown is still the talk of the country and it feels a little taboo to be out running, especially as I've gone by car. This isn't essential travel and while not illegal or wrong, I can't help but feel a little subconscious driving the dark empty streets through Didsbury. It's only a five kilometre journey through the back streets, but I couldn't face another long running 'commute' to my workplace on the streets.

So, after parking up just south of the River Mersey at 6am, I quickly distance myself from the car, as if some patrolling Victorian policeman will spot me, blow his whistle and follow me with his colleagues on a furious chase around the surrounding streets. It'd sure help my pace.

Setting off along Orchard Road West, I quickly leave the stereotypical 1930's semi-detached houses with their curved bay windows and peaked gables and drift into an estate with darker bricks and uniformity that reminds me of the curving roads of Wythenshawe to the south. Curving around onto a main road, I stumble across the crisp, white, Art Deco frontage of the former Forum Cinema, now the largest Jehovah's Witness Kingdom Hall in the country. Looping back and forth between Longley Lane, Palatine Road and Church Lane, I reach the small village green beside St Wilfrid's Church and Northenden's Conservation Area. This area is much prettier and much older, a relic of times long past.

Northenden's development is one of a rural riverside idyll repeatedly jostled and threatened by noisy neighbours. With the river, motorways on three sides, Sharston industrial estate to the south and the sprawling estates of Wythenshawe beyond, Northenden almost feels like an island looking in towards its village centre rather than outwards to the world. Mentioned in the Domesday Book as Norwordine, its name derives from the Anglo-Saxon for 'north enclosure'. For centuries, it was the farming village closest to the only place where people could ford the Mersey between Stockport and Sale. This led to it being on the major route for the transportation of precious salt mined in Cheshire, passing up through Manchester and northwards into Lancashire. It prospered on this passing trade throughout the medieval period, the village and surrounding farms part of the estate owned by the Tattons of Wythenshawe Hall. Tenant farmers used the water mill on the banks of the river to grind their corn for a fee. The mill owner just so happened to be the Tattons family of Wythenshawe Hall. I dare say the Tattons charged five groats extra per hessian sack at the mill checkout too. Or twenty-five groats for a wheelbarrow for life. Mill Lane, Boat Lane and a roaring weir are all that remain of the spot where the mill and a small row-boat ferry service once stood.

In 1862, Palatine Road gained a stone bridge across the river and suddenly Northenden was accessible as a place for the middle classes to commute to Manchester. A horse-drawn bus took passengers from the Church Inn to the tramway terminus in West Didsbury, from where they could travel to anywhere in the centre. The wealthy of Withington and Didsbury also headed in the opposite direction, travelling down to the river in their leisure time for a taste of country life. Northenden once more took advantage of this influx of visitors and reinvented itself as something of a local tourist destination. Pleasure gardens, boats for hire and cruises up and down the river thrived on this Victorian desire for rural escape. Farmers brought their fresh produce to sell to the visitors and a handful of pubs sprang up beside the water; the largest being the Tatton Arms (then The Boathouse) – built by the Tatton Family, who else. It has been closed since 2007 and derelict for over a decade, but finally might be saved and converted into apartments.

Further east and surrounded by a new estate is the Grade II listed mansion of Rose Hill. Now converted into flats, it was once the home of Northenden's most notable family; the Watkins. Absalom Watkin fought for voting reform and repeal of the Corn Laws, but it was his son Sir Edward Watkin, who led a far more interesting life. An MP for much of his life, he was also a railway entrepreneur who helped manage and build several railways in Britain and across the vast lands of Canada. He started to build a channel tunnel, before fear of a French invasion halted the digging. He also set up a vast pleasure garden and amusement park in 1894 outside London, with a railway link to bring the masses out of the city. Hugely successful for a while, the centrepiece was to be grand tower forty-five metres taller than the Eiffel Tower. Sadly subsidence and a lack of funds stopped it mid-construction. Later, this area was used for the British Empire Exhibition with Wembley Stadium built exactly where Watkin's Tower would have stood.

At the front of the house is a glacial erratic boulder mounted on a stand, brought here by Watkins in 1892 from nearby Woodhouse Lane

Farm. The Shar Stone, as it is known, gave Sharstone Hall its name and subsequently all of the surrounding area. I can't help think this is the rich grown-up equivalent of a boy bringing home a nice pebble he found on a walk. No doubt he would proudly point it out to many of the interesting and famous visitors to Rose Hill through the years, including three Prime Ministers and Charles Dickens. One can only imagine the tales told around the dinner table and over port and cigars inside Rose Hill.

Returning to my car in the morning gloom, I notice the motorway flyover soaring over the river and Palatine Road and recall that Doves recorded a B-side called 'The M62 song', which they recorded beneath a motorway close to their homes in Northenden. They called it M62, only later learning the motorway was now called the M60, but kept their mistake because it scans better. You know, I'm starting to think Doves can't be trusted at all when it comes to advice for this challenge.

A solid 58 roads caught by the river today.

Friday 5ᵗʰ March 2021 – 8.02km – Morse Code

In one of the least inspiring origin tales, Burnage is thought to derive its name from 'brown hedges', common around here in the medieval period. I'll be sure to keep an eye out for any still surviving. Burnage village is much further to the north, with this end suburban and filled with semi-detached houses from the 1930's and 40's. With the traffic thundering past and the main railway line parallel to it, the area has the air of a transitionary place, a place to pass through on the way to the motorway or into the city centre.

Having seemingly spent much of the last six months running in the dark, I hedged my bets by not only going out in the afternoon, but also on the way home from work! Parking up close to Parrs Wood and the border – no brown hedges - with Heaton Mersey, I step out into the bewildering light, self-conscious of the stares of random passers-by. Heading around a couple of roads in this corner of Burnage, I swiftly tick off a few roads around Burnage Lane, which at one time thrived with weaver's cottages, the residents making cloth on a loom in their homes. Heading along a side street, I step out onto Kingsway, the main dual carriageway at the heart of the suburb, named after King George V. I'm sure he was delighted.

Pushing on up the main road I reach one end of Lane End Road and divert along it to find the other. Here in 1906, next to what was once Lane End village, Swiss engineer Hans Renold built his factory manufacturing his great invention, one still used in machinery and bicycles today; roller chain. Employing upwards of 1500 people, his factory was at the centre of Burnage life for eighty years. Renold was an enlightened boss, championing workers rights by setting up a 'shorter' 48-hour working week, a canteen, social clubs, a sickness fund and even a golf course. The factory closed down in the eighties, with the site now home to a housing estate and a large supermarket. Yet, one hidden fragment remains in situ. Alongside Lane End Lane, as it heads past Tesco's and on into the Heatons area of Stockport, are some solid iron railings. Painted black and in good condition, they were likely made in the metal foundry within Renolds and retained when the supermarket levelled everything else. Interestingly, on each post, there's a small cross motif representing the flag of Switzerland, a tiny reminder of the Swiss man who made his mark on Burnage life.

Further north up the dual carriageway I find myself on Daneholme Road. It was here at number 2 in the 1940's that a famous actor was raised. The son of a lorry driver who was often away working and a mother who left when he was only seven and his younger brother five, he grew up fast. In a tight, friendly community, he and his brother were often left with neighbours or learnt quickly to look after themselves. Just around the corner from his house was the Odeon cinema and like many excited children across the country in the late forties and early fifties, he was a regular at their Saturday morning Cinema club. Unlike most kids though, this future star would get on stage and tell jokes during the interval, in a love of performing that would see him become one of most loved and missed actors of his generation. The actor was John Thaw and whether as D.I. Jack Regan in the Sweeney, Henry Willows in Home to Roost, James Kavanagh in Kavanagh QC, as Inspector Endeavour Morse in 33 feature length episodes of Inspector Morse or any of the scores of TV, Film and Stage productions; all those performances started here amongst the characters and community of Burnage.

Back down the other side of Kingsway I traverse the many cul-de-sacs between Parrs Wood Road and the railway line, seemingly running forever but making little progress southwards back towards my car. Beneath a cloudy sky on a grey day, I start to feel cold, hungry and more than a little tired. With one last push, I check my map and decide to bag one last street: Saddlewood Avenue. The most innocuous road in all of Burnage, it's a pleasant cul-de-sac and no doubt full of good people, but it's a strider's idea of torture. At nearly three hundred metres long, I knew there'd likely be an alleyway at the dead end to provide me with a shortcut back onto Kingsway.

There was no alleyway, there was no ginnel, snicket, passage, walk or lane. There was no shortcut back onto Kingsway, not even a hedge. Crushed, I turned and staggered wearily back the way I came. Sometimes I wake up with a start at night as I'm still running along Saddlewood Avenue. It wasn't my finest hour nor the best running scheduling, but 24 roads isn't a bad reward for forty weary minutes of work.

Sunday 7th March 2021 – 26.49km – Paradise Lost?

After this pandemic is all over, the graves festooned with flowers and the new world begins, we might reflect on the cultural and historical losses buried deep under the devastating headlines. Today, I saw just such a relic of the past, quietly and irreplaceably condemned, putting to a close a place of beguiling wonder dating back to 1834.

Running every street in Manchester brings with it many surprises and little nuggets of history faded from all but the memories of a few. Some areas in Manchester require a little more digging, a little more sifting through the layers for the stories and news of what shaped a place's fortunes or failures. Then there's Belle Vue, a name synonymous with fun, excitement, wonder and joy.

Parking up on Northmoor Road, I sit in the car. It's 7am on a Sunday morning and -2C (Real-feel -6C). Safe to say, I'm not greatly enthused at leaving its warmth. Nonetheless, I prise myself out of the door and start a bone-chilling stomp around the nearby streets. Turning onto Kirkmanshulme Lane, I'm reminded that Ethel 'Sunny' Lowry lived on this street; one of the first women to swim the English Channel back in 1933. That must have been truly freezing. She completed the feat on her third attempt and after nearly sixteen hours in the water. This coming after her support boat lost her on her first attempt the year before and only found her because they glimpsed her red hat when lightning illuminated the skies. A tough, brave woman, I channel her resilience and head up onto Hyde Road. Here, opposite the aptly named Belle Vue Street, I find a plaque on the site of the former entrance to the epicentre of entertainment in the North for over a century.

Belle Vue began as a small zoological gardens in 1836, but rapidly expanded, adding a boating lake, firework displays, staged battles, wrestling and boxing bouts, concerts, dancing, tearooms, grottos and mazes in the formal gardens. They also got more and more exotic animals such as bears, monkeys, kangaroos, lions, hippos, giraffes and rhinos. A star attraction was Maharajah the elephant who provided rides for children around the zoo. Originally bought from Edinburgh Zoo in 1872, he was due to travel by train but duly destroyed his carriage with his trunk. I'm not an animal expert, but that seems like a firm 'No!' to rail travel from Maharajah. So instead, he and his keeper walked to Manchester from Scotland in a journey that took ten days. The mind boggles. In a time of little concern for animal welfare, the animals were more living exhibits than part of the breeding and conservation programs of modern zoos. Nonetheless, for the children and adults of smoke-filled streets and black and white films, this must have seemed as alien and exciting as a visit to the moon.

After the First World War, Belle Vue changed ownership and direction, developing into an amusement park alongside the zoo, with attractions such as the dodgems, flying seaplanes, a ghost train, caterpillar, a scenic railway and a water chute. Then came Bob's; the iconic wooden coaster that rattled, thrilled and terrified visitors for the best part of fifty years, its latticework hills and curves a striking part of the Manchester skyline. Innovation followed innovation, Belle Vue gained several ballrooms, put on a big-top circus and built the country's largest bingo hall. The athletics ground built in 1887 for football, cricket, rugby league, baseball was converted in 1929 to become the first purpose built speedway track in the country. Another new stadium at the other end of the site became the first place outside America to put on oval-track greyhound racing. Meanwhile the grand Kings Hall, used as tearooms and for exhibitions and dances also held concerts from the likes of Nat King Cole, Johnny Cash, The Rolling Stones, The Who, Led Zeppelin and Jimi Hendrix. At its height, Belle Vue was getting over two million visitors a year.

The decline would be gradual as attitudes changed to animal welfare and transport to better zoos and theme parks such as Chester, Blackpool and Alton Towers became more accessible. A couple of fires in the fifties and sixties didn't help, with the remaining attractions now looking old-fashioned and tired. The gardens finally closed in the late eighties, a hundred and fifty years after it first opened.

After three-quarters of an hour grafting around the suburban streets south-east of Annie Lees playing fields (named after the city's first socialist woman councillor), I return to Kirkmanshulme Lane and pass the old greyhound stadium, still standing, but condemned by the lockdowns to demolition and replacement by a housing estate. Faced with no paying customers, no appetite for virtual races nor governmental support, it and the racing community it supports are no more. It's only duty during the pandemic that finished it off – somewhat ironically – has been to host a walkthrough Covid test centre in its car park. This last standing piece of the north-west's colourful wonderland will shortly crumble and leave its legacy only in the memories of those who found here a fantastical escape from their humdrum world, if only for a short while.

Yet, while Belle Vue and all its lakes, rides, animals and stadiums might be gone, its name lives on next door at the National Speedway stadium, built in 2016 and home of the Belle Vue Aces – the club formed in 1928. With 72 completed roads complete, I leave the area with a sense of melancholy and wonder and a faint tang of regret that I live at a different time to when Manchester had its own terrifying rollercoaster.

Monday 15th March 2021 – 13.74km – Opportunity seldom knocks twice

Parrs Wood for the stars that could and those just misunderstood...

With my list of roads still to be run seemingly as long as ever and 13 months already flown by since I started, I realised I had to get out more than I was doing. While my tired legs didn't want to run after a long day at work, if I mentally could, then I physically must. So after a quick change in the car Clark Kent would have approved of, I clambered out onto School Lane for a wee pootle around and about East Didsbury.

Beneath the kind of cloudy blue skies only seen in the Simpsons titles, I loosen up my tightening muscles around a couple of roads of semi-detached houses before reaching the crossroads of Parrs Wood Road. Here, where a modern apartment block stands opposite the Parrs Wood Pub, is the location of the Capitol Theatre. Built as a cinema in 1931, it's real place in cultural history comes with its conversion into television studios for ABC Weekend Television in 1956. They filmed early episodes of hit British espionage thriller 'The Avengers' here; with Patrick Macnee as the sharp suited and bowler-hatted John Steed. As was the talent contest show 'Opportunity Knocks' hosted by Hughie Green. Long before Simon Cowell and the big red crosses, it was this black and white show with its audience 'Clap-o-meter' and weekly postal voting that catapulted acts from the pubs and clubs circuit to nationwide fame. The glory and fortune of national television could lead to a Royal Variety performance, their own television show or more likely a summer season on the pier in Great Yarmouth or a pantomime stint in Hull or Doncaster. Oh no it wouldn't. Oh yes it would!

I would know, I saw a fair few of them as a child; Bobby Crush, Little and Large, Michael Barrymore, Max Boyce, Billy Pearce, Les Dennis, The Grumbleweeds...

My therapist says I'm progressing and the night terrors will stop any decade now.

Far more interesting, to me at least, is a list of the acts that were obviously stars of their own heads and had a go. Women like Gladys Brocklehurst – a buxom cotton-mill girl who supplemented her singing act by her grabbing her husband Norman's hair and slapping him in the face, 'for the fun of it.' Some of the acts on the show at the Capitol theatre really do conjure up a sense of what constituted as entertainment at the time. Their names throw up a lot more questions than answers: The Brass Tacks, The Army Drill Team, The Almondbury Handbell Ringers, The In-Sect, The Original Vikings, The Foggy Mountain Ramblers, The

Defenders with Deirdre, The Crazy Tramps, The Blackpool Gamblers, The Pendlebury Legionaries Trad Jazz Band, The Crackpots, The Small Four, Dick 'n' Twink and Renaldo the Rebounder. So many studded and sequinned costumes still gathering dust in grandparents' wardrobes somewhere.

Manchester Polytechnic later bought the studios and made it the home of their theatre and television school, seeing performances from the likes of Julie Walters and Bernard Hill. Comedians Steve Coogan and John Thomson also studied here as drama students in the 1980's. In their free periods they would often head to the Parrs Wood Pub opposite, much to the annoyance and irritation of the local, hard-nosed boozers. The characters within and grief they got would eventually evolve into Coogan's student-hating character Paul Calf, with Thomson playing his friend Fat Bob in the subsequent TV series. After the theatre closed and was demolished, the school moved to a faculty on Oxford Road with its own 140-seat theatre. It retains the Capitol name.

Heading back along School Lane and in and out of the side roads, I soon find myself on a good pace and almost enjoying myself. So much so, I ambitiously head a little further over towards Wilmslow Road and sweep up and down the roads over there. Like a Pacman hungry for the nodes that mark out the roads I'm collecting, I ignore the growing heaviness in my legs and keep pushing on. Mistake. Heading east along Fog Lane and coming in and out of the long dead ends, I feel the familiar sense of weariness and know the easy running purring engine had spluttered to a halt and I was now moving onto the chug-chug-chug of the sluggish fat-burning diesel. So I stopped by Fog Lane Park to catch my breath and steel myself for what was going to be a long 4-5km on empty back to the car. As I take a picture of a crèche of lost gloves lined up along the metal fence, I'm reminded that this park was also the football playground of the young Gallagher brothers from Burnage. In the music video of one of Oasis' first singles – Shakermaker - Noel and Liam play on the football pitch in the park.

Digging deep, I start the trudge along Fog Lane, cursing my equal traits of stupidity and stubbornness. I've never been more than a kilometre from my car, yet I know I would regret cutting my run short. A quitter I am not. On another day, I might have marvelled more at another interesting lodge guarding The Drive, a remnant of the driveway leading to a long-demolished grand house that once stood here surrounded by extensive gardens; Catterick Hall. Built at the beginning of the nineteenth century, the Red Cross used it as a Hospital during the First World War.

Fighting my own battles, I find myself nearing the car just as the schools kick out, all the pavements filling with mums with scooters, dads with pushchairs and tired, hungry munchkins desperate to get home for some food. Even with a pleasing 47 roads gathered, I empathise greatly.

Sunday 21st March 2021 – 17.90km – A Tale of Two Cities

I set off today on the faint trail of two stars. One born in Rangoon, Burma before becoming one of Britain's most loved sitcom actors and another person so famous and influential, he made the Time magazine's list of the most important people of the Twentieth Century. But, before we get starry eyed at these tales of rags to riches, we must get back in our lane.

In the Nineteenth century, Great Britain was a nation of strict classes; of landed gentry, middle management and then the dispensable workers, horses and livestock. The last three not necessarily in that order. Upward mobility was rare and somewhat frowned upon. The rigidity of the right education and upbringing excluded the masses from a world of different rules and etiquette. Yet in Manchester, the rapid development of the cotton industry meant floods of money poured into the city from around the world, making many business owners fabulously wealthy in a short space of time. While the long-term wealthy had their country estates to escape the smoke and steam, there was a market for providing these 'nouveau riche' with somewhere to live. And so the Victoria Park estate was born.

Originally laid out in the gap between Manchester and the township of Rusholme in 1837, it was an ambitious scheme to build large mansions and villas on a private seventy-acre estate. Fraud, drainage problems and an economic downturn meant it was a slow sell, but gradually this gated-community (entry to the estate incurred a toll) took off as a place for professional classes to escape the grime and boorishness of the common hoi-polloi.

Stretching my legs on Daisy Bank Road at the heart of the estate, I'm immediately struck by the elegant row of Georgian villas set back from the road with their manicured lawns and mature trees to the fore. Unlike Didsbury where the atmosphere was one of secrecy and hiding away, these are bold houses flaunting their wealth. I get the sense that as this estate grew, it was a chance for the architects of the day to show what they had learnt and what they could do. The area of Victoria Park has twenty listed buildings including the Grade-I listed First Church of Christ, Scientist designed by famous Arts and Crafts architect Edgar Wood. I stop as I pass it, taking in the expressionist, art-nouveau church. It's unlike any other I've ever seen, yet nearly 120 years after it was built, it still looks modern, interesting and inviting. Famous residents of Victoria Park included political activists Richard Cobden and Emmeline and Richard Pankhurst, conductor and pianist Charles Halle – who formed the Halle

Orchestra in 1857 and pre-Raphaelite painter Ford Madox Brown.

Ford Madox Brown's is responsible for Manchester's answer to the Sistine Chapel in the Great Hall of the town hall. His masterpieces were the twelve Manchester Murals telling the story of Manchester. Begun in 1879, it would be fourteen years before they were complete, Brown dying later the same year, aged 72. Hidden away in the town hall for so long, it's hopeful these magnificent works of art get their due appreciation when the Town Hall completes its visitor centre for tourists in 2024.

Heading north up Anson Road onto Upper Brook Street, I once more get a melancholy feeling as I pass the hospital. The Manchester Royal Infirmary has been on Oxford Road since 1909, but its history dates back to 1752 and a hospital built three years later on Lever's Row - where Piccadilly Gardens is in the city centre now. Over the last 112 years, the current hospital has expanded many times, taking away some delightfully named streets, albeit a collection of names sure to trigger some people's OCD. For on one side of the main road, there was a terraced street called January Street, to the south and running parallel was February St. Further down the road we get March St, April St, May St, June St, July St and then the town planner obviously lost faith in calendar months and crossed the road to start on seasons. Here we get the wonderful Spring Street, the bright Summer Street and the wistful Autumn Street, before yet again the town planner leaps onto grains grown in the UK. Rye Street, Oats Street, Wheat Street and Corn Street follow, but no sign of Barley Street. I can't help but think this town planner probably struggled at Crosswords. After so many changes over the last century, the only surviving road yet to fall to the bulldozer is Autumn Street.

Turning away, I nip in and out of several roads around a pretty, little park and come out onto Plymouth Grove. Here on the corner of Swinton Grove is the home of a literary giant. Described in her obituary in 1865 as 'one of the greatest female novelists of all time', this was the family home of Elizabeth Gaskell. Most famous for her novels; North & South, Mary Barton, Ruth and Cranford, she also wrote the biography of her friend, Charlotte Bronte. A large Regency-style villa, it is well-preserved as a museum where visitors are encouraged to sit, touch and linger in the rooms where the likes of Bronte, Halle and Charles Dickens – yes him again – came to visit or stay.

Leaving Victoria Park behind, I cross Plymouth Grove and Stockport Road to a small Ardwick estate synonymous with a failed solution to a familiar problem. Unlike the wealthy, the working classes were reliant on the Council to improve their living conditions, which they did with gusto between the world wars. Clearing slum after slum, the city for a time was the greatest builder of council houses in the country. Alas after World War II, when the country was effectively broke, the rot set in and the city admitted nearly 70,000 of its homes were 'grossly unfit'. The solution was the bulldozer and bright ideas. Unfortunately, instead of replacing like for like with modern improvements, the council seemingly tapped into its vanity. A simple problem therefore required a radical solution displaying how the old leaders on the council are modern and enlightened. Or at least more modern and enlightened than their peers in neighbouring towns and cities. So, houses and traditional bricks would never do, instead they chose high-rise towers and 'streets in the sky' built with brutal lines in concrete.

Here on Coverdale Crescent was one such monstrosity; a pebble-dashed undulating wall of maisonettes climbing up to ten storeys high and looking like the architect had just heard of Minecraft and Tetris. Built in 1972 from pre-cast components like a cheap, flat-pack wardrobe, locals were less than impressed with its stark skyline, labelling the imposing block, Fort Ardwick. Worse still, this was the seventies Britain, so sadly new buildings were about as reliable as new cars. Within a decade, the roofs leaked, steel components were rusting, concrete panels cracking and window frames rotting. The only happy inhabitants were the vermin and fungus on the walls. By the late eighties, the council sent the bulldozers back in and pulled the whole lot down. Running these clean, meandering streets amidst modest red brick homes and plenty of greenery, it seems unfeasible that this was once a place of hi-rise misery, broken promises and such an ugly vision of the future.

On down New Bank Street, I run past the endlessly long engine sheds of Longsight railway sidings, the rumble of a locomotive creeping out ready for service filling the air with its diesel fumes and roaring engine. I can't help but imagine the daily racket of clanking, puffing and whistles as the old steam engines shunted carriages to and fro in the nineteenth and twentieth centuries. It's here that two very different, but strangely similar famous people stayed, one much longer than another.

The first was a Londoner who was the son of two musical hall performers in a difficult upbringing. At the age of 9, he was touring the country's music halls as part of a popular clog-dancing troupe called Eight Lancashire Lads. During this tour in 1899, he stayed for six weeks at 64 Morton Street (roughly between Edlin Close and Martindale Crescent today) and attended a nearby school – see July 18th 2021 entry. This young dancer had loftier comedic aspirations that would eventually take him from the stage to the silent silver screen and worldwide stardom. His name was Charles Spencer Chaplin.

The second star was born in south-east Asia but moved to live with his Aunt in Ardwick after his mother died when he was just eighteen months old. Growing up on Earl Street (now known as Cochrane Avenue) before moving to Wythenshawe, he became an actor starring on television and in films such as The Bargee and Carry On Screaming. His most famous comedic role though was about someone at the bottom of the pile aspiring to rise up and better himself, but always foiled by life, society and his cantankerous dad. Star of Steptoe and Son, he was Harry H Corbett.

Just two stories of tens of thousands, these two made it away from the noise and grime for a different life of wealth, comfort and respect. As I leave the ticking engines of the sidings behind and return to the peaceful birdsong on Daisy Bank Road, I'm reminded that even less than a kilometre apart, people can live very different lives in very different cities and rarely do the inhabitants change lanes. 54 streets added to the total, none of them built in the sky.

Wednesday 24ᵗʰ March 2021 – 19.41km – Halfway

Baguley has a strange, tenuous connection between an eleventh century French knight's squire and a Hollywood male gigolo. Now, there's a sentence you weren't expecting!

Before six and it's already the murky twilight of an overcast Mancunian dawn, the kind where the sun creeps in late while the teacher's still writing on the board, hoping no-one will notice. I'm in the oldest part of this south-western suburb of Manchester amidst a couple of rows of farm labourers cottages and bigger houses. Everything has a pleasing solid, old, weathered appeal and if you ignore the tram stop on one side and the sprawling council estate surrounded all the other sides, you could be back in this once rural hamlet. Squinting also might help. This tiny hamlet is old, very old, in fact it was mentioned in the Domesday Book of 1086. So long have people dwelled here, its name comes from old English, from the words for Badger (Bagca) and Wood (Leah).

Like many places, it's history hides in plain sight, captured like a fly in amber in its street names. Here there's the standard town planner staple of roads named after pretty English towns and villages; Cranleigh Drive, Ferndown Road, Winterslow Ave, etc. But, amidst these evocative names of sleepy rural idylls, we find New Forest Road, Blackwood Drive, Brownwood Close, Maple Road, Woodlands Drive, Fairwood Road, Green Oak Drive, Woodwise Lane and Rowan Avenue. If only there was some kind of common theme to link all these together, some connection of sorts. I can't help but think it's staring me in the face, I'll maybe come back to it.

Baguley was one of several manors in the area granted to the squire of a Norman baron killed in Shropshire in a subsequent battle after the Battle of Hastings. Hamo de Mascy was there on the day William the Conqueror invited himself over to Britain for a permanent palatial holiday in 1066, the new king rewarding him with a small parcel of his new kingdom. Changing his name and basing himself in the village of Dunham, he became a baron; he and his descendants lording it over Agden, Bowdon, Hale and Little Bollington from Dunham Massey Hall for centuries. In the early 13ᵗʰ century, one of his descendants - Matthew Massey - was granted land in Bromhale, Duckenfield and Baggiley (Bramhall, Dukinfield and Baguley), moving to Baggiley and taking up the name. Later in the late 13ᵗʰ century, a William de Baggiley was already a well-thought of member of the aristocracy, backed by the wealth from his family's Cheshire salt mines when he took a further step upwards. Marrying Lucy Corona, one of King Edward the First's

146

illegitimate daughters, he gained a knighthood for his trouble. This, if I recall correctly, was an option my school careers advisor failed to tell me about. To be fair, he was still struggling to explain how no qualifications would have any bearing on my designs to be a Ghostbuster.

Of course, Baguley is no longer a tiny hamlet on a baronial estate. Manchester happened. The 1930's Cheshire land grab happened. Wythenshawe happened. Over the centuries, the Baguleys married themselves widely through the well-to-do families of England and beyond, leaving one strange cultural quirk that I hinted about at the beginning of this run. In some colonial quarters of England's own extended visits abroad, the name Baguley gave way to a different spelling; Bigalow. Which brings us to the Rob Schneider film of 1999 – Deuce Bigalow: Male Gigolo – of which the least said the better, I think.

Being Wythenshawe, albeit the nearest part to Sale and Timperley, it's not a run that will live long in the memory. Hardly any of the roads are straight, they curve and curl and twist and turn, seemingly for their own amusement. That said, after a long and drab winter full of depressing news and isolation, there's a sense of optimism in the cherry blossom, daffodils and budding trees. Life goes on, nature has little interest in our woes and runs to its own timetable, come what may. Popping out of the looping estate, I hit the straight-as-an-arrow Brooklands Road. Which until recently, had the strange distinction of being the only road used by the Manchester Marathon that is actually in Manchester. (The cancelled Marathon this year has a new course taking in more Manchester roads in Chorlton and the City Centre, but when I did it 2019, it was nearly all in Trafford). Heading up Brooklands Road, I keep a close eye on my map and GPS, until just north of Cheswick Close, I find what I'm looking for. Marked by nothing grander than lichen-covered stone walls on either side of this busy road is Baguley Brook. This, and two Brooklands Road street signs opposite one another mark the boundary between Manchester and Trafford, but also the most westerly section of road in Manchester. It's not the most spectacular vista, but at least I'm not staring into a bush this time.

More importantly, this run of 57 roads means I've smashed through a significant milestone in my (lunatic) quest to run every single street in Manchester. With 3155 roads complete and *only* 3120 still to do, I'm officially past the 50% mark. I'm halfway there! Well done me. Or as a certain visitor to these parts might have said nearly a millennia ago, tres bien!

147

Tuesday 30ᵗʰ March 2021 – 10.07km – Sunshine at the Biscuit Border

Willy Wonka's factory (spoiler alert) doesn't exist, but a close second in real life comes on the border between southeast Manchester and Stockport.

Another afternoon run today as I try to nudge my total of streets gained each week ever upwards with an after-work run. While running on pre-fatigued legs is supposedly where the good stuff happens regarding muscle development, fat-burning and running efficiency, it has so far been a largely less than happy experience. It's more about enduring than endurance. Still, the sun is out, the sky is blue and I feel that spring optimism of a wonderful summer laid out before me. There's a wonderful aroma in the air too, but we'll get to that later.

I park up on the wonderfully inappropriate Hardicker Street on the edge of Levenshulme (An unfortunate derivation of Hardacre, West Yorkshire, if you must know). This area is on the border of Manchester and Stockport; the two areas divided by the almost overlooked ribbon of water, the Black Brook. Like so many of Manchester's old waterways, lined with thirsty trees, it snakes it's way between back gardens and businesses, culverted under estates and factories, only noticed when the rain is so torrential it bursts it's banks. Capturing all that liquid sunshine round here and in neighbouring Heaton Chapel, the Black Brook heads west, connecting to the Cringle Brook, which connects to the Ley Brook, the Platt Brook and on into the Chorlton Brook, before finally spilling out into the River Mersey some eight or nine km away.

Stepping out, I take a glug of much cleaner water and set off into the sunshine. Working my way north up a ladder of roads between Livesey Street and Henderson Street, I soon warm up. It's only 18C but after so many cold months, it feels good on the skin and great to be back in short sleeves. I am not alone on the streets. Many of the local kids are playing outside, their mothers chatting and basking in the summery conditions. Feeling a bit awkward making my way between the stabiliser bikes, discarded dolls, balls and hula-hoops under the querying gaze of protective parents, I put on my best harmless idiot smile and plough on.

On the other side of Stockport Road, with sweat beginning to pour off me, my run becomes a bit of a trudge down Broom Avenue, bordering Highfield Country Park. This oasis of woods, ponds, pathways and escapism amidst the streets and houses started – like so many local green spaces – as a scrape for clay. The growing city having an endless hunger for the rock mineral to manufacture bricks. More interestingly besides the Brickworks, this was also a site of the UCP Tripe Works. Unthinkable

148

today, the stomach lining of cattle or sheep was big business and with the likes of oxtail and cowheel, a godsend to the poor as a source of cheap, nutritious meat. How big a business, you ask? In 1906, there were over 250 Specialist tripe shops in Manchester alone and even in the 1950s United Cattle Products had 146 restaurants across the North of England. First and last date anyone?

Thankfully, the air today around these parts smells much sweeter and enticing. Heading down to the traffic lights on the border, I look across the border to the McVities biscuit factory in the neighbouring town of Stockport. Originally a Scottish biscuit maker established in 1830, it was the First World War and the supply of biscuits to be sent to the soldiers in the trenches that saw the company open its third factory in the UK, here in Heaton Chapel in 1917. Today this factory solely makes Jaffa Cakes, Digestives and Penguin chocolate biscuits.

All of the McVities' Jaffa Cakes you've ever eaten were produced in this one building on a winding production line over a mile in length. Running day and night, seven days a week, it produces four thousand cakes a minute! That's two billion a year. Two billion(?!). Or if you'd rather; 60 tons of Jaffa Cakes a day and 15,000 tonnes a year (the equivalent weight of 30 Jumbo jets). Such is our insatiable appetite for these treats the cakes are usually packaged and boxed aboard a lorry within a couple of hours of production.

Leaving behind this Mecca to the king of cake snacks, where the air is thick with the delectable aroma of baking biscuits and warm chocolate, I feel tired and dehydrated. I need a lift, a sugar boost and something to bring me back to life. With 35 streets added to the total, I stop off on the short drive home to spend nearly as much in the co-op biscuit aisle, mainly on a particular moreish cake.

Thursday 1ˢᵗ April 2021 – 23.53km – Jams, Consumption and Fake Bird Poo

All Fool's Day. What better day to parade your eccentricities with a health giving run around a grimy industrial estate and a bustling hospital.

Back to Baguley, I parked up on Shady Lane, the real Shady Lane, not all the other Shady Lanes that are just imitating... I stood up out of my car for another trip around what's fast becoming my nadir of running reports; Wythenshawe. Hopeful rather than optimistic of discovering something interesting and insightful in the brief time this area wasn't entirely populated by a smattering of farmers and several dozen cows called Daisy, Tinkerbell and Maureen the Moo. It's only just gone six on a weekday, but it's decidedly colder than earlier in the week, the hazy skies trapping none of the heat overnight. With the mini-heatwave over the last few days coinciding with the easing of restrictions, there's been concerns of too much too soon ruining all the sacrifices made so far. Yet simply being out in the sunshine – albeit weaker this morn – is such a morale boost, I'm not surprised the parks and beaches have been so packed. The roads of Baguley, well we'll see...

Bounding around the small estate south of Altrincham Road to get warm, I soon clamber up a small rise to a bridge over the Cheshire Main Line where Baguley Railway Station once stood. Opened in 1866, it sat on the line running from Stockport to Altrincham and on to Liverpool via Warrington. Closed as a station as part of the Beeching cuts in 1964, the line still runs today but with no stop in Wythenshawe, making it the largest town in Europe without a railway station. Although promised a new station since the 1990's, several campaigns have come and gone without success. Even the likes of rock star's Johnny Marr has failed to nudge the powers-that-be into action. The latest proposal sees a HS2 (High Speed Rail) link being built out to the airport from Manchester with a station in Wythenshawe to help link it to the rest of the country.

With 7km of running around the deserted closes and pretty gardens of suburbia, including a brief mistaken dalliance across Fairywell Brook into Timperley, I head back along Altrincham Road, past Wythenshawe Town Football Club and the back-to-back supermarkets of Lidl and Tesco. Turning right, I head down Southmoor Road, collecting some side streets on the way and an unwelcome return to the joint-jarring concrete roads. Across the tram tracks and the busy road as the daily commute in car and on foot gets up to speed, I reach Wythenshawe Hospital.

Before the government launched the National Health Service in 1948 or even before the council mooted the idea of a community hospital in Wythenshawe in the thirties, this site was home to a Sanatorium. Built in 1902 for the treatment of the Tuberculosis – which largely amounted to bed rest and plenty of fresh air – Baguley Sanatorium initially had 150 beds, with the windows and doors open day and night to aid ventilation. The Sanatorium expanded until changing focus with the Second World War, treating soldiers and civilians with horrific new injuries and pioneering many new procedures for what we now call plastic surgery. After the war, investment came and the hospital expanded over the decades into one of the busiest hospitals in the North West. I self-consciously run a little way into the Hospital grounds, past a car park, bus stop and on to the helipad where the Air Ambulance lands in medical emergencies. Back out, I rush past the medics, nurses, visitors and patients milling around outside, feeling decidedly like a stranger who shouldn't be there amidst the morning traffic.

Heading north, I'm on the homeward stretch, but first I have a rather large obstacle in my path; Roundthorn Industrial Estate. It's not my first Industrial Estate, but it is my first on a weekday. I plunge myself into a world of traffic, fumes and the smells of engine oil, acetone and hot metal. I also garner the wary stares of mechanics, engineers and scaffolders at a burger van, who must wonder what the heck I am doing running these grubby, industrial streets where honest work and hard graft is the order of the day. I find Duerr's factory; the Manchester company that has been producing jam, marmalade, preserves and sweet spreads for over 130 years. Over the road is a car park which back in 2007 was the site of a film set for the Manchester-based television comedy; Shameless. Originally filmed on-site in West Gorton, local teenagers and random idiots constantly interrupted the cast and crew. So the production company rebuilt an exact replica of the fictional Chatsworth Estate here in Wythenshawe for a quarter of a million pounds. To give it an authentic appearance they had to spread over a ton of litter, plant grass and moss in the paving cracks and even drop yoghurt on the roofs to simulate bird droppings. Filming lasted for seven more series over the next six years before demolition in 2013.

Feeling tired and underestimating just how far away I was from my start point, I shamelessly trudge back to the car on heavy legs, but happily burdened with 56 Baguley streets bagged.

Monday 5th April 2021 – 25.27km – Hey Abbey Hey

'Tis Easter Monday and I have arisen.

Although I'd rather wished I hadn't. The wind had been howling most of the night and the temptation to remain in the snuggled oblivion of bed was nearly overwhelming. The inner caveman managed a powerfully persuasive argument of 'Warm good. Outside much bad!' Which was not only convincing from my soft, toasty abyss, but a compelling argument for all the days we've staggered through this last year or so. Alas the same Caveman would have me eat Pizza, chips and Jaffa Cakes until I was large enough for a Channel Five documentary and as such cannot be trusted. Besides, if I don't go out and run, I won't wear out my shoes and need to buy new ones. Runner's logic and desire for shoes in ever-brighter colours trumps all, so naturally I got up and drove to Abbey Hey.

Situated in the East of Manchester, nudging up to Gorton Reservoirs and the border with Tameside, the Gorton Township consisted of several hamlets separated by farms and fields, Abbey Hey being one such place. Although the meaning of the name is lost to time, it's known that residents with the name Abbey were recorded in the area back as far as 1320. As for the rest, Hey, your guess is as good as mine.

Nowadays, it is an area still awaiting the magic wand of regeneration. There are pockets of new houses here and there – identical but for their burgundy, olive or navy front doors – but it remains street after street of terraced houses. A sure sign of lack of interest and funds seems to manifest on the paved roads where the potholes reveal the smoothed cobbles beneath. Yet much worse lurks underfoot. On Walmer Street, a car drove into a sinkhole in the middle of the road in January. By the end of the next morning, the front of four houses had collapsed and would need demolishing, with the council, water board and fire brigade all pointing the finger elsewhere.

Hopeful for more solid ground, I alight from my car and instantly grimace. It's just 2C, cold even for early April. With the wind chill, it's a numbing -5C that stings the face and bare legs. I am just about warming through after five kilometres when I discover to my horror that my Strava is paused. My Strava is...bloomin'...paused! Sensing the inner caveman chortling heartily, I have to swallow back the disappointment, avoid being too hard on myself and spend the next twenty-five minutes re-running the same streets all over again. The sun rising to illuminate the grimy, overcast sky only adding to the thought I should have stayed in bed.

Travelling around these streets, again, it's easy to see the fight that must have gone on for the souls and minds of this industrialised community. With the local cotton mills of Gorton Mills and the nearby wadding works, the ceramics factory of Abbey Hey pottery, the leather works on Tan Yard Brow and the railway locomotive works of Gorton, this was a place of hard manual work and long hours. The two conflicting pillars of society in Victorian Britain were the Church and the Pubs. The church doors rarely opened, the latter's doors rarely closed. Running here, I see endless pubs in amongst the houses, some surviving through these lockdowns, some long since closed and converted into flats, but their shape and bricked up corner entrances unmistakeable. One can only imagine the raucous scenes on payday, ale supped by all these colleagues, neighbours, friends and enemies. Eternal friendships found at the bottom of tankards and bloody scores settled outside in the street beneath the gaslights. I find several buildings of ecclesiastical nature amongst the drab houses, although again the enthusiasm for these places has waned and they too have succumbed to the conversion to apartments. It's easy to imagine the sermons and prayers, the angst for relatives and spouses who fight, curse, philander and are led astray by the demon drink. The amount of gossip that must have endlessly swirled through these streets, the endless melodrama and scandal. And we both know who's worst for that, don't we? I say, have you heard...

Curving around a long S-bend, one of the few none straight roads I negotiate all day, that used to round the perimeter of the large Gorton cotton mill, I come across an innocuous brick bridge. Looking over the edge, I find neither a road nor railway, but a footpath on what was known locally as the Lanky Cut.

Built in 1797 and connecting the Ashton Canal to Stockport for easier transportation of coal from mines in Werneth and Denton, this was the Stockport Branch Canal. Less than 8km in length, it was nonetheless soon lined with mills and industry south of Gorton, desperate to base themselves on this superhighway of the age connecting them directly to Manchester and the world beyond. In the early years, it even carried passengers to Stockport. With the rise of rail in the early twentieth century, it fell into disrepair and by the thirties was largely derelict and overgrown with weeds. By the sixties and seventies, the canal was abandoned, filled in and grassed over. Still there is hope that one day, it will be resurrected as a canal, so visitors can once more glide serenely into the canal marina at Broadstone Mill in Stockport.

Running up a steep hill back from Hyde Road, I'm once more on a remnant of the ancient salt road running from Cheshire to Lancashire, the same route I last encountered back in Northenden. Climbing up past the listed pub on the climb; The Vale Cottage, it started hailing, not the soft kind of hailstones, but the hard, I-can't-even-open-my-eyes kind. At the top of the hill and as I head out along a country road past some allotments, the hail eased a little and switched to a snowstorm! In April! It maybe only lasted ten minutes, barely enough to cover the ground and me, but no sooner had it started, the clouds drifted away and as I reached my car, the skies were blue and the sun dazzlingly bright. Truly, four seasons in Abbey Hey.

Collecting in a rather splendidly ridiculous total of 101 completed roads. I left Abbey Hey a true Centurion of road gathering.

Friday 9th April 2021 – 24.78km - Hulme is where the Art is...

At the far north of Hulme and to the west of Deansgate Railway Station is the old ward of St George's, an area of Manchester that was once completely out of control.

The Bridgewater Canal curves through the north of St George's. Built in 1761 to bring coal from Worsley to the heart of Manchester at Castle Field Wharf, it rapidly brought coal-hungry industry to its banks in the form of textile mills, clothing factories, printers, flourmills and a brewery. With it came low-standard terracing for the masses in the surrounding streets. Haphazardly thrown together for profit rather than resident welfare, the place was rife with disease and overcrowding. In 1844, the overwhelmed council had to step in to forbid the building of any more houses in the area. Yet by the 1920's, still the people came, cramming themselves into the area; as many as 136 people were living per acre – just over half a football pitch -, four times the Manchester average. Nearly all of these rotten homes and slum communities were cleared in the 1960's and replaced by better housing in more spacious surrounds. Only with fewer workers in the area, the industry drifted away too and a slow spiral of decline set in over the following decades. Leaving the car at home I headed north this morning for a mundane housekeeping run around Hulme, picking up streets I've missed and others previously closed for building sites. Often overlooked or simply passed through, this part of Hulme has a notorious place in Manchester history as both the home of those with much blood on their hands and where a clandestine ball shocked the Victorian sensibilities of the nation.

Heading north from Chorlton, I must stray into the neighbouring borough of Trafford. The border carves deep into Manchester territory up Upper Chorlton Road and Moss Lane West before receding North West back towards Cornbrook and the Manchester Ship Canal, as if from the spoils of an inter-council war. Feeling very much like I'd dipped behind enemy lines, I assumed the steady pace of a native Trafford runner, avoided eye contact with the locals and nervously attempted to blend in amidst the foreign buses, dog-walkers and passers-by.

Once up into St George's, I find the streets an eclectic mix of houses and apartment blocks of so many styles and designs, although leaning more to the functional than the flamboyant. It's not excessively daubed in graffiti or plagued by fly-tippers, but it lacks any sense of an identity. Several apartments look new and inviting, but are often situated next to a street you'd rather not visit after dark. With the new apartments

155

going up and the tower blocks being re-clad, it feels like another area in transition, gradually getting better and awaiting the tipping point when the estate agents start sending editorials to the media about the ten reasons its now the next up-and-coming area. Running amidst these building sites and quiet streets, the world rewarded my cynicism with a chance to invite in the awkwardness.

Rounding another corner onto an obvious dead-end, I'm faced with around sixty builders of varying ages all in hard hats, heavy boots and oodles of High-Vis. Seemingly waiting outside their building site to start their shift, they chat and chomp on sandwiches for their breakfasts. I hesitate as many look up quizzically at me. Putting on my best far away stare, I plough on, weaving through the now quiet groups. Past the last one, I run the last thirty metres to the brick wall at the end of the road, the puzzled glances burning into the back of my neck. Stopping at the impenetrable wall, I sigh inwardly and turn to return through the crowd. Being odd is such a burden sometimes.

Talking of which, there's one street here that's notoriously linked perhaps to Manchester's most famous crowd. Barrack Street, south of Chester Road once led to a cavalry barracks built in 1804, that housed several hundred men and horses. In 1819, it was the 15th Hussars of Hulme Barracks that charged onto St Peter's Field to disperse the crowd of sixty thousand at Peterloo. Housing nearly thirty battalions over the 19th century, the cavalries of Hulme barracks fought at many battles including Waterloo and in the Crimea, before closing in 1914. Men stationed here included Prince Louis Napoleon, Prince Albert Victor – grandson of Queen Victoria, and Winston Churchill. All that remains today is the Grade II listed Officer's Mess, where it's said many royals dined through the years, although the interior has long since been converted to apartments.

Further north from these changing estates of social housing, I reach Chester Road, a major thoroughfare once known for its abundance of public houses serving the mill-workers in the 19th and early 20th centuries. Before the First World War, it was common for some of the pubs to open early to serve rum and coffee to the women workers on the way to their 6am shift. Other pubs had unusual enticements for their customers, such as the Egerton Inn where drinkers went in to converse with the champion-talking parrot on the bar. Or head to the Star Inn with its aquarium built into the wall of its best room. Outside in the street, barrel organs played music and an Italian man wandered around with his pet bear, who'd perform for customers for pennies. These weren't pubs for visitors or small groups of friends around a single table. These were places where everyone had their spot and conversation, banter and song included the whole room.

Running along Ellesmere Street parallel to the canal, I find a resurgence of investment, with the old mills now all apartment blocks and newer ones springing up alongside them. The trendy shops and bars arriving to serve this growing community of young professionals. Money awash where there once was none. Yet on the other side of Chester Road, much of that struggle to make ends meet continues. Such is modern life, such is Manchester.

At the end of Chester Road, the ornate Gothic Revival Church that gave the area its St George's name remains as a significant landmark next to the Mancunian Way as the western gateway to Deansgate and the city centre. Converted to apartments at the start of the new millennium, the three-storey tower apartment with bedroom in the belfry was last on the market in 2015, for a cool one million pounds. Now looking a little isolated beside such wide, bustling roads. In the 19th century, the dank, narrow cobbled streets of the mill workers surrounded the church on all sides. Running these streets would have been arduous, long-winded and no doubt dangerous, especially when the police were on an infamous stakeout.

Opposite the church, where the Mancunian Way underpass cuts through the Chester Road roundabout was roughly where the Temperance Hall on Hulme Place once stood. It was here on 24th September 1880, that the hall was booked for the "Pawnbrokers Assistants Association" Annual ball. Although the blinds were drawn and windows almost totally blocked out, the 47 lemonade-sipping revellers within (it was a Temperance hall, after all) were being watched by policemen perched on a nearby outhouse roof, looking in through a small gap in the windows. This was the culmination of a nine-month crackdown on vice after a Victorian tabloid sex scandal broke of local councillors and prostitutes in the Town Hall a year earlier. A story, perhaps best kept for another day. I mean, if I'm glossing over that, just imagine the scandalous Victorian rabbit hole down which we're about to plunge?

Back at the Temperance Hall, the 'disgraceful' scenes of harmonium playing and dancing were meticulously logged on the privy roof, while other officers lurked in alleyways nearby. The Police waited and waited as the hours passed and the revelry inside grew more raucous. Finally after waiting inexplicably for five hours for any late stragglers to arrive from as far afield as Liverpool and Sheffield, the police moved in at 2.30am. Bursting into the Temperance Hall, they shockingly caught the 47 men dancing with one another, some dressed in historical costumes and

157

around half of them dressed as women. They arrested all of the men except the harmonium player hired for the evening, who was blind and entirely unaware of what was happening around him. That or he was the quickest-thinking guy in the room. All of the arrested spent a night in prison and then charged the following morning, two received £25 fines (£2500 in today's money) for their moral outrage, many stood in court still in their dresses. Worse still, the national paper's of the time not only printed the men's names, but also their ages, occupations and addresses. Thankfully, theses prudish attitudes and the shame of the City's Victorian authorities are long gone and Manchester's thriving LGBTQ community celebrate this historical moment, linking it with their own annual 'Drag Ball'.

Without dragging out this enjoyable run much longer I detoured to snaffle a few more stranded roads and take my total for the day up to 63 more streets, before heading south down Princess Road and cutting back through my favourite park to home.

Saturday 17th April 2021 – 24.77km – Skates, Fate and Counterfeits

This was not just a run, this was an old Warehouse run...

Another day, another yin and yang explore, this time north of the city centre. The run took me around the clean and tidy new-build streets of Cheetwood, before dipping down Great Ducie Street into the shameful, litter-strewn, awfulness of Manchester's rag-trade.

Cheetwood is an area north of Strangeways and nudging up to the irregular border with Salford. In the late 19th century, this area was largely a smattering of terraced streets and Synagogues – Cheetham Hill as a whole still has a large Jewish population – built around a large undulating patch of land. This housed several clay pits and brickworks, baking the boulder clay in the hot kilns to feed the city's insatiable appetite for more houses, mills and factories. Gradually this area and the terraces were cleared, a modern suburban estate built in its place. The pinkish-brown bricked houses with their simple grass gardens and undulating curved roads and avenues made for a pleasant start to a dawn run.

I did have an awkward moment though. Running up Waterloo Road, I passed a lad in a black hoodie who obviously thought it was good sport to sprint past me and show me his pace, me obviously being an 'old' plodder. Only of course he then stopped, because running uphill is hard work and less than ten seconds later I pass him again. Fifty metres further on, I have to divert into a three-pronged cul-de-sac to tick it off my list. Returning to Waterloo Road, I see my hoodie friend now only twenty metres ahead. Again as I pass, Insane Dolt decides to go all hare on my tortoise and runs on, this time flexing his guns when slowing to a wheezy stop. Unperturbed, I pass this weird native for a fourth time and divert into another cul-de-sac. At which point my double-knotted shoelaces both inexplicably came undone at the same time and I sadly had to spend a good ten minutes retying them. Whilst squatting behind a car out of sight...because of...erm...the breeze, yeah that's it, the cold breeze.

Disappearing without a trace wasn't the fate of one Joseph Hyman, a Russian Jew fleeing persecution in his homeland at the beginning of the 20th century. Sadly, his original plan to start a new life in America didn't quite go according to plan. Leaving his family in Manchester in 1912, he bought a ticket for New York, hoping to bring them across once he was settled. He bought a ticket in third class steerage aboard a brand new ship sailing on its maiden voyage. Walking on deck in a big Russian coat one night, he felt the ship lurch beneath his feet and turn off its engines, the rhythmic throb replaced by silence. He rapidly learnt the unsinkable ship had hit an iceberg. Yes, he was aboard the ill-fated H.M.S Titanic. In the ensuing chaos, he was asked to row one of the last lifeboats to leave the ship, before being picked up by the Carpathia three hours later. Safe in New York, he saw the thriving food scene and decided to take the idea back to his waiting family in the UK, although he understandably was petrified of ever getting aboard a ship again. His cousin came to the rescue by accompanying him and getting Joseph stinking drunk for the full length of the return journey. Safely back in Manchester, he set up Hyman's kosher deli on Waterloo Road in 1913. The deli was an immediate success and known locally as 'Titanics' for four generations until its sad closure in 2016. The Hyman name continues though as the only smokehouse in Manchester that sells Smoked Salmon, cured to Joseph Hyman's original recipe.

Leaving suburbia behind, I move down Great Ducie Street into what the police have called 'Counterfeit Street'. It's here amongst the modern world of Manchester's rag-trade that the illegal trade of fake clothes, perfumes, make-up, shoes and handbags, headphones, batteries and sunglasses is rampant. No matter how many times the police raid the suspected warehouses, seize goods worth millions of lost genuine sales and convict perpetrators, others simply step in and continue as if nothing has happened. Which gives you an idea of how big this industry for the gangsters and criminals the trade ultimately supports.

Worse still, for me at least, was that this criminality and contempt for society is reflected in the streets. I have never run anywhere as litter-strewn and dirty as some of the streets here. The gutters and pavements are strewn with rubbish, the edges lined with weeds as if a scene from a poverty-stricken area of a third world country. There are completely law-abiding, clothing companies and warehouses here but the bad ones hide in plain sight. Businesses have bright, shiny signs and hoardings above fences with about twenty centimetres of rubbish sitting trapped behind the length of it. You can understand why no-one complains or wants any council clean-up crew to come visit for fear of further enquiries, so it all remains like the end of a outdoor rave or a street after a carnival. I ran like a demon around here, anxious to get away from the random spotters in loading bays and the huge guard dogs seeking a hole in their fences to get at me as I passed. Not Manchester's prettiest side, nor it's proudest claim to be the counterfeit capital of the country.

Which is a shame as amongst this mix of clandestine forgery and genuine fashion designers; there is on Derby Street both a relic of one of Britain's most-loved clothing manufacturers and a grand building known as one of Manchester's lost palaces. Amongst the modern fifties, sixties and seventies buildings on the other side of Strangeways prison, I find one much older warehouse with a distinct place in Britain's clothing heritage. Although Michael Marks and Tom Spencer's first Penny Bazaar opened in Leeds in 1884, it was here in Manchester ten years later that they moved from market stalls to opening their first store. Belarusian immigrant, Michael Marks felt at home amongst the Jewish community here and opened the store in the front room of his home at 20 Cheetham Hill Road (now roughly where the Park Inn Hotel is located). They closed the store in 1897 and expanded again to a new site on Stretford Road, but I'm here to see just how comfortable and confident they'd become in Manchester. Further up the hill and just off Cheetham Hill Road is Derby Street, where Marks & Spencer's purpose built their first HQ and Warehouse in 1901. The large four-storey brick warehouse looks a little faded and worn around the edges now, but happily it is still in use by other clothing companies, continuing the legacy of this very British institution of the high street.

Further along Derby Street is a huge clothes warehouse with an impressive stone and brick frontage. This majestic old lady of Cheetham Hill was built in 1910 and still adorns its original name proudly in stone high above its grand entrance; Manchester Ice Palace. Adorned with white marble and room for two thousand spectators, it was known at the time of its construction as the finest ice rink in the world. Hosting the National Championships in 1911, it would go on to welcome the best in the world in 1922 for the Ice Skating World Championships. One of the most popular social spots in Cheetham, it would eventually fall victim to rising costs and changing tastes, closing in 1967. Although it survives in some form to this day, English Heritage recognises it as a building of historical significance in danger of being lost.

All in all, today was a cold run around this odd mix of housing and commerce, but beneath blue skies and glorious sunshine and with just enough hills to keep it interesting, it was just the kind of run I needed. Another 87 streets bagged, nudging me over the 55% mark, which is something.

Monday 19ᵗʰ April 2021 – 25.95km – Heroes and Villains

Exactly 251 years since Captain Cook's crew first sighted the mainland of Australia, I set off on my own long voyage south to the inhabited land of Northern Moor in the suburban sea of Wythenshawe. It wasn't a good trip.

Setting off at first light on a Monday morning, I decided to run from home and multitask on the way. With letters in one hand, a stack of used books in the other and a pair of old running shoes around my neck, I set off through Chorlton looking like someone from a cheap copy of It's a Knockout. Gradually, I lightened my load at the postbox, at a charity clothes box and a neighbourhood free library. The latter is something I've seen more and more of through this pandemic and the lockdowns; people heartwarmingly putting games, books, toys and DVDs out in weatherproof containers for others to browse, swap and keep. Reminding others, they aren't alone.

Unburdened, I meandered through Chorlton Green and Chorltonville picking up an odd road or two I'd missed before crossing the River Mersey by Jackson's Boathouse pub and heading through the forbidden land of Sale Moor. All the way, I felt somewhat off, I sped up and slowed down, threw in a couple of 'strides' to reset my pace but I just couldn't settle into a rhythm, my legs fighting me whatever I did. Then after about seven kilometres, I turned off Sale Road at the border and entered the Kerscott estate in Northern Moor. Now collecting streets, I immediately found a suitable pace and perked up immensely. It bizarrely seems like I'm no longer able to enjoy a run unless I'm on new territory?! Pavlov would have a field day.

A pleasant leafy estate of modern houses built alongside the Metrolink tramline to the airport and on a former fruit farm of apple and plum orchards. Slightly ironic when the original residents of the Wythenshawe Garden City all got to choose either an Apple or Cherry tree for their back garden as part of a drive for sustainable, healthy eating and a grow your own mentality. Following a sinuous route with only an occasional side street to worry about, I could happily switch off and enjoy the running rather than constantly looking at my map. Emerging to Wythenshawe Road, I turn and head northeast through the estate to Button Lane where a certain local legend grew up.

Certain Mancunians allow the allure of fame and fortune to change their ways and never look back, especially those from the less glamorous areas of the city. Others bravely stand up for those less fortunate than them and take those injustices right to the very top. At 110

162

Button Lane, one such man stepped out of his comfort zone to do just that. Manchester United striker Marcus Rashford grew up here, playing football on the semi-circular patch of grass outside his home, long before the scouts beat a path to his door. Yet, he's gained almost as much admiration for his battle for free school dinners for the most poverty-stricken of children. A fight he took to Downing Street and won. Never forgetting his roots, he even has a tattoo of the cherry tree outside his home, under whose fluttering leaves his dreams of United and England first blossomed.

I'm often conscious during my visits to some of the poorer areas of the city or those with a less than appealing reputation of not coming across as something of a poverty tourist. I don't research before I run nor attempt to paint any area in a negative light, but others are not so choosy. In 2009, a production company sent the ex-royal Sarah Ferguson to Northern Moor for ten days as part of a documentary subsequently shown on ITV. Using all the negative angles they could attain, they painted the area as something akin to New York's Bronx in the 1980's with crime astronomically high and guns, drugs and violence endemic. It caused outrage amongst the locals, as yet again the area's name was dragged through the mud with wild exaggerations and falsehoods. The show's pay off was to then have the ex-duchess build a community centre to 'save' the neighbourhood, somehow missing the fact it already had one. The thriving New Dawn centre at the heart of the community the blinkered program hadn't noticed. I'm surprised it didn't end in a live telethon entitled Northerners in Need and a Whippet-Aid concert at Wembley stadium.

Crossing back over the M60 motorway and cutting through Wythenshawe Sports Ground, I begin the long five kilometre trek home, my tired legs returning to their restless state now I'm no longer on new ground. Wearily plodding ever nearer to a kitchen oasis full of food and drink, I am thankful that at least on the return leg, I am only burdened by a haul of 46 roads towards my total.

Sunday 25th April 2021 – 29.41km - Crumbs it's Crumpsall

On 18th April 1930, the BBC radio newsreader announced, "There is no news" before cutting away to 15 minutes of piano music...

Today I headed for a grand expeditionary tour of Higher Crumpsall and Crumpsall Green in Northern Manchester. Like many of the outlying areas, this is another of those rural village idylls swallowed up by the city's hunger for new streets and houses during the late nineteenth and early twentieth century. Some of the larger houses and villas remain, but it's predominantly a leafy area of terraces, semi-detached and the odd mature apartment block.

Setting off from a side street just off Middleton Road, I plunge myself into empty suburbia, seeing no sign of any locals or traffic. Circling Cheetham Hill Cricket ground, I work my way carefully and methodically north along the border with Broughton and Prestwich. It's close to perfect running weather; cool, still and fresh. After a damp night, the rising sun reflects dazzlingly off the tarmac as if the streets are paved with gold, the blue skies showing Crumpsall in a glorious light and equally brightening my mood.

Perhaps Crumpsall's most famous son is Sir Humphrey Chetham, the Manchester merchant born at the original Crumpsall Hall in 1580. After making his fortune from trading textiles, he came to the attention of the crown in 1631 as Charles I offered him a knighthood. Chetham declined and received a hefty fine for the insult to the monarch. At least he kept his head, something Charles failed to do just eighteen years later. In Chetham's later years, he donated money to set up Chetham's Hospital school for forty poor boys (later the school of music) and left money in his will after his death in 1653 to establish Chetham's Library – the oldest public library in the English-speaking world.

Some three hundred years later in Blackley, a different initiative was flourishing from nothing. Working my way north through growing undulations and hills, I take a turn off the main road, cross the River Irk – once labelled the hardest working river in the country – and reach Blackley Forest. Planted in November 1953, long before worries of global warming and carbon banks were en-vogue, it was part of a package of land bought by the council for a new cemetery (Blackley Cemetery). Only, this western fringe was too steep for graves and only fit for woodland. Somewhere in the midst of cost-cutting and positive spin doctoring, the council encouraged tree planting from volunteer members of the public and local schoolchildren during 'Arbor Week'. Many locals believed it was either to commemorate the dead from World War Two or as part of the coronation celebrations of the new Queen, the ideas taking on a life of their own. Whatever the reason, the local volunteers were many and enthusiastic, making it Manchester's first true community forest.

Back across Blackley Vale into Crumpsall, I make my way south through several undulating streets, my legs beginning to moan at their mistreatment as I'm faced by yet more long, grinding inclines. Digging in, I round Herristone Park; a small community park originally laid out in 1968 to give the children somewhere safe to play other than the surrounding streets. Opened by the legendary Manchester United manager Sir Matt Busby, at the fortieth anniversary celebrations, Sir Alex Ferguson continued the link with Manchester United managers by unveiling a commemorative plaque of the park's history.

Tiring badly as the hills keep coming - including a few inclines over ten per cent - I persevere and work my way down to Arlington Street, beside the large Tesco supermarket. It's here, close to the Egerton Inn that Russell Street once stood and the childhood home of singer and actor Don Estelle. Most famous for the role of Gunner "Lofty" Sugden in the now taboo 1970's sitcom 'It Ain't Half Hot Mum', he also had a No.1 hit single with 'Whispering Grass' in 1975.

Whispering something a little bluer as I plodded my way back to my car, I felt all of the 29 kilometres as my tight legs fizzed and throbbed. Yet, I was happy I got it all done and didn't cut off early. It wasn't the most inspiring area today, nor did anything too interesting happen, but I did gather in 82 streets. Naturally, the run took me past no milestones or any kind of interesting totals. As the BBC might say in these circumstances. 'Here's some light piano music instead...'

Tuesday 27th April 2021 – 17.95km – Get your Motor Running

Despite my best efforts, my map of runs across Manchester is strewn with anomalies. In areas completely coloured in, single un-run roads mock me with their hide and seek victories. So, today I parked my pride and sped off on another housekeeping journey up through Whalley Range, Moss Side, Hulme, Chorlton-on-Medlock and the Universities.

First, I'd like to welcome the impatient readers from the July 31st Run page who are probably skimming this page for the answer to the musical duo living in Longsight. Go down five paragraphs and if you guessed 'Dollar', you're not just wrong, I'm actually a little concerned about you too.

It's an overcast, fifty shades of meh, sort of morning. Settling into the run, I slow down my pace and concentrate a little more on improving my running form rather than my surroundings. Rounding Whitworth Park, the traffic takes a right and I enter the near deserted Oxford Road. The northernmost section has been only for buses since 2017 and for those that remember the churning traffic jam of queuing buses and commuters, the difference is stark. Now more like a Dutch or Danish neighbourhood of segregated cycle lanes and wide pavements, it is a place of serenity and clean air amongst the historical university buildings. It also reminds me that the fight to keep the traffic moving is not a new one.

Back in the late 19th century, Manchester saw terrible congestion from all manner of horse drawn vehicles from hackney carriages and delivery carts to omnibuses and horse-drawn trams. In a decision that sounds strangely familiar today, the council at the start of the twentieth century, decided the answer to their traffic problems was to go electric. Eschewing rival technologies of compressed air, battery or underground cable systems, they overhauled public transport and ordered 400 new electric trams. These rapidly became the backbone of Manchester's public transport. Being cheap, regular and with stops every hundred metres or so, they were extremely efficient. While air pollution from the factories and industry was terrible, the trams were not adding to it.

At its peak in 1928, the trams carried 328 million passengers in a year, compared to just 44 million on the Metrolink today. Then came motor buses – that were cheaper and made more profit – and according to the faceless money-men, better than the clean, efficient, electric trams, that they deemed old-fashioned. It's an irony that the same cost-cutting means the new smoother roads needed for the buses simply tarmacked over the old cobbles, most of the old tram tracks still in place under the surface.

Cutting through the University on Dover Street, amidst all the old school buildings of different styles and periods, I always get a mental lift. The bright minds and untapped potential within reminds me that no matter how terrible the news gets, these buildings and thousands like them are shaping the bright ideas of the future. Even then, academia doesn't just initiate new science, research and human knowledge, it's a melting pot of ideas and influences that sometimes conjure up a little magic.

Ed Simons came to Manchester to study Medieval History in 1989 choosing the city because of his love of the bands New Order and The Smiths. Tom Rowlands also chose History in Manchester for the music scene and the famous Hacienda nightclub. They met and a friendship grew around their mutual love of hip hop, techno and acid house, eventually DJ-ing together in 1992 as "The 237 Turbo Nutters" in reference to their student home on Dickenson Road. After a name change to "The Dust Brothers," they would eventually take their final name in 1995 and become "The Chemical Brothers," after which the stratosphere of fame and success awaited them. OK, everyone wave bye to the curious readers as they flick back nine months to that run through Longsight, oh we were all so young back then...

The University has of course taken over the whole neighbourhood, replacing blocks of houses, businesses and industry. Looking at old maps, it's striking just how integrated and crowded together these different land uses can be. As I stray across Upper Brook Street into the social housing estate of modern and brand new homes with their curved roads, gardens, parking spaces and closes, I reach a remnant of the past. On the wonderfully named Polygon Avenue, thirteen of the old terraced homes stand stoutly on the pavement with their recessed doorways under simple embellished brick arches. These solid workers homes have stood for more than a century. At one end of the road is a row of shops of a similar vintage, but beyond their tiny backyards – where the new estate now stands – there used to be not just a saw mill but also a cooperage. One can only imagine the whirr of the saws, the clatter of machinery, the banging of hammers on curved wooden staves and hot metal hoops, the rolling of barrels and the constant coming and going of horse-drawn carts along cobbled streets. Then there's the furnaces, steam engines and belching chimneys. It's a wonder it wasn't called Tinnitus Street.

Another small factory nearby, just off Brunswick Street and equally crowded in by housing was a "Carriage and Motor Manufactory". This harks back to the turn of the twentieth Century when the move away from horses into use of the combustion engine sparked a revolution of

167

innovation. Industry's need for faster, more efficient and economical transport opened up a new exciting market while the more affluent sought a motor vehicle as a symbol of status. Being an industrial city, Manchester was not left behind in this scramble for modernization with several companies handcrafting motors. At the start of the First World War, the city was one of the biggest motor manufacturers in the world. Sadly many of these company's shone only briefly before going bust, production moving elsewhere or being bought out by a more successful company. Unlike the revolution a century before, the city failed to capitalise on its successes and by the outbreak of the war in 1939, there were no longer any factories building cars in Manchester. With so many cars nowadays with foreign brands and models, the names of Manchester cars still evoke a different age when you could be driving a Wilbrook, Belsize, Imperial, Horbick, Hercules or Empress. Or riding a Royal Ruby motorcycle.

Speeding home with all the care and ebullience of Mr Toad from the Wind in the Willows – as voiced by David Jason in the 1983 Cosgrove Hall feature length animation – I celebrate my 32 road haul with an exuberant 'Hey, hey, hey-hey! Poop-Poop!'

Friday 30th April 2021 – 30.15km – Come Run with Me, let's run, let's run away

The trouble with adulting is there are no adults to stop you doing the strangest things and before you know it you're running in places otherwise forbidden.

The City of Manchester is full of all manner of business parks, residential districts and industrial estates. Running every single one naturally brings a variety of experiences and unusual sights and sounds, however I'd be lying if I said I'd given much thought about the airport. As part of the 1930's Mancunian land grab that saw Manchester build the Wythenshawe Estate and expand its border south into Cheshire, an airfield was proposed in the parish of Ringway. Construction started in 1935 and it took three years to convert the agricultural land into grass runways and a rudimentary terminal. Opening on the 25th June 1938, it operated for only a year before conversion for war service as a place for plane repairs and parachute training.

Interestingly, the first airplane to use the airport landed a full year before it was open. On 17th May 1937, a De Havilland Hornet Moth flown by Duncan Menzies was searching for Barton Aerodrome over in Trafford but couldn't find any landmarks on the ground due to thick fog. Living in Wilmslow and knowing about Ringway's ongoing construction, Menzies swooped down and put his biplane safely down onto the grass. No doubt causing some surprise and confusion amongst the builders working on the half-finished hangar and terminal at the time. In a joyfully symbolic bit of whimsy, the very same Hornet Moth returned in 2012, circling the airfield before swooping down once more onto the runway to celebrate the airport's unofficial 75th birthday. Sat beside the pilot was Menzies' son Peter, repeating the landing of his father all those years before.

I wasn't looking forward to this run for a couple of reasons. Mainly because unless I wanted to pay for parking or risk my car getting towed, I'd have to park a good distance from the Terminals and commute in on foot. Secondly, although I was more than used to people staring and thinking I was weird, those people don't normally have anti-terrorist training or access to people with machineguns. I mean sure, these are public roads and there's no reason not to drive on them or run them, but I did wonder if mid-run I might not get a police car pull up for a little chat. Probably paranoia, but then again as the airport was technically closed, they would have little else to do. Maybe the sight of another human would be novelty enough.

169

Heading south from a street in Woodhouse Park, I make my way across the quiet roads onto Ringway Road. I pass the interesting Airport Pub, with its beer garden right next to the runway and planes landing or taking off every two minutes; it's normally as popular with plane-spotters as families. On I run in the early morning air beneath lightening skies. The car parks are relatively empty and a line of Ryanair planes stand close to the fencing by Terminal Three. It's here that the airport has its own tales of the supernatural. From as far back as the 1970's people have reported seeing a ghostly airman wandering around the Departure gates in uniform and pilot's hat. Only once they turn and look back, he's no longer there. Doors are heard slamming late at night and other reports claim a night watchmen who died on-site in the 60's is still heard patrolling, his footsteps echoing around the empty floors.

Moving swiftly on, I loop around the roundabouts and side roads, the eerie feeling of isolation growing, like being in a post-apocalypse movie where the disaster just happened, but the weeds have yet to grow. On I run into one or two of the surrounding hotels and down back roads leading to service areas. Many of the roads here have names like Chicago Ave, Malaga Ave, Toronto Ave, Palma Ave, Sydney Ave, Melbourne Ave and the tropical sounding Terminal Road North. On the dual carriageways, I have to run both sides and embarrassingly seem to have timed it just as a mass crowd of builders walk in from the car park to their building site. Not only do they encounter a weirdo runner coming from the airport, five minutes later, he's running back past them. There's looking lost and then there's looking lost, at the closed airport. Leaving the mocking comments and stifled laughter behind, I tick off all the adjacent roads and finally go for the big one.

Following the big blue road-sign onto Atlanta Ave, I find it ominously closed to cars. With no pavements and bright double-yellow lines on either side, I'm reminded that there are probably cameras watching my every move. Blinking hard, I pass on between the traffic cones and creep up the curving slope. I had the sense I'd just passed the velvet rope and was sure there'd be a security guard somewhere ahead to shepherd me back down the hill. I keep moving, soft padding onwards, climbing away from the surrounding roads, ahead only sky. At the top, the road curves to the left and levels out into the all so familiar dual lanes and lay-bys, zebra crossings connecting to the multi-storey car park opposite. As I reach the roof covering the road, I slow to a stop, marvelling that I'm here, running through the deserted Terminal 2 Drop-off zone at Manchester Airport.

It's a long run too, a good two hundred and fifty metres or so before sloping back down through some barriers to another roundabout. Realising that seeing it this eerily deserted, in daylight, is a once-in-a-lifetime experience, I slow to a shuffle and drink it all in. The lights are on beyond the Terminal doors but I resist the temptation of stepping inside. Halfway along, there are several cars and vans and as I pass I get a few stares from people carrying lights, cables and equipment inside. It seems the Airport's closure has left an opening for some television or filming in the Terminal without the random travellers in the background. I loitered full of questions, but everyone looked busy, normal and uninterested at my arrival, so I made my departure.

Leaving the passenger airport behind, I found a fence overlooking the concrete apron close to the terminal, spying row upon row of Thomas Cook and Virgin planes mothballed and waiting for the flyers to return. It was a strange sight. Leaving Terminal 2 behind, I began the long journey around the perimeter fence to the Freight Terminal. Unlike the passenger side, business here continued unabated; the car parks full, loads arriving and departing. In my travels across the City, I've sometimes wondered if there's any street where I'm the first person ever to run it. York Drive must be a contender.

The main road through the Freight Terminal, it's little more than a road through a loading bay, with only painted green pavements cutting through the lorries, vans, pallets, forklift trucks and high-vis marshals. Drivers and workers stared, as well they might, as I really had no reason to be there. Stoically wearing a smile and nodding to all who I accidentally made eye contact with, I gave a wide berth to anything moving, heavy, noisy or scowling and got the heck out of there as quick as I could.

Onwards past the Romper pub, I head down Wilmslow Old Road to the Runway Visitor Park where one of the last remaining supersonic passenger planes is housed. The retired Concorde here is a sad reminder that sometimes we progress forward and sometimes we take a step backwards to a slower, more mundane future. Coming back the way I came, I am immediately led into a huge empty car park that City Strides insisted was a road. Already more than sixteen kilometres into this run and getting a bit twitchy about how far I was from the car, I blew out my cheeks and nonetheless ran around the perimeter for a full kilometre before returning to the entrance. Crossing the main road, I added a couple of streets around the huge Amazon warehouse before plunging into the country road of Sunbank Lane.

Passing between tall trees and thick, lush hedges dividing the

171

fields, the sound of traffic receded and birdsong filled my ears. I breathe deeply and remembered that I used to run in green places for just such moments of tranquillity and calmness. My mind wandered as I occasionally emerged to a pair of old farm workers cottages or a converted barn, daydreaming of life now and in the past, here amongst the greenery, meadows and horses grazing in their paddocks. Cutting through an ancient wood complete with steep slopes and a babbling brook, I get a little lost en-route to my last road of the day, Mill Lane. Eventually emerging onto it, I find myself stop-starting all the way along this busier country road. With no pavements and the occasional passing truck, I hugged trees and made intimate friends with several hedges along the way. Passing the site of the 12th century Ullerwood Castle – now buried under a private residence behind trees and a hedge – I continue winding my way downhill to a small bridge over the River Bollin. The road climbs up on the other side, but this is the end of the road for me as beyond this trickling ribbon of water lies the forbidden county of Cheshire.

Twenty-three kilometres in, I ignore the pleas from my legs and push back up the hill I've just descended, knowing I'm still not done for the day. Emerging back from Mill Lane onto the main road, every fibre of my weary body urged me to turn left and trudge homeward. With a heavy sigh, I turned right down Wilmslow Road on a short out and back. Downhill and knowing what that meant on the return, I head alongside the main road into a long, gently-curving tunnel, the pedestrian and cycle-path separate from the traffic. After four hundred metres, I emerge into the daylight in a cutting no more than a hundred and fifty metres long. Ahead the dual carriageway disappears into another curving tunnel. Here in this hollow, between the two runways of Manchester Airport, is the most southerly point of the Manchester road network. Beyond the high, black-wire fences on either side of the road are jungles of thick, dense bushes. Of course there are bushes.

I take a moment to half-heartedly celebrate before turning around and beginning the long journey back to the car. Running on empty and climbing most of the way, this was something of a low point. Brain rebelling, a slight stitch and legs made of lead, I did my best to keep moving, even if at times it was only a shuffle. Returning the way I'd come also meant there were no distractions to keep me going, nothing to see I hadn't already seen. I counted breaths up to five hundred and then started over again. Suffering with all my being as my body ran out of fuel. It was a long effort, but I ticked off every corner and in the end, my car appeared in the distance. Clambering into the driver's seat, I sat for a long time before I had the energy to chew my snacks, let alone drive home.

All that distance for only 33 streets is scant reward for a grand day out, but the memories of random adventure will live on long after those of weariness and fatigue. Juliet, Echo, Tango, Lima, Alpha, Golf...proceed to afternoon time, you're cleared for drinking.

Sunday 9ᵗʰ May 2021- 27.14km – Hell's Teeth, it's Newton Heath

The joys of spring mean so many things to different people; the strengthening of the sun and lengthening of the days, the floral and arboreal rebirth of nature, the fleeting glimpse of sunglasses, short sleeves and the waft of an optimist's barbecue. Or, a chance to target an insalubrious area of Manchester with a dawn raid like some kind of street-bagging ninja. I acknowledge I might be alone on this one. Yet my athletic endeavours are rather apt, as for a period in the middle of the 19ᵗʰ century, Newton Heath could rightfully claim to be at the centre of the running world.

Newton Heath sits five kilometres northeast of the city centre, long being an area of industry and movement of people. French Protestants settled here in the 16ᵗʰ century amidst the farms and hamlets, fleeing the persecution of Huguenots by the Catholic faith across Europe. They brought their cotton weaving and bleaching skills with them and a cottage industry flourished. This knowledge and the skills passed down through the generations would make the leap into mechanised cotton mills in the area, centuries later, much easier. As Manchester grew in importance in the 18ᵗʰ and 19ᵗʰ centuries and rival cities across the North became more industrialised, the desire for swift, economic travel became ever more important. Not just for the supply of raw materials but for trade with the burgeoning populations across Lancashire and Yorkshire. The 18ᵗʰ century turnpike road of Oldham Road with its tollbooth was the main route from Manchester to Leeds and is still a busy artery into the centre from the east of the city. But horses, carts, muddy roads and hills were never going to be quick enough for the industrialists.

As the whirlwind of the 19ᵗʰ century industrial revolution hit Manchester, Newton Heath watched the battle for trade shift from the eighteenth century technology of horse-drawn barges on the canals to the high-speed efficiency of steam-powered railways. The Rochdale Canal cutting through the suburb, opened in 1804 and at its peak in the 1840's carried nearly a million tonnes of freight. The Manchester and Leeds Railway arrived here in 1841, carving through Newton Heath and slashing journey times from days to hours.

The area's less than desirable reputation is not a recent problem. The usual mix of low-paid work, ill-maintained housing and underfunded councils sees the scourge of crime, drugs and anti-social behaviour overshadow the quiet efforts of the majority to build a community. Even then, a brief look at the Manchester newspapers from the 1880's and 90's shows the amount of assaults, thefts and murders were far worse in the

174

past. Hard drinking men and women, dark streets and the fact many boatmen were just passing through all meant death was rarely a stranger. Many a body accidentally or deliberately ended up in the murky waters of the canal, workers headed to the mills finding them floating in the first slithers of dawn light.

Even setting off this early on a drab, drizzly Sunday morning, I was not totally alone. Wary of standing out on these sort of clandestine runs, I eschew normal runner rules of fluorescent colours, head torches and reflective strips. Instead, I dress in dark clothes and gloves, although my pale legs and the odd circling moth possibly ruin my desire for stealth. Still, I'm more visible than the shadows I pass in the initial gloom. Dressed head to foot in black, with hoods up and a shifty purposeful walk, I see four such strangers in the first ten minutes of my pre-dawn Sunday run. Maybe Newton Heath is simply Goth central, maybe black is the new black, maybe they were up to no good or maybe they too just didn't want to be noticed. Who am I to judge? I'm the weird one running and round here perhaps that has more negative reasons than positive.

With a wee nip in the air, I take a while to warm up, wishing the glowing superpower I'd temporarily felt after my first Covid Vaccination hadn't worn off so quickly. Two days walking around like the Ready Brek kid after a nuclear accident sure would have come in handy. Regretting my lack of internal fusion, I push on and find the 1832 Newton Silk Mill on Silk Street just as the dawn brings light and a whispered promise of warmth. Converted to offices for the NHS bigwigs, the mill almost looks too new and modern. But for an original stone plaque high on its frontage, you'd easily pass by without a second glance.

From there I speedily headed southeast and crossed over the canal into a mix of roads lined with 1970's houses and much older terraces, all sandwiched between the water and Brookdale Park. Rounding up these roads in good order and with no-one around, I settled into making my own entertainment. I had a little cough in Rothman Close and congratulated myself with an awkward robotic dance for hitting May street at the most apt time of year. Probably best not to discuss openly what I did on Flash Street, but suffice to say I've never seen a ginger cat move so fast.

Talking of animals, after returning past the shops of Old Church Street and re-crossing the canal, I noted a line of Canada Geese maintaining a two-metre distance in an orderly queue outside Lidl. They eyed me as dubiously as the grey-haired grandma with a tartan shopping trolley I passed. I got the sense all of them would beat me to a pulp if I got any closer.

I carried on to Great Newton Street where there's now nothing but a couple of empty car parks, yet this was once the scene of a great tragedy. On the evening of 14th January 1899, three families living together at number five were sitting down for their tea when their world collapsed around them. Strong gales had been blowing across the north-west for much of the day causing damage to many trees, roof tiles and large buildings. Sadly, one such vulnerable structure was the tall chimney at the disused mill behind their small terraced home. Without warning at 5.45pm, the upper portion of the chimney broke off and smashed down onto the house, reducing it to a pile of rubble. Of the 11 people in the home, four died and three received serious injuries. Surrounded by housing the chimney could have fallen at any time or in any direction, but fate dropped it on number five and in a split second, changed their lives forever.

Leaving behind a scene that must have devastated the community, I head for one that was designed to bring it together. At the end of Old Church Street, I pass where the once impressive Failsworth Industrial Society stood until earlier this year – a three-storey co-operative store once at the heart of this community. A brick palace of retail, built over a hundred and thirty years ago with such obvious pride, its long-derelict state and subsequent loss is a sad reflection on how an area's heritage can slip through the community's fingers. Without buildings, places and communal memories that span generations, community often fragments and loses its cohesion. Heading west along the 1970's estate between Oldham Road and the canal, I find a place clinging on to its place at the heart of the neighbourhood; the Grosvenor Arms on Eldridge Drive, known locally as the Glue Pot; one landlord apparently claiming it was because the locals tended to stick to the walls come closing time. One of its drinkers is famous around the world because of a picture of Manchester on New Year's Eve in 2015. The picture of him lying down in his blue suit and reaching for a bottle of beer as police arrest another man amid onlookers went viral across news and social media. Many likened its composition to a renaissance painting, full of drama, light and strong expressions. I'm sure he's not had to reach for a beer since.

Further west, I pass a small commercial estate of businesses, car dealerships and a Holiday Inn. It was here that the Royal Oak Hotel once stood. Together with the Copenhagen Tavern further back along Oldham Road (closed but still standing...just), these two pubs were at the centre of the Manchester's love affair with the mile. When pubs were so commonplace, they had to compete for their customers. Many entrepreneurial landlords turned to sport to guarantee custom through spectators, gamblers and drinkers. Both these pubs developed large running enclosures behind their pubs. The Copenhagen grounds opened in 1857 with room for a thousand spectators. Six years later, its success prompted the Royal Oak to build a first class arena complete with a circular 595 metre cinder running track, grandstands and room for 20,000 spectators. Yet while similar enterprises in London leaned toward long distance races upwards of 3 miles, Manchester became the home of the mile race attracting 'spinners' – as the milers came to be known – from across the country. With regular meets and an annual mile championship over a measured course, the best professional runners became local legends and celebrities, their exploits the first official world records over the distance. On the 2nd of July 1864, over 30,000 spectators crowded the arena, nearby rooftops and fence-tops to glimpse the country's foremost runners compete. Alas, the gambling and money involved became the sport of Pedestrianism's downfall. As the constant need for record-breaking and high drama became more important for business, some results became questionable. Amidst rumours of race-fixing and altered timings, the working classes lost interest and faded away. In their place, the middle classes took running from its prize-orientated origins and developed the respectable amateur sport of Athletics.

Opposite the Holiday Inn, at the corner of Monsall Road on Oldham Road, there is a large timber merchants right next to the railway. This was the old site of Heenan and Froude Ironworks; an engineering firm and foundry who in 1882 were contracted to supply and construct Lancashire's own homage to a similar structure somewhere in France; the Blackpool Tower.

With tired legs and an uphill false-flat grind back along Oldham Road, I firstly detoured about a kilometre to grab Swinstead Avenue – a missed cul-de-sac from a previous run – and then diverted to a place of Manchester football history and pilgrimage. On a new spacious business park, opposite the shiny new headquarters of Greater Manchester Police is a small red plaque on the side of a brick and glass office block. This is where Newton Heath LYR F.C used to play their football matches in the 19th century on North Road. Playing their games on a pitch opposite the smoky industry of the Lancashire and Yorkshire Railway carriage works and between an old clay pit and Monsall Hospital for Infectious Diseases, it's a mystery why they ever wanted to move elsewhere. But they did, first to Bank Street in Clayton and then out of Manchester completely (much to the continued mirth of their blue rivals). This was long before the Heathens changed their strip from white shirts and blue shorts to the more familiar red and white and renamed themselves Manchester United.

It could have course been so different, if it wasn't for a Saint Bernard dog called Major, who saved Newton Heath from bankruptcy. In 1902 after surging up the leagues, the rising costs of players wages and travelling the country to play meant the creditors were circling for their money. Fundraisers were organised by the club captain Henry Stafford, including a fete in a village hall, where his dog wandered freely with a collecting tin round his neck. Escaping to wander the streets, the lost and confused dog was taken in by a pub landlord and immediately showed affection to a certain man in the corner of the bar. He was John Henry Davies – the Managing director of Manchester Breweries – who subsequently bought the friendly dog from the landlord. With the police notified of the missing dog, Davies found out and met with the footballer to return Major to his rightful owner. Both immediately formed a rapport over the mischievous dog's antics. Shortly afterwards the brewery-man with a group of wealthy friends paid off the debts of Newton Heath and put new managers in place on one condition. The football club must change its name. Rejecting the likes of Manchester Celtic and Manchester Central, they became majorly United behind their new name.

A champion 77 streets that are definitely still in Manchester take me up past the 60% complete mark. And...I didn't end up in the canal. Even more importantly, those shifty-looking Geese didn't follow me home.

Thursday 13th May 2021 – 21.24km – Danger and the Endangered

'Unexcited run in the Baguley area. Please remove yourself from the Baguley area...'

You know you're not really enthused about going out for a run, when you check the weather and curse your luck that it's not raining. A white opaque sheet of overcast indifference hung over Manchester offering no glorious sunrise nor hope of movement in the heavens. Sometimes a glimpse of gleaming blue between shifting clouds is all you need to kid yourself of an incoming change. But not today. The skies have been whitewashed and it's plainly in for the day.

Turning my search internally, I am disappointed to find I have not become lame, diseased or bedridden overnight. Nor has the entirety of my running clothes spontaneously combusted in my wardrobe. There is no Geese-led siege of my home. Even my horoscope fails to mention any ambulating portents of doom. Seemingly with all plausible excuses exhausted, I gave in to that smug inner voice and headed once more out to Baguley, Wythenshawe.

Parking up just south of Wythenshawe Park, I headed around the western perimeter of the park into Northern Moor through three small micro-estates that perfectly sum up the Wythenshawe area. The first consisted of nine roads of 60's and 70's social housing centred around a couple of tower blocks on Bideford Road. After a man in his twenties was shot in the foot whilst cycling here last November, seemingly gang-related, the Manchester Evening News gathered several memorable quotes from local residents including:

"You do sometimes get the odd robbery or something like that on the street but nothing like this."

"I heard two loud bangs and a lad shouting 'ow, ow, ow.'"

"I was on the sofa about 7pm and I heard a massive boom. I don't know how my dog didn't have a heart attack."

The neighbouring area was a new estate of 3 roads with Lawnhurst Ave circling the other two. Made up of modern Wimpy-style homes with pale sandy brick and dark brown roof tiles, it looks thoroughly modern with its lush evergreen hedges and black railing fences, immaculate tarmac and perfectly placed fruit trees. An architect's drawing come to life, this would be an obvious place for young professionals, couples and slick estate agents with clipboards.

The last five streets were peak suburbia with post-war semi-detached houses, lush front gardens, cars on driveways and mature trees towering over the curving roads. Even the names of Cherry Tree Road and

179

Nan Nook Drive have a charming, pleasant ring to them. A place for families and retirement, good neighbours who make jam and put your bins out when you forget.

Yet these three different worlds rub shoulders with one another, just as they do all across this part of South Manchester. The majority live their happy lives in these pleasant, leafy suburbs without ever seeing or hearing about the dark underbelly that occasionally surfaces in the local newspaper headlines. To paraphrase another Wythenshawe resident, 'I've never seen any trouble and I've lived here for five years. Although, there was a shooting a few doors down last week.'

Cutting back through Wythenshawe Park and briefly delighting in the dank aroma of damp woodland after the rain overnight, I continued my way around a largely forgettable run, along the curving, meandering avenues and closes of Baguley. With my desire to be out running unchanging, I lowered my chin and picked up the pace, determined to get it over with as swiftly as possible. Finding the same mix of social housing, post-war and modern areas and plenty of my favourite knee-jarring concrete roads, I worked my way south beside the M56 Motorway to the edge of Hollyhedge Road. Eventually circling back northwards towards my car. On the way, I found what I was looking for all along, part of Wythenshawe that is truly special.

Wythenshawe Hall and Park is well known in these parts, but nearby on Hall Lane and almost hidden in plain sight is the Grade-I listed Baguley Hall. Looking a little forlorn amidst a disinterested housing estate, this is a grand 14th century timber-framed house, buttressed by later brick extensions. Yet it sits locked up behind high fences, with barely a second glance from passers-by. Built by Sir William Baguley who gave the area its name, it is probably the oldest timber great hall still standing in all of England. It sits in stasis. Part of a working farm as late as 1930, the incoming new estate left it overshadowed for interest by its neighbour, Wythenshawe Hall with its large park and gardens gifted to the public by the Tatton family. Major restorations in the 1970's and 80's stopped Baguley Hall's decline, but it remains closed to the public. Currently owned by the Government, English Heritage maintains and preserves it, but it awaits the funding to show off this national treasure to the wider world.

With another hard won 48 streets added to my Citystrides total, I find a new feature proclaiming my 'Global Rank' as 92nd in the world. I'm not sure what's more worrying, that I've run so many streets or that there are 91 crazier runners than me! Today was a kindly reminder of that running mantra that you don't have to go far, you just have to go.

Sunday 16th May 2021 – 27.90km – Bossing New Moston

'Y'all not fromt rand deese parts, arr ya boy...?'

After a few too many runs around the south and east of the city, I once more headed far across the city to the northeast of Manchester. Here I headed to the top right of my map, the sticky-out bit (sorry for the technical terms) of New Moston. Hemmed in by the Failsworth and Chadderton areas of Oldham, I really didn't know what to expect. Would it be like Blackley and Crumpsall or more like Moston and Harpurhey? Or would it be frontier country, a lawless borderland where I was the new running deputy in town?...Darn tootin', yeehaw, etc, etc.

It's not often a place can identify its birth to a single year, yet we know New Moston was born in 1850. Laid out in plans drawn up by Elijah Dixon - businessman and agitator for political and social change, dubbed the 'Father of English Reformers' – and colleagues of his new freehold society. They aimed to provide land for housing and allotments for workers away from the polluted perils of the inner-city slums. Much like the 'model' village of New Lanark in Scotland, it was seen as a way to bring order and design to a world that had exploded into industrial and capitalist chaos. Setting out 230 plots of land and building the roads for access, the area soon took off as a desirable new village sandwiched between farmland and the Rochdale Canal. By 1863 the New Moston Inn was opened on Dixon Street, cementing the new community around an alehouse. A success in his lifetime, developers expanded the area into the surrounding farmland at the end of the nineteenth century after Dixon's death.

Running these streets, I needn't have worried about any anti-social areas or lack of local pride. Working along the semi-detached suburbia of Nuthurst Road and the side streets, I pass Nuthurst Park and turn south. Heading into a dip in the leafy valley, the road bridges over Moston Brook. This meandering stream marks the strange jagged border between Manchester and Oldham in these parts. Looping back up the hill, I veer right into the oldest part of New Moston. Here signs proudly proclaim the area's success in the North West in Bloom competition. Headed between the old houses and mature trees, there's a real sense of being in a tight village community far away from the faceless city, plus there are other runners! It's been a while since I saw anyone else out so early on the streets, I always take it as a good sign I'm in a friendly neighbourhood.

It wasn't always so genial in these parts though. Being on the fringes of the city meant there was more space and fresher air than in some of the crowded areas, something scrupulous businessman were only too happy to exploit. Much like the Copenhagen and Royal Oak pubs in Newton Heath, running as entertainment also had a foothold up here. The Railway Hotel, just across the border in Chadderton, Oldham built a recreation ground in 1875 called Moston Park. With a 732-yard cinder track, the professional running enclosure sold tickets for what they then called the sport of Pedestrianism, frequently attracting up to fourteen thousand spectators. Cycling, shooting, horse and dog racing, hare coursing, wrestling and other pugilist sports all featured at the sports ground, as well as music and agricultural events. Only one minute from Moston Station, it led to crowds of drunken men flooding the area and upsetting the locals. So much so, when the Hotel alcohol license was up for review, the local rector Rev Thomas Wostencroft, fought hard to oppose it claiming third-class train travel on the day of an event was unfit for females or any respectable man and that the sports crowd were a rough lot. Much like Newton Heath however, the Park's success was fleeting, being sold and demolished in 1885. Pedestrianism would simply have to run along elsewhere.

Sadly, I slightly over-estimated how much I could pedestrianise today and ran out of legs before I could tidy up the map. Heading west of Lightbowne I managed all but a handful of roads of a new estate (little knowing this would come back and haunt me in a later run). At the time, I thought – quite rightly – that the extra couple of miles would have tipped me over the edge from supposed fun to cursing choredom. So I congratulated myself on knowing when to throw in the towel, even if so tantalisingly close to a hundred roads.

Besides, at the top of Lightbowne Road, facing the large Greengate Roundabout is the Gardener's Arms. This pub claims to be the highest pub in Manchester. And before any regulars laying wasted on the floor of various notorious back street pubs across the city can say hold my bong, I'm basing that fact entirely on its geographic Elevation, the pub being a massive 110 metres above sea level.

Still, that's 98 roads completed today and with no sign of a pursuing gang of outlaws from the badlands across the border, I can at least say I go out on a high.

182

Sunday 23rd May 2021 – 22.98km – Suck City

Wherever there are Streets...I'll be there.

Wherever there is injustice...I'll...I...I might be there.

Wherever there is suffering...I'll...I mean if it's on an unrun street and I'm passing...

For I am StreetMan! (Don't call me).

Sadly my only superpower today was to make a 23 km run around Levenshulme feel more like 29km. Setting off from beside Greenbank Playing Fields on a breezy, overcast morning, I wound my way around a grid of several terraced streets, warming up after a cool start. The terraces here are a little different to other parts of the city; a local byelaw stipulates they all must have a small front garden and alleyway access at the rear wide enough for a horse and cart to gather waste and refuse. Heading west along Manor and then Barlow Road, I'd reached Stockport Road before a glance at my Strava revealed it was still paused at the beginning.

The sinking feeling of wasting thirty minutes sucked all the enthusiasm out of my body as I realised the ambitious route I had planned was now super elongated. With much cursing and some digging deep, I retraced my steps. Normally I'd put the disappointment behind me and push on, but seeing the same familiar streets so soon only underlined my mistake.

Almost back where I started, my revisit is reminiscent to a rebellious return to the land right here on the 6th of July 1906. At a time of much poverty amongst the working classes, a dozen unemployed Levenshulme men took direct action in an extraordinary way. Bombs, guns and violence weren't their weapons for change, instead they set about a revolution against societal injustice with...2500 cabbages.

On six acres of unfenced Church land between Lonsdale Road and St Oswald's Road, the Levenshulme Landgrabbers stripped the turf from the land and sewed seeds to grow their own food for the community. Building a fire and later a turf croft, they had men guard their cabbage patch day and night, their escapades inspiring similar land-grabs in London and Bradford. Thousands of people enthusiastically visited the site, bringing seeds and food for the outlaws and making a carnival-like atmosphere. They gained widespread coverage in the national press and even worldwide with reports in the socialist U.S. Paper; the San Francisco Call. Through the long hot summer, these vegetable Robin Hoods remained on site growing their crop until the inevitable happened. With the socialist leaders of the Labour Party doing all they could to pretend the land grab hadn't happened, the Church decided the best way they could help the hungry poor in the community was to demand their grassy waste land back. Six weeks after the vegetable plotters began, the Reverend sent in a solicitor, backed by the police and twenty men armed with picks and shovels to escort the Brassica squatters away. Faced with unbeatable odds, the poor men retreated. Standing with the rest of the community, they would watch on as the hired heavies destroyed the plants, straw bedding and the local's temporary hut. Amen.

While the Levenshulme Landgrabbers lost this battle and their food, just the following year in 1907, Parliament passed the Small Holdings and Allotments Act forcing all councils to provide land for residents to grow their own food, including cabbages.

Headed down Stockport Road amidst the shops, I dart in and out of several small dead-end roads next to the railway line with some unusual names. The likes of Farm Side Place and Farm Yard hint at the rural past, while the old dames of Alma Rd and Ethel Terrace show the changing popularity of forenames. My two personal favourites though are the oddly titled Elbow Street and the marvellously uninspiring Kevin Street.

Picking up a few stray streets at the southern end of Levenshulme, I then hop onto the F'Loop cycle path and head north-east for a couple of kilometres into Longsight, revelling in the novelty of heading in a straight line. After working several roads of a new estate, I head up Falshaw Way and once more cross the Nico Ditch, the ancient trench I first encountered much further west in Platt Fields. Here it is overgrown and runs between the new estate and old, with little to indicate it is anything other than what it obviously is; an overgrown ditch.

With these repeated streets beginning to hang heavy in my legs, I made it around several streets of semi-detached houses to emerge beside the forlornly overgrown Melland Road Playing Fields. These used to extend south of the Nico Ditch and during the Second World War the area now occupied by Melland High School was commandeered by the military. Initially – like so many open areas in Manchester - it contained a battery of anti-aircraft guns and spotlights. More interestingly, as the air threat faded towards the end of the war, it changed into P.O.W. Camp No. 126 – Mellands Camp. The camp held German Prisoners of war captured at sea and in the North African war. Much later, it held Italian Prisoners as the Allies liberated Europe. In 1943 when the Italians changed sides, the prisoners were given much more freedom to move around Gorton and Levenshulme, no doubt to the delight of the local ladies. The camp didn't close until the late forties, when all the prisoners had been repatriated. After the war, it became home to 165 Provost Company of Royal Military Police.

184

On I went, my legs growing leggy and then leggier still. Knowing I couldn't finish all the streets I wanted, I concentrated hard on a logical route back to my car, not an easy feat. Fatigue can really confuse the internal computers. This is rather apt as I pass 272 Mount Road, once the childhood home of Glyn Geoffrey Ellis. Born in October 1945, he would sign a record deal at eighteen under the stage name Wayne Fontana, accompanied by his backing group 'The Mindbenders'. Two years later they would release 'Game of Love', which would top the U.S. Charts and reach number two in the U.K. It was only kept off the top spot by the hugely forgettable 'I'll Never Find Another You' by The Seekers. The Mindbenders would never trouble the top of the charts again despite several revivals, eventually working the sixties nostalgia circuit. Sadly, Glyn left us last August, losing his battle against cancer, aged only seventy-four.

With legs of lead, I crossed a continent back to the car, leaning on the park fence for several minutes before a thin slither of energy and alertness returned.

Wherever there is suffering...I'll...be right there at the front.
Wherever there is injustice...I...I'll be too tired to even notice.
Wherever there are Streets...I'll be there, possibly twice.
For I am Tiredman
74 hard won streets today. (18 of which got a double visit.)

Tuesday 25th May 2021 – 12.23km – Lively streets and Murder Lane

I head back once more to the indistinct border area between Longsight and Levenshulme in the early afternoon. After so many dawn runs on a Sunday, I'd forgotten how busy places can be just after lunchtime. I'd totally forgotten how annoying it is when other people are awake! There were people walking on pavements, shoppers stepping in and out of shops, buses consuming and disgorging the miserable masses, randoms stood jabbering into their phones, cars rushing past on the roads, what is this lunacy!? What are these people doing here, don't they know I have important nonsense to do!?

With the drama of Sunday's fiasco still lodged in my brain as well as my legs, I return after work on the Tuesday to right the wrongs. And the wrongs kept on coming. After the lost kilometres of Strava-gate, I reviewed my run and checked the map of the area covered. This always brings up a frisson of fear that I might have missed a street. I click on Fernwood Avenue and let out a hearty groan. This uncompleted cul-de-sac shines out from the middle of my last run, surrounded in every direction by kilometres of completed streets.

Bad words, many, many bad words.

Parking up beside Crowcroft Park under grimy grey skies, I reluctantly turn away from this green oasis and head for the tarmac instead, hopeful that the blustery winds don't sweep even darker clouds in before I'm done. Crossing Stockport Road, I get to work meandering my way back and forth along several redbrick terraced streets, dodging cars, pushchairs and many people eyeing me suspiciously. I quickly realise it's another one of those areas runners avoid, well surprise, here I am, get a good eyeful won't you, as I won't be back.

Rapidly collecting several short streets, I dart back across Stockport Road in a break in traffic, round the south end of the Park and head past the unusually sandy-coloured brick terraces of Stovell Avenue. Emerging onto East Road, I find Longsight Cricket Club. Originally formed in 1848, the club played an Australian cricket team in a couple of matches in 1878 as part of the Aussies first official tour of the country, four years before the match that spawned the Ashes urn. Longsight won one match and drew the other, with none other than W.G Grace's brother George sealing the victory with a second innings of 42 runs. Sadly, the ground was sold up for housing in 2012, but the club remains with its bowling green and its place in cricket folklore as the second English team to ever beat Australia (after Nottinghamshire).

Further up Northmoor Road, I find the rather splendid Beswick

Cooperative Society building. Built in 1912, it is a beautiful centrepiece towering over the neighbouring terraced streets. Obviously built with such ostentatious pride, it is a gorgeous mix of red brick, terracotta, jade-green glazed tiles, embellished friezes and ionic columns the colour of patinaed copper. With shops on the ground floor and a grand entrance at the centre to the first floor Assembly Rooms, it even has a tower at one end adorned with four stone eagles. The impact on the surrounding streets at its opening must have been immense. It continues as shops, a community centre and apartments, safe from change or the wrecker's ball. This grade II listed building reminds me that the line between a building finding a second life and being condemned like the Failsworth Industrial Society building in Newton Heath is a narrow one.

Having put it off for long enough, I struck out for the stray, cutting across the boggy wilderness of Nutsford Vale Park, a wonderfully wild area much richer in insects, birds and plants than the wide open grasslands of parks like Crowcroft. On I plod, the enforced three-kilometre detour like a punishment for my previous carelessness. Worse still when I get there, I can't believe how I can have missed it. Running all fifty metres of it, I let out a sigh and return the way I came. Crossing back over the park, I turn into new territory, settle into a steady rhythm and look forward to getting this whole area put to bed.

Hoovering up some more tightly packed terraced streets at the rear of the Cooperative building, I find myself headed up Pink Bank Lane to a notorious part of Longsight. Past what was Gorebrook Iron Works, I cross the brook - once one of the most polluted in Manchester – and reach a street known for many years by locals as Murder Lane. Opposite Melling Street is Nutsford Vale; a lane that once ran between a Tarpaulin factory and a Dye Works. At the eastern end, it ran beside the brook and emerged on Buckley Road beside some Sewage Works. Without streetlights or housing nearby, this eerie shortcut between Longsight and Gorton would have saved a long walk around the fields to the north or south of the factories. On the evening of 12th of May 1909, it would prove deadly. The following morning, when ladies of the Tarpaulin factory headed for work, they came across the body of Emily Ramsbottom, strangled with a handkerchief on Nutsford Vale. The 27-year-old had just ended a tempestuous four-year relationship with her boyfriend, Mark Shawcross, who naturally became prime suspect. He confessed, then changed his mind and claimed his innocence. With witnesses seeing them out walking together that evening, the jury at his trial disagreed and found him guilty of murder. His hanging at Strangeways Prison, Manchester came just three months later.

The dye works is long gone, while the Tarpaulin factory is now a series of motor garages and M.O.T centres; the already narrow street lined with cars, car parts and all kinds of rubbish on either side. I blink hard and head down here, past the open garage doors where machinery whirrs, grinds and radios fill the air with their mainstream melodic ramblings. Weeds and bushes grow tall on either side in the muck and grime in the gutters.

I pass two guys talking beside a car who wonder where the heck I'm going.

I run on, also wondering where the heck I'm going.

I head past rusted steel gates, barbed wire atop railings and several abandoned oil drums. On I go as the road narrows, the aged brick and corrugated steel walls closing in on either side. Up ahead cars block the road up to a solid barrier wall. It's the end of the road. Even with the obvious signs of life nearby and the total change of use, the eeriness of Murder Lane prevails, hanging over the place like a shadow. Turning around, I begin the run back, a mechanic doing a double-take as he checked for any cars but saw me bouncing along instead. I pretend I haven't noticed or that I really don't belong here. This is a place of work and oily hands, of behind the scenes deals rather than customer-orientated razzmatazz. That said, my imagination cannot help painting stories onto this dark canvas. At any moment I expect to see a guy with two heavies arrive, a briefcase handcuffed to his wrist. Or hear a muffled banging and cry from one of the locked car boots as I pass. The two guys by the car watch me go by, one saying something I didn't quite hear. Let's assume it was 'Good form, nice hip extension, well done my friend, remember to relax your shoulders...' and not 'Hey Joey, we got some kinda wise guy here, disrespecting our neighbourhood. Joey! Get me my murder gloves and my favourite handkerchief...'

Keeping good form, relaxing my shoulders and nearly bursting a lung, I made it back to the car in about eight seconds. 33 streets added, and no murders, although I still prefer running empty streets.

Sunday 6th June 2021 – 18.81km – John Sorensen uses his loaf

Two subjects dominate the road names on this modern estate in Beswick, linking the road names together. The first list is easy and reflected in roads such as Stadium Drive, Athletes Way, Arena Drive, Olympic Street and Commonwealth Avenue. The second less obvious group is reflected in Lloyd Wright Avenue, Paxton Place, Rylance Street and Wren Way. Neat to feel like I was running through a word search.

I took a weekend off running last week. Never outrun your love of running is sage advice, as sometimes not running is better than tiresome running. Nonetheless, even after a long week at work, I was mentally raring to get back out there to de-stress after a week and a half. Today I headed for a new area in east Manchester, one with something of a poor reputation. Rolling up super early to Beswick, I targeted an area between Ashton Old Road and Ashton New Road. An early night and a half five start meant unsurprisingly I had the area I'd chosen all to myself. I needn't have worried either, no doubt parts of Beswick are as rough as they used to be, but near Ashton Old Road there is a new estate of modern brick homes and some eye-catching white and grey stylish town-houses with slanted roofs looking more like something from Spain or the south of France rather than Manchester. It was here where I found the group of roads celebrating the stadia built just north of this estate for the Commonwealth Games in Manchester in 2002. The other group of roads were of course named after famous architects, give yourself a pat on the back.

Out on the main road and nipping in and out of little side roads, I came across a familiar building, albeit not as grand as its successor over in Longsight. Here was another branch of Beswick Cooperative Society built in stone and brick in 1899. With shops on the busy road and apartments above, it's not listed but it looks safe and secure for now. Turning right before the curving railway viaduct, I dip back through the modern estate with its architectural quirkiness and abundant greenery.

The area further north is a trip back to the 60s and 70s style of social housing. Here the flavour of the week when it came to naming roads came from an obvious inspiration with Biscay Close, Fairisle Close and Viking Close; all sea areas used in the shipping forecast. There are a few weeds in the gutter and broken glass underfoot here, putting me a little on guard. More so as I round a corner and see a pushchair simply abandoned at the side of the road, thankfully empty. Eyes wider, I notice a few gardens also look overgrown. Suddenly this isn't a place I want to linger, thankfully my legs have loosened and I pick up the pace.

189

Back to the south and I'm on Blackrock Street where the old really meets the new. Three streets of back-to-back terraces crammed into this area at the turn of the nineteenth century remain, still looking in great condition for their age. Opposite, on the other side of Blackrock Street, they are building twenty-two new homes with heat sinks, triple glazed windows and no gas – the first net zero carbon social homes built in the UK. In the neighbouring Grey Mare Lane area, more money is going into making it a low carbon estate, some of the first steps to Manchester Council's somewhat ambitious commitment to be a zero carbon city by 2038.

Just over a century before that council target, someone else in Beswick was using his loaf. John Rahbeck Sorensen was born in Denmark in 1893, arriving in Manchester from Australia in 1932 he set up a baking equipment supplier in Hulme. Three years after this success, he expanded and set up a bakery in Beswick making all manner of cakes. Only one had the public queuing down the street though, his delicious Malt loaf. The fruited loaf rich in raisins and vitamins from the malted barley flour made for a great snack for the hard working people of Manchester, with the bakery delivering to shops up to five miles away. By 1938, his fame was such Imperial Bakeries (Manchester) came and made him an offer he couldn't refuse for his bakery business. John's legacy would live on to this day however, his Malted Loaf Cake still sold today under the name Soreen, in honour of its inventor.

And now I'm really rather hungry.

45 Streets completed today with not a great deal to see, but it felt good to get it done, especially as I had the sense - for once - to stop before doing too much.

190

Monday 14ᵗʰ June 2021 – 21.46km – Raise the White Flag

Not wishing to go too far today, I could have surrendered to laziness, but instead headed south once more to one of my top 500 favourite areas in Manchester; Wythenshawe.

Yesterday afternoon, England did a Sterling job of winning their first match of the Euro 2020 Football tournament 1-0 vs. Croatia (which is now being held in 2021, but is still Euro 2020 because it's not about money, but they have already printed all these t-shirts...). I only open with this fact as the game coincided with a lazy, beery afternoon of shouting at the television and generally making my best impression of an inebriated oik.

So here we are, the morning after the afternoon before and I'm up early for a refreshing rain run to start the week. Alas, the weatherman was about as accurate as Croatia's shooting and it was another warm day, hitting the high teens already before 6am. A very slight breeze helped move the warm air around a bit, but I knew at least it'd give me chance to sweat out all the beer and salty snacks from the day before.

This time in Wythenshawe, I was visiting the north end of this sprawling suburb, to Benchill, Sharston and the place that wants nothing to do with the W-word; Northenden. Channelling the I-Spy books of my childhood and recalling a certain political furore involving a labour front-bencher derisorily tweeting such an image, I spent most of this run spotting houses festooned with England flags. When it comes to sporting patriotism and coming together to support the national football team through the highs and lows of a tournament, I knew the salt-of-the-earth people of Wythenshawe wouldn't let me down.

Heading north through the pleasant suburban estate beside the busy Princess Parkway artery into Manchester, I get one of those moments of joy where the streets are empty, the air warm and the running good. I'm awake and alive, devouring the curving and swirling streets in steady and efficient fashion. Today my internal computer is totally on it and I'm knitting together a complicated line around these streets with a minimum of fuss. Sometimes finding a route with a minimum of retracing your footsteps is like solving the conundrum of the Seven Bridges of Konisberg (Literally, one maths geek just squealed in delight).

Crossing a long arching footbridge over into Northern Moor, I pick up half a dozen missed stray roads before returning to Northenden and on down into Sharston Industrial Estate. Filled with the usual soulless mix of warehousing, offices and car parks, I pound the straight, concrete roads with little enthusiasm. Until, that is, I find the old Grade II listed

Sharston bus garage. Built to house 100 double-decker buses in 1942 for the populous of the large new Wythenshawe estate, the war office immediately commandeered it to make Lancaster Bombers. Now, the aged building with its large curved concrete roof looks more like a misplaced aircraft hangar surrounded by high fences and security gates, the space inside used for long stay parking for the airport.

Out onto Longley Road, I pass over the railway bridge, close to where Northenden Station once stood until the 1960's. Still in-situ though is a most impressive brick signal box. Built in 1881 in the usual functional style of a large shed with glass windows around three sides for visibility, what makes this signal box so unusual is its sheer size! The ivy-covered signal box towers up from the trackside beside the bridge to see over it to the junction down the line, a full five storeys high!

South of the Sharston Link - connecting the M60 motorway to the M56 - I cover some roads in Benchill, as well as the site of Sharston Hall on a gentle corner of Altrincham Road. A manor house built in 1701 by Thomas Worthington – an early Umbrella Tycoon – was at the time described as the finest Georgian house in all of Manchester. After the Worthingtons died out with no male heir in 1856, the house passed through the hands of several industrialists and merchants before David Leopold Quixano Henriques and his wife Edith moved there in 1918, the house's last residents. Descended from prominent Jamaican Jewish merchants, their stay at Sharston would be cut short when in 1932, a faulty axle in their motor car sent them crashing into a tram in Hazel Grove. David (66) and Edith (63) both died on the way to hospital in Stockport. Later the grand hall seemed to follow the all too familiar path of being bought by the council, used for a few decades, fall into underfunded disrepair, get vandalised, partially collapse and get demolished. Today, where this once glorious treasure stood, there stands a private cosmetic surgery hospital. Designed in a mock 18th century style, it only underlines how little time or money we can spare embellishing our modern buildings.

48 streets added. 19 England flags spotted. 1 more area ticked off.

Wednesday 16th June 2021 – 18.67km – Some Might Say...

Half the world away from home today, with a supersonic trip over to southeast Manchester. I rested up yesterday as my hip was still a bit niggly, but the importance of being idle every now and then, can't be underestimated. The gorgeous early sunshine was so dazzlingly bright too, it cast no shadow on my phone at times, which made my planned navigation all around the world of Burnage hard work! But, whatever, I'll get through it, little by little, the masterplan will slowly come together. Some might say this challenge is utter lunacy, but you don't live forever, the days soon slide away, so roll with it while you still can. Although I will acquiesce to it being a little bonkers.

Yeah, I did, our kid, 13 times I did. A Gallagher brothers inspired run deserved as much, right? D'you know what I mean? Ok...call it 14.

Today I headed for Burnage and I could hardly run in these parts without paying due homage to the Oasis siblings, I mean they're practically Mancunian royalty. Parking up on the border with Heaton Moor on Barcicroft Road, I headed methodically north-east up the wide Burnage Lane, dipping into the side streets on either side. Burnage is largely an area of social housing, many of which are now in private hands. Like Wythenshawe, it is a green and pleasant suburb of Manchester with many more nice areas than rougher areas, but it only takes a few idiots to spoil things. As with a few places in Manchester, I'd run these early each morning all year, but I wouldn't be back running around these parts in the evening or after dark. A chance meeting with one of the bored crazies or even the imagined thought of it wouldn't lead to a relaxed run.

As I reach Burnage Academy for Boys (Formerly Burnage High School), I'm reminded that although the newspapers might like nothing more than stories of knife crime and drugs, the success stories here don't stop at two football-mad, rock-star brothers. Some of the footballing talents to be educated here include Wes Brown, Darren and Jason Beckford and most notably Roger Byrne; Manchester United and England full-back who tragically lost his life in the 1958 Munich air crash. Other sporting stars include Menelik Watson who played as an Offensive Tackle for the Oakland Raiders and the Denver Broncos in American Football's NFL. Lamin Deen also attended the school before becoming a Grenadier Guardsman with the army, his sporting moment coming in 2014 as a Winter Olympian, piloting the 2-man and 4-man bobsleighs. The Gallagher's original bassist also attended Burnage High School. As did Aziz-Ur-Rahman Ibrahim; guitarist most notable for his work with Simply Red, the Stone Roses and Ian Brown.

Rather more interesting is the story of Bernard Morgan, the 96 year-old Burnage WWII war veteran and code breaker. After arriving on Gold beach in Normandy on D-Day, he was stationed close to the front lines encrypting and decrypting messages. In May 1945, he received and printed out the first official Telex from headquarters declaring the fighting was to end in 48 hours. He was the first soldier in Europe to know the war was over, a whole two days before V.E Day. It was a secret he would keep from his family and friends for 50 years, the Telex still proudly in his possession, despite museums falling over themselves to get their hands on it.

Touring so many identical roads and avenues with their semi-detached homes, verdant hedges and wheelie bins spectators, my mind wonders to internal matters and not everything is going so swimmingly. The camber on the roads has taken its toll on my body, causing me more than a little hip pain. Running so much, I get plenty of niggles, aches and pains but this feels a bit more than a momentary grumble. It's not yet enough for me to stop and is helped a little by running on the left side of the road instead, but it's something I'm going to have to manage while it repairs itself.

On the way back towards the car, I briefly stop for a selfie at Oasis Close, where naturally one of the road signs was missing, no doubt sold online and now adorning some fan's bedroom wall. Then as my run comes almost to a close, I reach Cranwell Drive. It's here at number one – where else? - that the Gallagher brothers grew up before forming Oasis and recording 23 top ten hits, 8 of which went to the top of the charts. Even after their split in 2009, both brothers continue to have successful solo careers. A humble semi amongst hundreds of others, it's also a good reminder that great things can come from small beginnings.

61 streets added on a beautiful day in Burnage.

Saturday 19th June 2021 – 25.87km – Gorton Bennett!

'The name Gorton means dirty farmstead.' Thanks Wikipedia, but I'll take it from here.   Another trip to East Manchester today, to the not so dirty, not so farmsteady area of West Gorton for a milestone run past Manchester's 'Taj Mahal'.

In fact, it's more likely Gore Brook gave Gorton it's dirty name. Gore in Dutch means dirty, so it's a simple leap to imagine the Anglo-Saxons using the name for this dark-coloured stream fresh from the surrounding peat-land. Mind you, if they thought it dirty at source, one can only imagine what the locals called it during the Industrial Revolution when all manner of pollutants and waste washed into it. Like so many of Manchester's waterways, it's now largely hidden from view in culverts and behind houses, which I suppose at least keeps it free of shopping trolleys and traffic cones.

After the less than dramatic 0-0 draw between England and Scotland in the Euro 2020 group match the evening before, I found little signs of life in Gorton before six o'clock in the morning. Parking up just north of Hyde Road on Crossley Street, I closed my car door quietly, sure that there would be many a sore head in the surrounding bedrooms. Thankfully, I wasn't one of them, the allure of a dawn expeditionary run to a new area more appealing than another pounding hangover of regret. I do sometimes wonder who I am these days.

Heading in a loop back down to the main road, I find Yale Road and Harvard Road. So if any American asks, I think it's fair to now say I went to Harvard and Yale. If they ask what I studied, I'll just say mainly street-maps before quickly walking away to avoid any further questions. Leaving my debatable U.S. university education behind, I head north, meandering up the eastern side of Gorton Park and onto Gorton Lane. It's here I am confronted by the glory of the Church and Friary of St Francis, more commonly known as Gorton Monastery.

An unlikely place for a Friary of Franciscans, they arrived in this working class suburb at the height of the industrial revolution in 1861, gaining help in their endeavours by a large local population of immigrant Catholics fleeing the famines in Ireland. There was little money available but the Friars and their burgeoning flock pitched in with fund-raising and free labour to build a small chapel and then an adjacent Friary. By 1866, with more sponsors from wealthier benefactors, they laid the foundation stone of a new church. The architect was the renowned Edward Welby Pugin, son of celebrated Augustus Pugin who designed much of the Gothic detail in the new Houses of Parliament in London. Edward

195

continued his father's Gothic Revival style and with two large catholic churches in Manchester already in his portfolio, he was the perfect choice.

His masterpiece stands narrow and tall above the street and neighbouring houses, the gothic style of the medieval age built with modern red brick and contrasting pale sandstone. With a steeply pitched, thirty metre high roof and a small green-patinaed copper spire reaching even higher for the heavens like a rocket, the sheer size of it in a residential area gives it a real presence. One can only imagine the influence it had on the mill workers and hard drinkers in the cramped surrounding terraced streets as this colossal house of god stood tall amongst the smoky skyline of large mills and belching chimneys.

Like so much change and buried history in Manchester, the slum clearances almost did for the Friary. As the congregation moved away and the population density reduced, so the church grew short of funds and fell into disrepair. After the Friars left in 1990, the church was deconsecrated. Soon afterwards, the roof fell in and circling profiteers were looking to convert it into apartments. Thankfully, a few volunteers set up a charitable trust in 1996 and began the long journey to gain lottery funding for a thorough restoration. Since returning to its original beauty, it has become a community space for events, weddings and tourists.

Leaving the Monastery behind, I work my way west through areas of social housing and a few tight terraced streets, surviving long after their neighbours have been bulldozed. The sun is shining between scattered clouds, the temperature is in the low teens and I get a rare moment of Zen-like running. I feel like I'm on rails, cruising along effortlessly with power and purpose, a broad smile on my face.

Rounding West Gorton Youth Centre I head down Belle Vue Street, working the streets on either side before emerging on Hyde Road opposite a pile of rubble where the Showcase Cinema used to stand. I recall going there once to see a film on a weekday afternoon and sitting with my friend in a vast and completely empty 400-seat cinema. I like to think this says more about the business than my taste in films, but then again I once went to the cinema to watch G-Force; a live-action Disney film starring four secret agent Guinea Pigs. I may or may not still be scarred by the experience.

This pile of rubble coincidentally sits on the site of Belle Vue, itself reduced to rubble in 1989. Standing across from the empty site now, it's difficult to imagine the rollercoasters, rides and zoo animals all just across the road. I take a moment, thinking of the laughter and joy of families heading inside, of the thousands of kids pulling excitedly on their parent's arms to cross the road and the beaming smiles as the troubles of daily life fade away.

Heading east along Hyde Road, I still feel good and with little pain from my hip, I decide to push on and head past the large supermarket and Gorton market into the neighbouring estate. Map-reading as I go and trying not to do too much in any one direction, I loop up past St James Church and the surrounding suburban streets before heading back to the car with an extra eight kilometres in my legs.

Knowing I was close to the milestone, I knew this extra work would definitely get me past the line, for indeed, toot all the horns, ring all the bells, I've made it past 66.6% completed roads in Manchester. I'm 2/3rds of the way through my challenge! And if any indication were needed of just how big all this nonsense is...my last milestone was 50% complete back in March.

84 streets today. One missed road I'll have to detour back to...but you can't win them all.

Sunday June 27th 2021 – 22.49km – Just Visiting

To show my affinity and support for my fellow England football fans as they build up for their big knockout match against Germany, I too have chosen a route taking me straight to Prison.

Heading once more to the north of the City Centre, I find myself a white plastic garden-chair's throw from Victoria Station in the decidedly unglamorous surroundings of Strangeways. The area's name derives from the Anglo-Saxon "Strangwas"; meaning 'besides a strong, flowing stream', although today it is largely synonymous with the prison of the same name. Having had my porridge, I was well up for doing a stretch around these parts, keeping my head down and doing my time. The irony of flaunting my liberty so near to locked-up criminals is not entirely lost on me, but I'm guessing most inside would only run the streets of Manchester if there were sirens and accompanying flashing blue disco lights. Besides, these people are obviously terrible at rolling the dice and collecting streets; Do not pass Go, Do not collect £200...

After parking further north up Bury New Road, I looped around Elizabeth Street to collect a few stray roads from a previous run before finding myself on Collingham Street, south of Manchester Fort Retail Park. Half hidden at the end of a grubby, unglamorous road used and abused by garages and wholesalers is a community unlike any other in Manchester. With bungalows surrounded with caravans, mobile homes, large lorries and trailers, this is a traveller's site rented from the council with a difference, for these are the homes of Showmen, past and present. Created nearly fifty years ago as winter quarters for the off-season, this is now a close-knit community of current and retired fairground workers, people who know what it is to make a living selling fun and excitement whilst almost constantly on the road. I didn't stray too far inside this private estate, but far enough to glimpse the amazing fairground artwork on trucks and rides not currently in use.

Heading south, I meander through the grid-like rag trade warehouses and factories east of Cheetham Hill Road and down into the notorious Red Bank area. Here beside the windy River Irk and the wide bounding arches of the railway viaducts leaving Victoria Station, there are tall, shiny apartment buildings full of professionals and comfortable living in the freshly marketed Green Quarter. The contrast between this slick present and the grubby past of this location is stark. It's here in the 'Old Town' of Manchester that the Jewish immigrants from Eastern Europe settled on the banks of the stinky, oozing Irk, between the filthy factories and beneath the soaring viaducts of the railway. It's was also one of worst slums in Victorian England where German Philosopher Friedrich Engels studied the shocking conditions for his influential book 'The Condition of the Working Class in England'. At the time, Britain shook the world into the industrial age and Manchester was at the vanguard of that revolution. It was said where Manchester led, the world followed. Yet amidst this enviable capitalism, power and wealth that so appealed to other countries, the invisible workers and underclass fared little better than raw materials or animals. Books by the likes of Engels highlighted the dire state of the crowded, dilapidated houses with their earthen floors, the unsanitary disease-ridden conditions and the appalling pay and conditions. It also influenced him and Karl Marx to write the Communist Manifesto that ultimately shaped European and Russian Communism.

From Red Bank to Red Square, if you will. I just did.

Yet, despite the shortcomings of their new home, these entrepreneurial Jewish settlers didn't descend into the criminal and drunken escapism of neighbouring slums populated by the British and Irish. From Red Bank, a special Jewish community grew that influenced the wider Manchester society, building synagogues, schools and a free library, not to mention championing the Union movement and radical action for the improvement of conditions and pay of workers. Many of these buildings such as Cheetham Town Hall, the Union offices and several Synagogues remain on Cheetham Hill Road, albeit used for other businesses or as a Jewish museum. The Jewish community in Manchester continues to thrive further up the road in Cheetham Hill.

Before being the road to Cheetham Hill, this road climbing away from the River Irk was known as York Street. At number 141, on the 24th November 1849 a woman was born who would go on to beguile and bewitch generations of children long after her death. Frances Hodgson Burnett was the daughter of a successful Deansgate Ironmonger who sadly died from a stroke when she was only three years old. Her mother Eliza continued the business, but with five growing children, they slowly fell on hard times, eventually emigrating to Tennessee in America in 1865. It was here that Frances' imagination would come into its own as she married and gained success as a writer of popular romantic novels. Yet it is her children's stories that keep her name alive in books, on stage and in films. Known for A Little Lord Fauntleroy and A Little Princess, it is perhaps The Secret Garden that she is most well-known for, with it being made into a film four times, including last year in 2020 with Julie Walters and Colin Firth.

Nearby on Empire Street, I find Empire Brewery, the home of Joseph Holt's beers since 1860. Founded in 1849 and briefly brewing in the Northern Quarter, it's been in the same family for six generations. The beers are made using water from a borehole over five hundred deep and the historic Holt yeast strain that dates back 172 years. This true survivor of a depleted Manchester brewery trade is still going from strength to strength. Its Sixex Strong Ale, brewed from a century old recipe has won a gold medal at this year's International Brewing Awards. As I traverse around these roads either side of Cheetham Hill Road, I note a few random drunks and scallies out early this morning who definitely wouldn't be able to handle such a moreish dark ale. With the pubs and clubs shut for so long, I'd almost forgotten about people staying out all night and crawling home stinking of sweat, booze and weed. Seeing them noisily arguing beside minicabs or looking moody and dishevelled at 7am, I remember I'm not always the oddest sight on these city streets.

Nudging west, I pass the back of where the Boddingtons brewery used to brew the Cream of Manchester here beneath its iconic chimney and yellow and black livery. In 1992, it was also one of the first beers to sell a can with a widget in it to release carbon dioxide when opened and therefore form a thick, creamy head atop the beer as preferred by Northern beer drinkers. A revolution rapidly copied by its competitors. Its part in making bitter a trendy drink at a time when real ale drinkers were typically bearded, nerdy and old enough for painful hips, cannot be underestimated. The current thriving market of niche craft ales continues that popular trend with hipsters, who are typically bearded, nerdy and young enough to be painfully hip.

Past the new apartments on the site of Strangeways Brewery is the prison synonymous with the area, not least because of the international headlines it conjured in April 1990, a notoriety that even made it change its name. Built in 1869 with capacity for a thousand inmates, thick walls and an iconic seventy-metre high brick ventilation tower, Strangeways was a place of imprisonment and execution. One hundred prisoners were hung at the prison from its opening to the cessation of capital punishment in 1965. One year earlier, at 7.59am on the 13th August 1964, the hangman Harry Allen led Gwynne Owen Evans to the gallows inside Strangeways Prison. Fifty kilometres away his co-conspirator Peter Allen also shuffled from his death row cell to the gallows in Liverpool's Walton Prison. Both had been convicted of murder during a bungled burglary in Workington, Cumbria in April. At exactly 8am, both sets of trapdoors opened and the prisoners fell to their deaths. These two would be the final two hangings in Britain.

Strangeways also has the macabre claim of the fastest hanging in British history. On the 8th May 1951, notorious executioner Albert

Pierrepoint led murderer James Inglis from his condemned man cell to the adjacent execution room, put the noose around his neck and pulled the lever. Urged by a prison guard to go quietly and without delay, Inglis took him at his word. From his cell door to the trapdoor opening took only seven seconds. Pierrepoint's assistant Syd Dernley says in his memoirs, Inglis practically ran to his execution.

The most famous event in the Prison's history though took much longer. Back in 1990, a riot in the prison over overcrowding and living conditions led to the prisoners taking charge and barricading themselves inside. Causing millions of pounds of damage and smashing their way out onto the roof, they soon hurled roof tiles at any guards or police below, the standoff and negotiations took 24 days to resolve. Sadly, one prisoner died and a guard died in hospital after a heart attack. Repair, rebuilding and modernisation took three years and cost £80 million, reopening as H.M.P Manchester in 1994. Famous inmates include mass murderer Harold Shipman whilst on remand, singer Ian Brown, footballer Joey Barton and television antique expert David Dickinson.

68 streets notched onto the cell wall today in a place of dark ale and darker history. Strange ways indeed...

Friday 2ⁿᵈ July 2021 – 24.27km – Wythenshawe Wander

Simon Gregson - Steve McDonald in Coronation Street - was born and raised in Wythenshawe; once Europe's largest council estate. Aged 4, he pooed himself on a helter skelter.

Hoping for no such scatological issues today, I reluctantly returned south of the M60 once more. It's not that it's particularly a bad area or oppressive or that it holds a grip on you like some other areas I've run. In some places, the helplessness hangs in the air like an invisible smog of desperation and abandonment. The unavoidable commercial propaganda of the Haves dripping unaffordable shiny desires onto the awestruck Have-Nots and Never-Haves leaves many with anger and mental health problems. The masses struggling with the basics of food, heating homes and a real sense of being left behind and no one listening or caring. Little wonder things get broken. Yet, even given Wythenshawe's reputation and the occasional negative splashes across the newspapers, I've never felt in any danger or any hurry on its streets.

No, my selfish reluctance and lack of joy for this sprawling mass of suburban housing is that as it was built on farmland as a garden city, it has little in the way of history, old buildings or character for me to waffle on about. It's simply a long, long montage of identical social housing, semis, garages, green verges, buses and trams. All very pleasant and all very zzzzzzzzz. It comes to something when I get excited at seeing a postbox. Look, look, something different, something red!

Starting just off Greenwood Road on Alders Road in Benchill, this was an ambitious run to complete the area north of Simonsway and East of the M56 motorway. After twenty-odd minutes finishing fifteen roads in Benchill, I started the long traverse down to Peel Hall. Sure, this was only around three kilometres – including a couple of stray Closes en-route – but it felt very strange. I've been grabbing streets for so long, that heading in a straight line past side streets and without looking at my map every other minute is an uncomfortable novelty. This was a throwback to 'normal' running with all its distractions of internal monologues, searching questions and imagined twinges and niggles. Worse, the feeling of deja vu, of wasting energy on streets I already recognised only made these kilometres drag ever longer. Some people dread treadmill training because the view is always the same, it seems I've taken that one stage further!

Meandering west through many streets that won't last long in the memory, I reach the Civic Centre, the focal point of the town. Built in the sixties as a shopping centre with a large Co-Op and many smaller shops, it's now dominated by an Asda supermarket and a brutally dreary concrete multi-storey car park. Next door is the Forum, complete with swimming pool, library, cafe and leisure centre. In 1976 it was home of the World Snooker Championships, sharing the honour with Middlesborough town hall in a strange two venue format. It wasn't the first time Manchester had hosted Snooker's top event, with the 1974 tournament held at Belle Vue and the 1973 tournament held at the City Exhibition Hall (Now the Air and Space Gallery of the Science and Industry Museum). Back in '76, Wythenshawe held the grand finale with Welshman Ray 'Dracula' Reardon beating Alex 'Hurricane' Higgins 27-16 in a marathon 43 frame final across four days. Never mind the cushions on the table holding up, the audience would need equally durable pillows. The following year, the World Championships moved to the Crucible in Sheffield, where it remains to this day.

From 1968 until 1982 the Civic area also contained the Golden Garter theatre restaurant; the self-proclaimed 'Showplace of the Stars'. Opening with Bruce Forsyth, it would host many famous singers and comedians through the years like Lulu, Dusty Springfield, Cliff Richard, Eartha Kitt, The Hollies, The Bee Gees, Roy Orbison, Gene Pitney, Tony Christie, Des O'Connor, Morecambe and Wise, Freddie Starr, Tommy Cooper, Bob Monkhouse, Ken Dodd and Ronnie Corbett. Sadly, the disco age replaced the desire for cabaret and the stars headed for television, pantomimes and summer seasons on the coast. Nine years after it closed, the building was gutted by fire and it's now a Bingo hall. Although as I run pass, it looks ominously like it has permanently closed its doors, another victim of these strange times.

With a little bit left in my legs, I decide to head west along Simonsway and up and over the motorway into Newall Green, before meandering north up Firbank and Hollyhedge Road on the long way back to my car. A few slight gradients along the way almost made it interesting, but in the main, like the rest of the run, it was hardly out of this world.

It wasn't always as such. Sixty years ago this month, the first man in space, Yuri Gagarin visited Manchester for a civic reception at the Town Hall - three months after he blasted into space. Arriving at the airport, he took an open top car through the streets of Wythenshawe, waving and beaming to the crowds along the way. His only stop on the way was to receive a bust of Lenin from the Amalgamated Union of Foundry Workers in Whalley Range. Truly a different time.

I don't know if Yuri pooed himself as his Vostock 1 rocket blasted him into orbit. But, I think if ever a code brown is justified, he gets a free pass. 51 soporific streets added to the list.

Saturday 10th July 2021 – 31.44km – Nightmare in Blackley

Blackley derives its name from a dark wood that covered much of this area at the far north of the City. If I'd been paying attention, I might have seen that as the portent of doom for what lay ahead.   Still, with Covid restrictions due to be lifted on the 19th and England somehow into the Euros final, the country has been glorying in the warm muggy glow of positivity this week. Although the sun was still avoiding us, I headed north with a bounce in my legs and smile on my face. It wouldn't last.

Starting on Hill Lane, I stomped upwards, the ramps and sharp rises soon devoured as I headed north, welcoming the change after the decidedly flat and dull roads of Wythenshawe. Early on a Saturday morning and running along smooth tarmac amidst the red brick terraces, semis and green hedges, I was in my element. Running streets far from home was what I do and these streets were going to get collected. Changing my route from my original plan, I worked my way west, with my headphones blasting out some tunes and the simple joys of problem solving a route keeping my brain happy and occupied.

I spotted the Co-op Academy – which is presumably a school where corner-shops go to grow up to be small supermarkets – and the vast Blackley Cemetery – whose long internal roads thankfully don't count towards my total. The Cemetery is relatively new, having been a Golf course into the 1950's. It is the last resting place of local comedian Bernard Manning and the remains of some 114 executed prisoners exhumed from unmarked graves at Strangeways when it underwent its renovations in the early nineties. (The extra 14 – for those paying attention - came from executions at Knutsford and the New Bailey prison, the bodies moved to Strangeways when these jails closed down.)

Retracing my steps from the cemetery gates and turning onto Crab Lane, I step back in time. This old road looks as if it has somehow hidden itself from the developmental highs and lows of the rest of Manchester. Named after a nearby orchard that grew crab apples, it is a settlement once surrounded by farms and fields. With rows of terraces for farm labourers and their families alongside sympathetically built modern homes and a quaint old church and community pub at its centre, the atmosphere is still that of a rural village where little has changed in two hundred years. Thankfully, a conservation order put in place in 1983 means little more will change in the future either. Climbing the narrow road as it winds its way up and over a small hill, I spot the cobbled gutters and the mock-Victorian gas streetlights, details everywhere only adding to the tranquil atmosphere. The village shop, thatched roofs and original leaded windows may all be long gone, but this street retains all the charms of a life in Manchester and its surrounding villages before the fire-breathing industrial monster scorched the ground and devoured its inhabitants.

Returning to the present I continue along rural sounding roads like Tweedle Hill Road, Plant Hill Road and French Barn Lane. The latter of which was a road I was going to have to run there and back. Not usually a problem, only as I turned onto it I found it was flat for around eighty metres before plunging over a cliff edge down a nine percent slope for a few hundred metres. Oh the dread and trepidation as I free-wheeled down that slope, before reaching the edge of a previous run. Turning with heavy legs and a heavier heart, I swearily ground my way back up. I like hills, but there are hills and then there are hills like Barn Lane. If you'll pardon my French.

Passing within a few hundred metres of my car and feeling a little leggy, I shook off any ideas of splitting the run in two and pushed on. Heading on a long protracted route to the junction of Victoria Avenue and Rochdale Road, I crossed the long bridge over the M60 to the edge of Rochdale – a new forbidden land for my list. Trudging back across into Blackley, I paused on twenty-one kilometres to eat a gel and drink some juice. Decision time. To my left was a long out and back with a few side streets and an estate around the base of several tower blocks, I estimated maybe four or five kilometres of running. Straight ahead, it was probably little more than one kilometre back to my car. So far from my home, I didn't really want to have to return just for a tiny slither on the map of maybe ten roads. My hill-frazzled legs made their strong protests known but my logic and stubbornness won out. One final push and I'd complete the top of the map in Blackley.

Big mistake.

Just two kilometres later, I hit the wall hard and slowly fell apart. My energy levels plunged over a French Barn Lane precipice and no matter of slowing, drinking or stretching was going to help. Three long kilometres later and I was down to effing and jeffing my way around the tower blocks on Moorway Drive. Alternating between speed walking and slow jogging, I felt dreadful and desperate to get back to my car to the food and drink that would hopefully revive me back from a shuffling jelly baby to a partial human being.

Incidentally, whilst in the deepest dark depths of drudgery, I passed a significant location. The Temple at Heaton Park claims to be the highest point in Manchester with spectacular views across the city from a hill measured at just under 108m above sea level. Yet here on Moorway

Drive, I find myself a further 9 metres closer to the skies at 117 metres above sea level. Granted the views are somewhat limited opposite the Cartmel Court tower block and there are zero markers, cairns or lines of Tibetan prayer flags near the car park or on the pavement, but nonetheless I have now officially climbed Mount Moorway.

Suspecting it must be the thin air atop the Mancunian world upsetting my constitution, I trudge on, back to the junction where my brain had overruled my legs and sent me into this perilous low oxygen death zone. Turning for my car, I rush mostly downhill, sucking in the delicious thick air as I return to more sensible elevations under the 100 metre mark. Deep in a land of fatigue, the last little kicker after a two kilometre trudge was a seven percent steep hill up Kerr Street to Hill Lane to finish. Staggering up the last few metres and turning the corner at the top, I've never been so glad to see my car in all my life.

Changing as quick as I could so as not to get cold, I ate all I'd brought and glugged a bottle of water before leaning back in my seat and welcoming back the feelings of life, strength and control. I'd messed up, miscalculated the elevation, underestimated the sapping mugginess and got over ambitious. A fine cocktail of minor errors, shaken and served, had delivered a draining punch that made a hard run much tougher than it needed to be. It was chastening to remember even though I've been doing this for a long while, I'm not immune to messing up. Running is easy, except when it's not. Disrespect the distances at hand and those distances will readily bite your legs off.

94 hard-earned streets added today and a healthy dent to my running self-esteem. An ego too far, it seems.

Sunday 18th July 2021 – 16.76km – Blood, Sweat and Fears

Today, I headed for a sticky West Gorton on the trail of violent gangs, railway ghosts, football roots, judgemental dragons and a murdered policeman. So, nothing much out of the ordinary.

As England valiantly lost in the Euro's final on penalties and the country wrung its hands at the terrible scenes of entitlement and temper tantrums amongst the crowd, I shrugged and went back to my running. The streets might have beat me last time out, but today was another day.

Parking up on Ashover Avenue, just off Hyde Road, amongst some lovely new homes finished with dark grey brickwork and white rendering, I immediately realise I'm being watched. An old-ish man at the end of the road stands outside the one stop shop. At six o'clock on a Sunday morning, he certainly wasn't shopping, but he had indeed stopped. Perhaps he'd misunderstood the rules. Sadly I needed to go that way, so I did, my solo audience watching me with all the focus of an owl hearing a mouse sneeze three fields away. Passing him, somewhat widely, I went fifty metres along the road to Hyde Road and came back towards him, realised belatedly I'd missed a road and made a somewhat awkward about turn. Heading up Haverford Street and back around to my car on Ashover Avenue, I once more headed straight towards the increasingly confused old man outside the shop. Making eye contact for a third time, I had the very English urge to casually nod my head to my new acquaintance or cheerily mention the warm weather. Instead I did what anyone wouldn't do in such a situation and gave a little wave. He didn't wave back.

West Gorton hasn't always suffered at the hands of staring old men, in the late 19th century it was much, much worse. The first youth culture appeared in the early 1870's, with a uniform of bell-bottomed trousers, heavy buckled belt, brass tipped clogs and a neckerchief round their necks. They lived in a culture of extreme gang violence, one that terrified the local civic and religious leaders. This was a time of the Scuttlers. Territorial gangs of 14-19 year-olds with short hair and long 'Donkey fringes' would defend the honour of their slum areas in Manchester and Salford by fighting other gangs in the streets; striking them with knives, their clogs and belt buckles. Scuttler gangs were rife across Ardwick, Bradford, Gorton and Openshaw. Women gang members also fought one another, intimidated witnesses and assaulted police. This outpouring of violence born from poverty, poor education, ill discipline and despair went on for nearly thirty years. In one instance in 1879, the Gorton Reporter described a street brawl involving some 500 Scuttlers of rival gangs. At its peak in the 1890's, it was said Strangeways was home to more Scuttlers than other criminals. Something had to be done...

Heading along Clowes Street into a neatly laid out and well-designed new estate, I pass the site of St Mark's Church between the altered street's route and Beastow Road which confusingly follows the old path of Clowes Street. It was here in the winter of 1880 that the daughter of the Rector, Anna Connell and two Churchwardens set up a football team for the local youths and young men. Alongside a Rugby team and a Cricket team in the summer, the aim was to give them an alternative to the Scuttling gangs and the persistent lure of the Public Houses. Through several name changes, brief mergers with Belle Vue and numerous moves to new fields of play, St Mark's F.C. would eventually grow into the fifth most valuable football club in the world with an estimated value of over $2Billion; Manchester City F.C.

Making short work of this smooth tarmacked and easily navigable estate, I looped back around onto Bennett Street. Here on a Brownfield site of what was once Gorton brook Chemical Works and the Union Iron Works is the 17 acre, 8 soundstage TV and Film world of Space Studios. It's only a handful of years old, but its productions vary from Coronation street, Peaky Blinders and Devs to Sky's Intergalactic and Cobra to upcoming film Morbius and Steps latest music video. It is also the current home of all those nervous entrepreneurs sweating and puffing out their cheeks on Dragon's Den. Naturally I couldn't see much activity or filming going on from the road, but I did spy several trailers and motorhomes parked up behind one of the studios with some tables, chairs and a catering truck nearby. Pop back at lunchtime and like Steps, you could reach for the stars! Sadly, security may be called and at best it'll be awkward, at worst you'll get your arm stuck in the fence. More tragic than Tragedy.

Heading east along Bennett Street, I pass the impressive Church formerly known as St Benedict's. Much like the stunning Gorton Monastery, this tall brick church with its high gothic tower and huge stained glass rose window once served the densely-populated Catholic flock in the surrounding streets. Alas, the slum clearances and dwindling population meant it closed in 2002 and faced an uncertain future. Innovation arrived just three years later and changed it into Manchester Climbing Centre. With ample space for twenty-metre high climbing walls that curve, bend and overhang, it's a unique attraction within a listed building.

Heading down St Benedict's Square, I turn onto Reabrook Avenue, formerly home of Armitage Road School. On the 9th January 1899, the school took in a travelling performer who was lodging nearby, a

208

nine-year-old clog dancer Charles Chaplin. Not sure what they taught him about the world, but six weeks later, his act continued its tour of Britain and he was gone.

Returning to the western end of Bennett Street, we enter Ardwick and return to football history. Currently the Olympic Freight terminal for storage of shipping containers and soon to be a new housing estate, this pocket of waste land between Galloway's boiler works and the railway viaduct became a rudimentary football stadium. The Hyde Road Ground in 1887 was home to Ardwick A.F.C. (Formerly known as Gorton A.F.C, West Gorton A.F.C and before that – you've guessed it – St Mark's). By 1894, the club made its final name change to Manchester City.
One unusual feature of the ground was the small "Boys Stand" in one corner. This terrace had a railway line used by the boiler works running between it and the pitch! By 1904 the stadium had a capacity of 40,000 and as such was used as a neutral ground for an F.A.Cup semi-final between Newcastle United and The Wednesday. (The Magpies beat the owls 1-0, but lost 2-0 to Aston Villa in the final, if you simply must know everything!)

In 1920, the ground became the first outside London visited by a reigning monarch when King George V watched Manchester City beat Liverpool 2-1. (I hope someone got him a hot pie and a gold tankard of Bovril at half time.) By 1923, the club had outgrown the ground and moved to Maine Road in Moss Side, yet a small part of the ground is still in use today at The Shay in West Yorkshire; half of the roof of Halifax Town's Skircoat West Stand came from the main stand of the Hyde Road Ground.

Leaving Manchester City behind, I head for the site of a most heinous crime that became known as the Manchester Outrages. Heading westerly along Hyde Road, I pass beneath a modern concrete railway bridge, the overhead wires promising a thundering flash of a speeding train at any second. Here on the 18th September 1867 though, it was a different flash and bang that shook the chattering classes of the city. At a time of growing unrest between the British Rulers and Ireland, a group calling themselves the Fenian Brotherhood were attempting to incite an uprising on the mainland. Two of their leaders; Thomas J. Kelly and Timothy Deasy had been caught in Manchester and were being escorted in separate sections of a police van with three women and a 12-year-old boy to Belle Vue Gaol to the east along Hyde Road.

At this bridge, a gang of 30-40 Fenian sympathisers stopped the police van. After shooting a horse, the ragtag bunch of twelve escorting police officers fled, leaving one officer – Police Sergeant Brett - inside the stranded van with the prisoners. Hatchets, sledgehammers and prying bars could not open the doors, so they pleaded with Brett to open it from the inside; he stoically refused. Then fate dealt a cruel blow. One of the rescuers drew his pistol and placed it by the lock, just as Sergeant Brett stooped to peek out the keyhole. The shot killed him instantly and he became the first ever police officer in the city to be killed on duty. One of the women prisoners pulled the keys from his dying body and after handing them through an air vent, the Irishmen were free. They were never recaptured.

The police went into hyper drive rounding up anyone with an Irish accent and raiding houses all over Gorton and Ardwick. In the end, amidst a feverous anti-Irish atmosphere they got three people convicted of murder and hung outside Salford Gaol. To this day in at least a dozen places across Ireland, there are monuments and murals commemorating the sacrifice of these three Manchester Martyrs.

Heading up Devonshire Street North and the side streets of small commercial businesses around Chancellor Lane, I finish at an unlikely stop. Along an uneven cobbled street, through a tunnel with water-stained walls, I find the ominous entrance to Ardwick Station. Through a gate beside a large overgrown shrub, I walk a narrow path beside the railway viaduct, turn to climb some narrow steps, turn again to meander past a large electrical substation, climb up and over a rusted footbridge over the tracks and then down onto the ghost station of Ardwick. Built in 1842, it was once a busy hub in the Manchester network, yet now it only gets two trains a day (One in, one out) and a measly 1500 passengers a year. I stroll the full length of this island platform atop the viaduct. Stranded between the main line and a curving side line, it feels both abandoned and ignored, but there's a kind of beauty in that. Close by is the Ardwick depot and as I watch, a train creeps out of the sheds and crawls towards the main line and Manchester. I'm no trainspotter, but there's something beguiling at watching such a huge hulk of metal and energy move along at a graceful pace whilst filling the air with the earthy stench of fumes and hot metal. As it nears, I stand on the rusted footbridge looking out across the rooftops of Manchester, basking in the sunshine and the elation of a post-run glow.

I looked down at the driver and gave a little wave. He didn't wave back.

After last week's debacle and the air getting increasingly humid beneath a thick blanket of cloud, I kept this run much shorter, but still clocked up a decent 46 streets.

Sunday 25th July 2021 – 18.47km – Weary in Wythenshawe

After last week's thoroughly enjoyable and historically interesting run, it seems only right to balance the yin out with a healthy dollop of yang. And nothing comes more yang-ier than another trip south over the motorway, to the area formerly known as Cheshire.

With this challenge taking over much of my free time and free thoughts, it's little wonder some of those free radicals turn on me every now and then. Which is probably why I have a recurring dream where I'm giving guided running tours of Wythenshawe for tourists. I am sweating profusely as I know this is the least historic and interesting suburb I have run. I have nothing to say because there is nothing to see. So I do the honest, dignified gentlemanly thing and hurriedly try to run away...but sadly wherever I go, they all follow me. I speed up, they speed up, I cut down alleyways and in and out of cul-de-sacs and they follow effortlessly, laughing like crazed Olympians taking selfies with their phones. No matter which trading estate or identical concrete road I dart down they're there in hot pursuit...'Mr Man, who build this? Who lives there? Mister, where tram go? What they sell there? Hey, we go faster again now?'

It's been a long week working outside in the summer sun. Doing physical work in 28-30C saps the energy from the body like no other and I empathise greatly with those currently taking part in the 2020 Tokyo Olympics. Scheduled in the tropical heat and humidity of July, it seems lunacy to compete at such a time, no wonder many of the events are scheduled for an early morning start. Not feeling up for a long run, I tried to find a nice easy-ish loop to keep my roads tally ticking over before feasting on the action from sport's greatest show on earth.

Parking up just off Ruddpark Road in the Woodhouse Park area of South Wythenshawe, I forced myself out of the car; sleepy, empty and unenthusiastic. It was much cooler than earlier in the week, the skies open to the pale blue of early summer morns before the sun dazzles and steals the show. With a slight chill on the skin, I rushed the first few streets in an effort to warm up, settling into a breathy rhythm. There was little to see, most of my energy spent reading the map and working a logical route through the curving, winding roads where one junction looks much like another, the whole layout like a maze of houses, green verges and concrete roads. I won't miss them. Jarring the hips, knees and seemingly the very marrow of my bones, the mean streets of Wythenshawe hit back hard, seemingly indignant at being conquered.

After 9km of meanderings, I emerge onto Shadow Moss Road and head north before cutting across the adjacent tram tracks and dipping into the small Ringway Trading Estate. Further up the road, I head into the plusher corporate world of Concord business Park with its modern brick and glass offices set amidst leafy avenues and spacious car parks. It's here I encounter a quandary, a predicament of conflicting information. Approaching the offices for Virgin Media, my map tells me Threapwood Road continues in a long loop behind the offices. Yet, red and white barriers block the roads either side of the building. How disappointing to come all this way and have my task spoilt by an inaccessible route. Still, rules are rules and the barriers are obviously there for a reason. One cannot just walk where one wants, willy-nilly, trespassing through a company's empty car park, even before 7am on a Sunday morning, is not a matter to be taken lightly. So I ran round them instead. The most childish part of me wished a security guard had come out, so at least I'd have someone to race around those five hundred metres. Although encouraging them to keep up for a third lap would probably prove a tad self-indulgent.

Heading east along Simonsway, I pass Atlas Business Park with its barriers, but my spree of petty trespass is over as my map sees no roads here. On a little further and I pass the 17th century farmhouse Chamber Hall, albeit behind tall hedges and hidden from view. The Listed building and small plots of farmland harking back to a sleepier rural time. The wooden building was encased in brick in 1703, retaining an original medieval roof beam and a 17th century studded plank door with strap hinges and moulded wooden handle.

I'm at the south eastern edge of Manchester here and see signs for the borough of Stockport ahead at Heald Green; which itself sounds like a wound that hasn't fixed itself properly. Turning away from this forbidden land, I head south towards the airport, ticking off a few more side roads before moving west past the lovely Tatton Arms pub in the tiny hamlet of Moss Nook. The area south of here was for centuries a peat bog called Shadow Moss. Dug up for use as fuel, locals each had an allocated patch of bog called a 'Moss Room' where they would dig up peat before carefully relaying the moss back on top. Later farmers used the fertile land for market gardening of fruit and vegetables. The hamlet of Heyhead, the farms and farmers are now all gone, the land used by the airport and long stay parking.

At the end of Ringway Road, I slow to a crawl and then stop. My willpower is at a low ebb. Drained, I sit on a fence at the end of the runway, watching several planes thunder down the tarmac between the shimmering lines of lights and soar effortlessly into the empty blueness over my head. It's easy to imagine the excited giddiness on board as the passengers escape these shores after so long being unable to go much

212

further than the nearest shops. As ever with these things, wherever there is the glory of technological wonder and innovation, tragedy is never far away. In this case, less than 50 metres from where I'm sat.

In the early afternoon of the 14th March 1957, a Vickers Viscount was approaching the airport for landing after a routine flight from Amsterdam. One mile short of the runway, it suddenly turned into a shallow dive to the right, the tip of the wing striking the ground before the plane burst into flames and crashed across Shadow Moss Road, demolishing two houses and killing all 20 passengers and crew on board, plus two more on the ground. In a terrible, gut-wrenching twist of fate, ex-airport fireman Wally Wilding had petitioned against the dangers of low-flying aircraft a year before the crash. His fears happened as the plane hit his home, killing his wife and young son instantly. The cause of the crash, like so many in those pioneering years of air travel was metal fatigue and a single faulty bolt on one of the aileron flaps. The safety of modern air travel is down to lessons learnt from all that has tragically gone wrong in the past. As I run past the rebuilt houses at the crash site, you wouldn't even know anything untoward had happened here. I leave with some sadness that this forgotten tragedy remains unmarked by a memorial or plaque to those who had their lives sadly cut short.

A respectable 55 roads run today, far more than I'd hoped. Now to nurse these aching joints and dream of gold medals for me and all my running tourists.

Sunday 1ˢᵗ August 2021 – 23.22km – Good Grief it's Newton Heath

Away, away-o to Newton Heath I head this morning for a run
filled with stories of strong-minded Women. After Wythenshawe last
week, it was nice to return to softer, tarmacked roads and actually have
things to see and enjoy. Even the subtle differences in architecture and
street layouts make a welcome change after the monotony of
Wythenshawe semi-detached cottage estates. With much of the far-flung
areas in the Northeast and Southeast areas of Manchester completed or
near completed, I have left a distinct gap still to do across much of the
eastern portion of the city. Running from Harpurhey and Moston down
along the eastern border, through Clayton, Gorton and Longsight into
Levenshulme and Burnage. This side of the city is where the bulk of these
elusive un-run roads remain, mocking me with their unexplored exitence!

With the cyclists, swimmers and divers doing us proud over in
Japan, music festivals back on and a massive 85million vaccines having
been administered in the UK, there's a real sense of summer optimism in
the air. Although as last week's heatwave slumps back into the mild,
broken clouded days and wet nights of an unremarkable Manchester
summer. I, for one, am not complaining in the change of temperature.

Parking up just off Berry Brow on Assheton Road – presumably
where they make electric car seats – I immediately saw this might be a
somewhat hilly run. Climbing steeply away from the level crossing and
the old Railway Inn beside it up Berry Brow though, the road rapidly
reached a plateau and I settled into a steady pace around several damp
roads with some respectable Victorian townhouses. This is Clayton
Bridge, a small hamlet at the eastern end of Clayton Vale built to house
the workers at the nearby Dye and Finishing works and various other local
industries such as the print works over at Phillips Park and rubber works
at Culcheth just to the west of here. All the industries attracted by the
meandering waters of the River Medlock. Here at number 18 Ingham
Street, near the centre of a modest row of terraced houses, I find the later
life home of Hannah Mitchell – a radical suffragette and socialist who
helped the Pankhursts in the fight for women's votes and rights. She
eventually worked for Keir Hardie - first leader of the Labour Party.

Further to the north, I briefly divert down another steep hill to the
border with Failsworth, over in the forbidden land of Oldham. Rebelling
against the natural conventions, I pass unseen into this other world of
foreign houses and roads for a hundred metres, climbing up to the next
bend in the road. Here I slowed and paused nervously, although I couldn't
see any onrush of armed guards, whirring drones, barking dogs or

growling tanks, I knew they must be on their way. Looking around with wonder, my imagination struggling to conjure the culture, language and decors that must exist within this foreign environment. With a last glimpse at the houses that look oh so similar to those just over the border in my own city, I flee hastily back across to the safety of Mancunian ground underfoot. Climbing back up the hill and chastising myself at such an unnecessary diversion, I grin with exhilaration at getting away with my brief adventure into Failsworth. I only hope I maintain my liberty from their secret service agents long enough to one day tell my grandchildren.

I skirt past Brookdale Park, originally the gardens of Brookdale Hall; the impressive two storey home of local industrialist James Taylor built in 1850. Taylor made his fortune with his partners with several mills including Newton Silk Mill nearby on Holyoak Street. Complete with stables, farm buildings and greenhouses, his home with its servant quarters and glass summerhouse sat in eighteen hectares of grounds. The Manchester Corporation bought it in 1900 and converted it to a park complete with sports facilities, pathways, sunken gardens and the obligatory bandstand. The Hall was sadly demolished in the 1960's in that period when there was little money for the past, only the follies of an imagined future.

Winding my way methodically west and north takes a while as the streets here are densely packed, cul-de-sacs and closes dipping into every gap between roads to squeeze in a few more abodes. I see as many new builds as old, as much unloved social housing as tidy gardens, places I'd love to call home and others I'd rather not. In places, I see hanging baskets resplendent with dazzling blooms and where every car seems in a competition to be the cleanest. In others, I appear to be ankle deep in litter, with plastic bottles skidding noisily away from my toes to the gutter. On the corner of Scotland Street, I come across a black car with four flat tyres and a huge splash of white paint across the windscreen and dripping across the bonnet as if a passing present from an ill pterodactyl. Someone has seriously upset someone else, emulsions obviously running high!

Heading down Briscoe Lane, I'm reminded that I'm not the first to have marched swiftly down this path. Pointed roughly northeast, this arrow-straight lane follows the Roman road originally built to connect Chester to York. I guess I should be grateful that doesn't still count as one road. It's also home to The Phoenix; a pub or club, which has certainly seen better days. With the P hanging off the peeling paint above the door and a burnt out car in the weed-filled flagged garden, even Brian Potter might call it quits on this one rising from the proverbial ashes. Looking decidedly closed and as inviting as a dose of anthrax, I check my map and rave on out of there. Shabba!

Moving gradually southward, I rush to and fro never really straying too far in any one direction before returning. Moving into an area of council housing and the four tower blocks of Croydon Drive, I reflect that for all hardships people suffer today, there have been worse periods to live through. Just nearby in Clayton Vale in the early twentieth century, the Manchester Corporation used the waste ground as a place to tip municipal waste and the ashes from the nearby Stuart Street Power Station. Regardless of this environmental disaster, the real hardship came in the impoverished 1920's when the Miners went on strike. There are tales of grubby children, men and women in their hundreds scouring this blackened, dusty ground for a nugget of unburnt coal, many with spades and shovels as if from a scene of a Californian gold rush. All for the hope of something to cook with and keep them warm into the perishing night.

As the drizzly rain returns, I find myself on Amos Avenue. It was here at number 79, almost opposite Christ the King Catholic Church, that Mancunian TV presenter and writer Judy Finnegan grew up. This would be in the 1950's and 60's, long before she married Ali-G impersonator Richard Madeley and presented the student and unemployed daytime favourite; This Morning. I pause in tribute by staring vacantly into the middle-distance like some of their viewers who were incapable of finding or working their television's remote control. It's the least I can do.

Meandering in and out of several roads at the edge of Clayton Vale, I find myself tipping over the rim of the plateau several times onto steep roads. So late in the run, I have to dig deep to lift my tightening legs and haul myself back up these telling slopes. I guess it's all good training even if you're not actually training for anything. Even though it was a little of a struggle at times on the steepest of hills, I still enjoyed that fight through the lactic acid, heavy breathing and the mind game of pushing hard over the top of a climb when others naturally slow to catch their breath. Many a time in races I've gained ten or more places amongst the staggering masses atop a climb. Heading downhill past the car and on one final loop down Berry Brow and back up a ridiculously steep narrow footpath, I called it quits as soon as the last road was complete. Walking back to the car with my sides aching, I felt that happy joy of the thoroughly exhausted but unbroken.

I got much more done than I'd hoped for too; 90 roads complete plus one extra street. After I'd finished and checked my results, I discovered one road I'd not run sticking out like a sore thumb amidst all the completed streets on my map. Lumbering back into a run 10 minutes after I'd stopped was much less glamorous, my stiffening limbs making me feel like the Tin Man from the Wizard of Oz. Serves me right as I'd missed it. Unlike the television show This Morning.

Sunday 8th August 2021 – 16.37km – Parrs Wood Paddle

Ah summer. A time to leap out of bed, throw on those light running clothes and bound into the warm embrace of the sun as it recharges your mood and bedazzles your spirits...

Manchester, as ever, fails to comply to the rules.

Hauling myself up from the mattress, I look out through a curtain of raindrops at a world even a goose might turn its beak up at. I didn't want to go. I reasoned it would be stupid to go out in such weather and make myself ill, besides no-one could make me go, I'm not a child anymore, I'm a 43-year-old man. That was the end of the matter, I wasn't going, I was being a normal, rational, sensible and logical human being and wisely going back to bed. Decision made. Final answer.

Thirty minutes later and I pull the car up on Parrs Wood Road at the eastern end of Didsbury. The rain has been here for thirty-six hours at this point, the skies the grey glow of a dirty skylight, the ground sodden and filled with puddles merging into small lakes. Passing cars sent up rooster tails of spray as they swished through the wet streets. Blackbirds landed on the grass verges for their morning worms wearing full yellow sou'wester hats and coats. A mouse passes in a small rowboat fashioned from leaves. There's two fish watching me from a hedge. A duck waddles past towards the river with a surfboard under its wing.

With all manner of lies to myself about skin being waterproof and enjoying it once I got going, I expected that at best this was going to be something of a misery-fest, at worse a tumultuous journey into quarrying new swear words from a pit of muttered profanities.

Despite myself, I settled into a dripping, soaked rhythm and with the occasional soaring leap over a puddle, actually began to enjoy the run. The rain bouncing off my head and shoulders eased to a strong persistent drizzle as I headed away from the suburban streets onto Wilmslow Road. Passing Didsbury Cricket Club, which traces its history all the way back to 1858, I reach the Towers Business Park. With its gaudy, oversized signs and frontage of modern glass offices, this small site hides an architectural treasure at its rear. Looping around the empty car parks and the brash walls of shiny glass, the first glimpse of the gothic splendour of The Towers is like looking upon a weathered film star at the head of a table of teenagers.

It took four years to build in red brick, stone and red terracotta, completed in 1872 for the cost of £50,000 (£5.7m in today's money). Once described as the finest of all Manchester mansions, the locals reputedly

218

called it 'Calendar House', because it was said to have 12 towers, 52 rooms and 365 windows - although more a flight of fancy than fact, it gives a hint of the scale of this grand old building. It's place in history is no less impressive. In the late 19th century, local businessmen faced increasing charges from the railway companies and Liverpool docks to access the Irish Sea and with it, the rest of the world. With cotton to import and goods to export, profits were being squandered and solutions were about to become radical. Here in June 1882, in the drawing room of notable engineer Daniel Adamson, the historic decision was made to undertake the colossal task of creating a wide waterway linking Manchester to the sea; the Manchester Ship Canal. After its opening in 1894, the canal would help the Port of Manchester to become Britain's third busiest port, despite the city being 64 kilometres inland. I wander a while around the building, resplendent even in the rain and envy the workers who can lunch and sit in its shadow.

Looping back through its grounds, I return to Wilmslow Road and head down Kingston Road past some lovely Victorian houses with a fine assortment of 4x4's and sports cars in the front drives. Back up Millgate Lane beside Fletcher Moss Botanical Gardens, I take a small detour inside this fine park to see the Alpine tearooms. In the 1880's this was a private residence known as the Croft and where the radical Emily Williamson lived with her husband. Only it wasn't the suffragette movement that caught Mrs Williamson's attention, rather the environmental shame of 'murderous millinery'. In 1889, at a time when feathered hats were all the fashion, Mrs Williamson pushed back and formed the fledgling Society for the Protection of Birds. Despite terrible mocking from the bird-brained patriarchy, within ten years the society had truly taken flight, gaining twenty thousand members across more than one hundred and fifty groups. It even garnered approval from Queen Victoria and granted a royal charter. Born here in Didsbury, the RSPB continues to fight for the rights and habitats of our feathered friends to this day. I show my gratitude with a thankful nod of the head. Or should that be a twitch...

Sightseeing over, I return to the suburbs and head to the end of Millgate Lane and back over some gargantuan puddles. Halfway down I cross a bridge over one of the flood overspills for the nearby River Mersey. The wide green trench looks like an old moat, with floodgates in the riverbank at the far end. Glad it's not yet required, I nonetheless push on a little faster. My clothes have soaked up almost all of the rain, sticking to my skin and hanging heavy on my shoulders. My fingers are becoming wrinkly and shrivelled as if I'd spent too long in a bath. One too many missteps mean my shoes and feet are currently wetter than a dolphin's handbag. Yet, as I reach a point where I could easily split this run in two and beat a squelchy retreat back to the car, I hear some inner Spock/Data tell me how illogical it would be to have to return to this part of Manchester simply because of some exceptional seasonal precipitation. I'm not sure I like inner Spock, I'm not a hundred percent sure he has my best interests at heart, but I know he'd only say there is no like, only do. So reluctantly, I do.

Cutting through an alleyway onto Kingsway, I head south, up and over the swollen, swirling waters of the River Mersey to the sign marking the forbidden land of Stockport. With little enthusiasm, I turn and work my way up through the streets just off this main road and across to Wilmslow Road, once more beside the Mersey. Here near the centre of the old stone Cheadle Bridge, there is a small, almost overlooked marker labelled 'L/C'. Rather than a misspelt memorial to someone called Elsie, it actually denotes the old boundary between the counties of Lancashire and Cheshire. Also marking my liquid-covered about-turn, I head back to the north to the huge Parrs Wood cinema and entertainment complex. Behind it and almost hidden in plain sight is Parrs Wood House, a Georgian mansion described by the architectural historian Pevsner as 'a poorer man's Heaton Hall.' It now lives on as the sixth form of Parrs Wood High School, known in 2008 as the fourth largest school in the UK with nearly 2,500 students.

Crossing the main road by the Wetherspoons pub, I head back down the opposite side of Kingsway, dipping in and out of no less than nine cul-de-sacs just as the rain turns into a heavy rain shower. 'Oh good.' I muttered, or something similar as I attached my snorkel.

The long slosh, squish, splash and splosh back to the car was not a parable of defiant positivity. There was no rousing inner monologue or orchestral score, no wide-eyed passersby or slow motion leaps over puddles full of fish. It was nothing triumphant, virtuous or inspirational bar a very northern sense of stubbornness in the face of misery. I am all mule, hear me whinny-hee-haw.

On a happier note, as I sat eating recovery snacks in a steamed up car – to hell with the twitching net curtains - I discovered my persistence had floated my total up 44 sodden roads to 75% streets complete. 4711 streets, roads, lanes, cul-de-sacs and avenues run. Only 1569 left to go. Whisper it quietly, but with a fair wind, I might even get this done before the year is out.

Tuesday 10th August 2021 – 14.8km – The Boy is Back in Town

Back on home territory, I go looking for Eric, phantom fish and a secret showbiz hotel.

With my shoes still faintly damp after the weekend drenching, I step out into the August afternoon sunshine, wishing they were damper. Another post work run and one of those days where I was already a little baked, tired and dehydrated before I started. I knew I had to bounce back outside from home immediately or the sofa gravity would get me big time. So with scant regard to fashion and more akin to a triathlon transition than a change of clothes, I was back out on the streets of Chorlton before my persuasive brain could begin its internal marketing presentation on the joys of rest days and biscuits.

Heading East along Wilbraham Road, I'm back on home territory, although the ticker-tape and waving locals remain imagined. It feels strange to be somewhere so familiar, yet also somewhere I haven't run for almost eighteen months. Beyond the shops and Morrisons Supermarket in Chorlton, I pass the rather underwhelming hidden start to that old friend and running route; the Fallowfield Loop. Over the bridge over the Tramlines, I divert off the main road and start picking up some of the smaller roads I haven't travelled before. These are the usual straight roads and semis of suburbia, albeit with a handful of dreaded concrete roads mixed in to sap the hot, weary legs. At the end of Ellesmere Road with its older, taller and more elegant villas, I pause at the South West Manchester Cricket Club.

Founded in 1882 at the height of the Victorian enthusiasm for sport and well-being, the club has two rather particular claims to fame, neither of which relate to Cricket. In 2008, this club was the site for the Ken Loach film 'Looking for Eric'; a comedy-drama about one man's escapism idolising Manchester United and its former star striker, Eric Cantona. A picture of the footballer pulling a pint at the club remains pride of place behind the bar. In the same year, the club's crown-green bowlers set a new Guinness World Record by playing bowls 24 hours-a-day for a full seven days. I dare say in this instance, any transfixed spectators would be excused for momentarily 'resting their eyes'.

Working east I reach Alexandra Road South in the heart of the Whalley Range Conservation Area. Much of the original layout of mature tree-lined avenues and tall Victorian villas of the suburb survive here, giving the area a pleasant, leafy atmosphere. This is also an area of various churches and exclusive schools, including Hartley Hall, which combined the two. Built in 1878, for the Primitive Methodist Church to educate its prospective preachers, its gothic clock tower and original railings and gates make it look like a school lifted straight from a Dickensian novel. It currently houses the K. D. Grammar School. Further north past the English Martyrs R.C. Church with its stunning stained glass windows, I run alongside my favourite park where this all started, seemingly thousands of hours ago. Here overlooking the park is St Bede's College – an independent Catholic school – in a building with an unusual past.

In 1874, this was the site of Manchester's first ever Aquarium. With sea creatures in 68 tanks filled with barrels of salt water brought in from Blackpool, this strange world of fish and crustaceans from the deep must have been a wondrous revelation to the local Mancunians. Or perhaps not. Despite the considerable expense, the Aquarium was something of a flop. Being so far from the centre in a suburb can't have helped either. Just three years after opening, the Aquarium closed its doors, the building bought by the college. Incorporated into the new building, a few hints remain of its watery past. In the plasterwork above the marble columns and arches are some plaster moulds of fishes and sea creatures. In other places, there are noticeable dips in the marble floor as a direct result of the sheer weight of the water held in some of the larger aquarium tanks. Granada Television has used the beautiful original interiors for filming 80's series Jewel in the Crown and The Adventures of Sherlock Holmes. Notable alumni include the sixth Dr Who – Colin Baker, The Word's Terry Christian, England Footballers Phil Foden and Jadon Sancho, Inspiral Carpet's Clint Boon, folk singer Mike Harding and the lead singer of Herman's Hermits – Peter Noone.

Something tells me I'm into something good, as I leave Alexandra Road South and the park behind to work my way down the parallel street at its rear, Alness Road. Here, on the quiet, leafy corner of Wellington Road in 1966, an Irish lady named Philomena took over the running of the Grange Park Hotel, otherwise known as the Showbiz Hotel as it was popular with all the singers, dancers, comedians and novelty acts playing late night at Manchester's Cabaret Clubs. As such, its bar only opened when they returned from work at 2am and closed at 6, with breakfast served from midday. Supposedly only open for residents, it nonetheless became a favourite late-night haunt for George Best and some local heavies known as the Quality Street Gang.

Only Philomena was no ordinary woman, she was the mother of Phil Lynott of Thin Lizzy fame. He often visited and was said to have befriended many of these local gangsters, to the extent his hit record - The Boys Are Back In Town – is believed to be written about his friends in the roguish Gang. A decade after she took over the Hotel, another band was making waves in an infamous television interview. When the Sex Pistols swore live on Bill Grundy's Today Show – which seems beyond tame now – they found every hotel in Manchester turning them away. Except Philomena's. Stood on her doorstep in the rain, she gave them a five-bed room and invited them down to the bar, where they were reportedly the nicest mannered lads. I dare say, sat amongst local gangsters and a powerful Irish matriarch who's given you refuge for the night...you'd be the nicest mannered too.

With sweat pouring and my lips parched, I head home from Whalley Range with my 32 scorched streets, ready for a cold shower and a gallon of juice. Whiskey in a jar will just have to wait.

Friday 13ᵗʰ August 2021 – 27.01km – Hammer and Clank at Gorton Tank

Nineteenth Century Manchester was a place of great industry with cotton mills and textile works filling the air with smoke and steam. Yet, Cotton wasn't all that Manchester was famous for at the time, the steam power that had revolutionised the mills was also being harnessed in ways that must have equally fascinated and terrified all those that saw it.

After last week's drenching and the turning of a significant milestone, I had to take a long hard look at where I was headed. At best, I had three and a half months before my job would enter the Christmas rush and become so exhausting as to render running on my recovery days as not just unwise but impossible. Despite my deliberate avoidance of time-frames or pressures on this challenge, I now realised I had a choice to make. It had taken me four and a half months to get from halfway to three-quarters of the way through this challenge. Continuing at the same pace and missing December out, I'd still be running in the cold and dreary months of February and March 2022. Alternately, I could push on and try to get this challenge completed before the enforced break at the end of November. I went into this challenge eyes wide open at the size and time it would take, but even I have to admit that having come so far, I was looking forward to seeing that finish line, no matter how far away in the distant future it may still be.

Gorton and Openshaw however were much closer destinations and the subject of today's exploration. Starting on Gorton Lane, close to the Steelworks Tavern, I head east, finishing off several roads north of Gorton market before dipping into a small industrial estate on a historic industrial site. As I breathe in the delectable aroma in the air of baked treats, I imagine the boxes of jalapeno cheese bites, vegetable samosas or mini pizza tarts as I find the Iceland food factory. Floating and drooling, I pass by this and several other businesses, somehow resisting the lure of a nearby burger van as the near irresistible aromas of sizzling bacon and fried eggs waft from its open hatch. Several happy punters in high-vis jackets and hard helmets take no notice of me as they gorge themselves on deliciously greasy calories. No doubt, the hard-working and hard-drinking men of Gorton who originally worked on this site equally required such hearty sustenance, for this was the site of Beyer, Peacock and Co, manufacturers of Railway locomotives.

With the vast Gorton Locomotive Works – known locally as Gorton Tank - on the other side of the railway line and B, P & Co. on this side at the Gorton Foundry, this part of eastern Manchester was synonymous with the railway industry. Built in 1854, Gorton Foundry turned out over 800 engines in its first fourteen years, many exported across the world to southern Africa and South America. Some of their greatest innovations included a condensing train for the London Underground, reducing the steam put out by conventional engines in London's tunnels at the time. Perhaps more impressive was the 'Garratt' - a powerful 200-tonne monster with a boiler spanning seven foot in diameter. Designed for difficult terrain along tightly curved tracks, this beast became widely used throughout Africa, Asia, Australia, South America and the South Pacific. Anyone seeing this hissing metal dragon rumble past on its diet of coal, fire and water must have been awestruck at how it could move let alone pull a colossal cargo behind it. Despite a diversion to produce heavy artillery during the First World War, Beyer, Peacock and Co. would continue building engines into the diesel and electric age before finally closing in 1966. By which time it had produced nearly 8000 locomotives, some still operating around the world to this day.

Running along Railway Street and heading north, I pass two more burger vans amidst the businesses here before reaching Ashton Old Road and heading west. On my left where Gorton Locomotive Works built over 1000 engines for the Manchester, Sheffield and Lincolnshire Railway Co. which later became Great Central Railway when it extended its network to Marylebone Station in London. More than manufacture, these works were used for maintenance, repairs, overhauls and refitting of trains and carriages, the great site once filled with railway lines like a spilled plate of spaghetti. It's now predominantly home to Smithfield Fruit and Vegetable market and the Openshaw home for GMP Traffic Police. All trace of the past has been long demolished or buried but as I worked my way west I found one little patch of the past showing through between two patches of overgrown waste ground. Here on Redby Street, a short side street running north to south from Ashton Old Road towards the railway line, is a short length of track set into an old cobbled street. This was part of a route running straight through the streets of Openshaw connecting Armstrong Whitworth's huge naval gun factory to the North Street steelworks some 250 metres away. The thought of pulling back the net curtains of your terraced house and watching a small engine shunting wagons of hot steel ingots down your street as the glass vibrated and pictures fell off the walls certainly must have made life interesting.

Crossing the main road into Openshaw, I pass yet another hot food van surrounded by white van drivers and even a small hole-in-the-wall eatery called the Butty Hatch serving a mechanic in oily overalls. The growling whale song from my stomach was seriously distracting my hunger for streets.

It was at this point I noted some of the streets were getting a little more unloved with several places scoring a fair to medium on the abandoned mattress Index. Whilst unsightly and annoying, I kept the rating low as the propensity for broken glass was light and there were no signs of any of the crazies turning up with their one brain cell and a box of matches. 'It burns, it burns, I make hot yellow-red!'

Moving swiftly on, I pass through another dilapidated industrial area filled with garages, litter, broken roads and badly weathered brick walls topped with barbed wire or weeds. Passing back under the railway I start a three-kilometre diversion down to Hyde Road and the old site of Belle Vue Gaol. Built improbably just along from the Zoological Gardens in 1845 to house up to 500 short-term male and female prisoners, it became synonymous with overcrowding and abysmal conditions. Alas, it wasn't the terrible life for the prisoners that caused the jail to close in 1888 but subsidence from underlying mining from the nearby Bradford colliery damaging the foundations. After the prisoners moved to Strangeways and the New Bailey in Salford, the building was demolished, with some of the stonework ironically purchased by Belle Vue to build a similar place of captivity for the rhinos.

Heading back up to Ashton Old Road and back alongside Smithfield Market, I feel my legs slowly turning into wood and my willpower waning even as I pitch downhill. Nearly done, the railway crossing Gorton has one last treat for me. Heading down Bessemer Street, there's a slight kink in the road as it passes under the wide spread of railway lines, giving no view of the exit at the other side. Through the darkness sits my car and the end of a weary run around 75 streets. Yet, here I stand in the dazzling sunshine, the dark entrance into this tunnel under the tracks looking as inky black as an entrance into the underworld and as inviting as a one way trip into an abyss. Of course it'll be alright, I tell myself, it's only a bit of darkness, nothing to be scared of. And that's when I remember today is Friday the 13th...

Sunday 15th August 2021 – 21.10km – Too Much or Too Little

Irish writer and Theatre critic, George Bernard Shaw once described today's location as the prettiest village in all of Manchester.

The football season has restarted and the crowds are back! After so many games behind closed doors and fake crowd noise played over the matches on TV, it feels like another step towards normality, towards people enjoying themselves again and not having to worry about doing so. Alas, the weather on this Sunday morning was not behaving as it should, still at least the rain wasn't cold. To be fair, the shade of grey and the temperature of the drizzle are what largely define Manchester's seasons. Still, 'liquid sunshine is character building,' said no one ever.

No one. Ever.

With all the puffed cheeks, sighs, bowed head and sagging shoulders of a stroppy teenager, I reluctantly headed out into the gloom behind my windscreen wipers. Totally not in the mood, I'd already shelved my planned long run in Blackley for an easy 5-10km saunter nearer to home. Compromise, I told myself. The rolled eyes and sigh of my scepticism was more telling.

Arriving in Burnage just as my car's heater sputtered out the warm breath of an asthmatic lizard, I parked up on Senior Avenue and appropriately hauled my cold-blooded bones out of the vehicle. Stepping my workload up to two or more runs a week on top of my physical job was going to take a little getting used to. I knew I could do it, but also knew it'd mean starting with a healthy dose of fatigue already in the legs. Still, 'fatigue is character build-'. Oh do...shut up!

Ladybarn is yet another of those pretty hamlets surrounded by old terraces surrounded by more modern urban sprawl. The mix is often confusing at first but the more I look, the more I see. From the unique shapes of old farmhouses and labourers terraces, often pointed at an angle or perpendicular to the road. Some substantial dwellings stand beside converted Wesleyan chapels and the school for the clergyman and schoolmaster. Even the embellishments and flourishes (or lack of) on buildings can tell you what type of people they were built for and their relative affluence at the time. The older buildings, the survivors often sit close to public houses and churches by important road junction, such as at the meeting of Mauldeth Road and Ladybarn Lane. Yet this junction is also a tale of three ghost pubs no longer serving thirsty travellers.

In general, pubs are dying. People are drinking less and staying home more and the pandemic has simply accelerated this decline. Those that adapt survive, those that don't or can't just fade away into people's memories. The Talbot Hotel on the aforementioned corner was a grand affair that survived until 2008 before making way for an apartment block. It's most famous landlord was Frank Swift in the 1950's. The former Man City and England goalkeeper ran it after retiring from the game, back in the day when football paid pounds, not millions. Sadly, after moving into sports journalism, he would perish in 1958 aboard the United team plane in the Munich Air Disaster. Around the corner is the Brewer's Arms, still standing but permanently closed due to the changing times. It awaits rescue, conversion or the wrecker's ball. More intriguing is the signpost further up Ladybarn Lane. Here in the front garden of a new residential house is a tall black pub sign for the Derby Arms, yet neither property on either side of it was ever a pub. A little digging revealed it was a pub accessed through a wide alleyway to Exbury Street; the next street over (the new property is built across the alleyway). The pub was converted to a residential property back in 2004, but the pub sign remains, no doubt confusing thirsty passers-by and runners ever since.

Working my way somewhat illogically through all these streets east of Parrs Wood Road, I survive a couple of downpours as the rain appears aggrieved by my continued presence. Yet once I'm wet, I know I can't become wetter. I have already attained peak wetness, further precipitous precipitation holds no fear for someone blowing drips off his nose. Besides, even the dog-walkers aren't out in this weather, I have the water-logged streets to myself. It's so wet, my phone case has steamed up and I'm largely winging it when it comes to map-reading. Still, I think I've bagged all I need in Ladybarn and head down Mauldeth Road, crossing Kingsway into Burnage.

Despite its reputation, or perhaps more because of the large swathe of social housing built there in the 1930's, in the late 19th century Burnage village was still a lovely rural idyll. The village was centred mainly just south of the junction of Mauldeth Road and Burnage Lane, (where happily the Victoria Inn still thrives), before the city closed in around it. It was indeed the beautiful village of Burnage that George Bernard Shaw was so taken with, much like any visitor today, possibly. Yet, for a brief time in the Edwardian era, this conflict between the spacious rural life and the dark gravity of industrial employment in the centre brought about a revolutionary desire for a suburban utopia.

Burnage Garden Village, just up Burnage Lane is one such attempt at providing a community estate that promotes healthy, affordable housing for workers in a green environment whilst still being close to work; the best of both worlds. The large notices at the entrance declaring the private roads, strict speed limits and the clamping of unauthorised vehicles initially strike me as a little excessive. So far, so unwelcoming. Nudging inside, I run this large square of roads, with its tennis and bowls club hidden behind the houses in the centre, a little unsure of where I am. There's something strange about the place, although at first I can't quite work out what it is. It's not until I'm halfway around that I notice not just that there is nobody around, there is no sign of anybody being around, no lights on or flickering televisions. Then I notice all the properties have tightly clipped hedges, literally every single one. The green verges have no tyre marks on them and all the cars are impeccably parked by the kerb. All the doors and window frames are white and there are no wheelie-bins in sight, not even in the gardens. It's a little like time-travel back to a place of working husbands and domestic housewives, of reputations to be upheld and finding respectability within society.

It also makes me think hard about the past. No doubt nowadays, these "norms" are brought about by strict tenancy rules, but in the past it would have been the judgement of neighbours and the fear of being outcast that kept people in place, complying to hidden rules. Perhaps the halcyon days of 'community spirit' were less about people watching out for one another and more people simply watching one another. No doubt this place has been alive with social generosity during Covid, but something about the lack of freedom of expression and a diktat of rules from above sends a faint Orwellian shudder down my spine.

Just one street away on Grangethorpe Drive, I'm reminded that the flipside of a society of indifferent individuals is no less frightening. Here amidst this tree-lined suburban avenue a former rockstar once lived. Guitarist Dave Rowbotham played in numerous bands in the 70's and early 80's including The Durutti Column and The Mothmen and as a session player for the likes of the Happy Mondays and the early years of Simply Red. Sadly, he would later turn his back on his musical peers and struggle with alcohol and heroin addictions. Tragically, in November 1991, he died in the living room of his flat here, murdered with an axe-like lathe hammer. Such was the lack of community and his recluse type existence, the police found very little known about him, his visitors, where he went or who he met. Media appeals came to nothing and the Police shelved the case. His murder remains unsolved to this day.

Not too long after visiting these two locations, my phone battery swiftly ran out of charge and turned itself off. Despite my fatigue and plans for an easier run, I surprised myself with another 79 streets ticked off in a bumper week. Mentally tired, soggy and drained, I take solace that I have no new niggles and as such, I must be getting fitter.

229

Tuesday 17ᵗʰ August 2021 – 8.44km – Wealth, Hope and Charity

Finishing work relatively early on the quietest day of the week, I headed for Cringle Park at the north end of Burnage. To keep my streets total ticking over, I knew I had to occasionally throw in a few short, afternoon runs on tired legs. Even if once again, the drizzle was falling from the grey, cloudy skies.

Starting just next to the Fallowfield loop on Errwood Road, I decided, as I wasn't planning on going far, I would go fast. Once I'd eased the stiffness from my limbs, I picked up the pace and gave my heart and lungs a good workout. It'd been a while since I'd pushed the pace it felt great as the houses and parked cars on the narrower streets flitted by over my shoulders. Alas, no sooner had I started my charge, I was dodging approaching cars, waiting for passing pedestrians and bouncing up and down from the kerb. Ah yes...afternoons.

Now home to some good-sized semi-detached houses, this area was once where several wealthy merchants and business owners built their grand homes. Joseph Dyer – a Connecticut born Englishman – made his money introducing several U.S. Innovations to England and developing important inventions that boosted cotton spinning's productivity. He lived out some of his later years at Cringle Hall in the 1840's and 50's. His devotion to economic, social and political reform stands him out amongst many of the wealthy Manchester elite at the time. This grand twelve-bedroom mansion with stables and coach-house sat in three acres of land, later becoming the Manchester Babies Hospital. Demolished in 1986, it lives on in the road name Cringle Hall Lane.

Just to the south, it will come of little surprise to discover that, Burnage Hall Lane is named after another grand mansion. This was an even larger, more substantial stone and brick mansion than Cringle Hall with larger grounds, ornamental gardens, orchards, greenhouses and a long driveway lined with lime trees. In 1836 it was owned by Henry Bannerman, part of the Bannerman clan who had steadily arrived from Perthshire, Scotland to their thriving textile mills here in Manchester. Bannerman and Sons grew wealthy specialising in shirts, calicoes, sheets and underclothing for export to the world. In 1848, Henry and family retired to Kent to grow hops on a 450-acre estate, employing some 50 people. Dying in 1871 with no heir, he left his substantial £120,000 fortune (£14m today) to his nephew Henry Campbell on the caveat he became a Bannerman. I'm not sure how many nanoseconds it took 35 year-old politician Henry to become a Campbell-Bannerman, but I suspect it wasn't many. He would go on to become the leader of the Liberal party in 1899 and Prime Minister from 1905 until his death in 1908. One can only wonder at the influence a certain passionate reformer neighbour had on this wealth finding its roundabout way to a great reforming mind and party leader.

Burnage Hall was demolished around the time Campbell-Bannerman was in power, the inevitable slither of Manchester's boundaries eyeing this spacious home for one family as the perfect site for homes for 430 of Manchester's busy worker bees. All would disappear in the name of progress.

Diverting back down Kingsway and across to Cringle Park to pick up some stray streets I'd missed due to the previous day's battery problems, I pushed even harder and even managed a rapid finish down the last five-hundred metres of Linden Park, much to the wide-eyed judgement of an old lady out walking her dachshund. Like me, I suspect that dog and all the others round here unknowingly mourn the loss of that beautiful avenue of Lime Trees.

Five miles covered in a little over thirty-eight minutes is a grand way to build an early afternoon appetite, but more importantly, it builds my streets total another 22 roads higher.

Friday 20th August 2021 – 11.85km – Wilting in Wythenshawe

I'm not saying today was a mistake but perhaps I should have taken note that my start point was at the junction of Tuffley Road and Wrekin Avenue.

Another after work run, I had it planned out before realising it was 21C and humid beneath a thick overcast duvet of stratus clouds. I could have postponed it and gone home but after some deliberation I diverted down the M56 into what has become something of my nemesis; Wythenshawe. Pulling to a stop in Newall Green, I guzzled some water and set off, tired and hungry but determined to simply grab a few roads and head home. Heck, even ten roads would help, it'd at least be ten less next time I was down this way.

I'd barely gone a kilometre when I hit trouble, the worst kind of trouble.

Heading down Kennett Road – a concrete road much like so many others – I spied them in the hazy distance; a group of youths. Fresh-faced young varmints playing football and enjoying the school holidays, but no doubt armed to the teeth with cutting barbs about stupid runners, rubbish trainers and the cumulative damage to knee joints caused by repetitive foot impacts on hard surfaces. Damn educated rapscallions! Why, they might even mockingly encourage me with references to the 1994 Academy Award-winning film, Forrest Gump. I slow and simultaneously nudge the peak of my cap up with one finger and reach for my six-shooter with other. Sadly, in the heat of the moment, I'd forgotten I am neither a rogue cowhand nor is this Arizona in the 1880's.

Unarmed, but noting they had yet to see me on the horizon, I wipe my dry mouth on the back of my hand and run on. I push forward in a steady positive rhythm that says I don't want no trouble, but if there is trouble, I'll give them double of the no trouble they were going to get anyway. As I near, one looks up and says something. I've been spotted. My breath catches in my chest, muscles tensing, but I run on, determined to show no fear. Another boy shouts and an arm is raised, the fresh-faced urchin momentarily pointing his stubby, nail-bitten finger in my direction. One of them puts his foot on the ball, his hands moving casually to his hips, watching me as I run between the impromptu goal posts.

I run on. They stare.

I run on. Someone sniffs. It may even have been me.

I run on. Nothing is said. They return to their game as if nothing ever happened and I do the same and simply run on.

Sometimes, despite the best precautions, you just have to stare extreme danger in the face, act on instinct and simply push through to the other side.

Miraculously unharmed, I push steadily on to the south, hitting some tarmac roads, the slight softer surface only ruined by the heat coming off the dark surface, swelling my feet and baking my calves. Not soon after, that pre-run glug of water came back to haunt me in the form of a stitch. More careless than anything, I only had myself to blame and endured the pain in my side, stretching my arms overhead and to each side whilst not wanting to slow my pace too much. No doubt to the amusement of anyone watching and thinking I was dancing to the Y.M.C.A.

With a route forming on the hoof, I ran the side roads on either side of Greenbrow Road like the branches of a tree before diverting out into the countryside. That's the strange thing in this corner of the Wythenshawe. The estate just stops. On one side of the road is social housing, on the other is a thick country hedge and farmer's fields. In this tiny rural corner of Manchester, there's also a little rat-run; a back roads route across to Hale and Timperley. For a driver it's a pleasant drive between tall prickly hedges, for me it's a 450 metre white-knuckle run along a busy road with no footpaths. Stop-starting my way along like some Frogger-type video game, I eventually emerge unscathed on the Old Trafford border, at the corner of the wonderfully named Roaring Gate Lane.

Heading north on a public footpath, I have the briefly remembered joy of running off-road. Before all this began I used to run trails a lot, drinking in the peace and quiet, listening to the birds and buzzing insects and revelling in the greenery. I realise I miss it, but I have little time to get sentimental. Half a kilometre later, I am heading east back along another country road towards Wythenshawe Hospital. At least this one briefly has a footpath, until I hit Floats Road and Clay Lane and then I'm routinely back in the hedge. From stitch to stitched up, I return from my jaunt into the countryside to run back along Greenbrow Road, I'm never more grateful for the sweet, baking pavements under my weary feet.

34 hard won streets added today and a timely reminder that not all roads give in easily, not all roads are equal, but they all count the same.

Saturday 21st August 2021 – 19.65km – Ghost Streets of Clayton

Openshaw derives its name from the old English for a coppice or open wood; from a time when coppiced wood was an important crop for building fencing, furniture, tools, weapons and making charcoal. Before the swirling chaos of smoke and steam descended on Manchester, this largely rural area was known to be occupied by people employed making hats. The area really thrived though in the second surge of the industrial revolution at the end of the 19th century. With neighbouring Gorton, this was a place of heavy, dirty industry and bubbling vats of chemicals. It was a place of great fiery forges building equipment for other great industrial enterprises, the buzz of electrical engineering, the growl of internal combustion engines and motor cars and the careful manufacture within a government munitions factory.

It also must have been a somewhat pungent place to live. Into the smoke-filled heavens, the local Aniline chemical Works (used in dyeing and medicines) would have added the smell of rotten fish. With rubber works, oil works, a coal tar soap works and a malt vinegar brewery also nearby, one can only imagine the heady cocktail wafting down the streets depending which way the wind blew. With these great labouring workforces came a greater labour movement, where the ills and wrongs of their forefather's lives were met with the collective strength of trade unions and a devotion to socialism that has never left Manchester.

Back to back runs always seem such a good idea before the first run. Currently I think my legs must feel much like Roy Keane's dog. What, we're going out again...? Still, I know I've done 60 and 70 mile weeks before now, so I don't fear the distance, I just have to be careful about the turning, making sure to slow right down, especially in the cul-de-sacs. Moving straight, my muscles can handle it, it's the twisting of knees and hips on tarmac, the abrupt stopping and starting that puts the lesser tendons in the firing line. Taking wide lines and gentle accelerations are the order of the day. Giving myself an extra hour in bed for recovery, I headed once more to east Manchester, slowly closing up that gap and creeping my front line above the Ashton Canal for the first time.

Not sure what was left of this industrial powerhouse, I parked up in west Openshaw, just north of Ashton Old Road at Openshaw Park. It was grey, humid and wet underfoot, dry but threatening rain if I as much as looked at the sky funny. Starting my watch, I headed west past the Heaven on Earth yoga centre – which may or may not be run by Belinda Carlisle – and almost immediately stumbled upon an old friend in the terraced back streets. A corner shop branch of the Beswick Co-operative

Society – much smaller and simpler in design than the previous two - built in 1905 and still with its tiled name above the door. It lives on as the home of a niche church group. To the north, I enter a small industrial estate and regret that extra hour in bed.

I find Sheldon's bakery and I'm definitely in his spot. With delivery lorries and forklifts all around and the air full of a divine baking smell, I head seemingly towards the entrance to their bakery site. Several glances at my phone show this dead-end is in fact a public road with other warehouses and companies on it, but as the bakery seemingly own properties on both sides, I feel like I'm apologetically tiptoeing through their loading yard at peak time.

'Sorry, so sorry, my bad, humble apologies...'

Running down the middle of the road past the first awkwardness, I immediately spy another some two hundred metres away. Sitting on a wall, watching my approach is a single man in high-vis. As I near, the brick wall and barbed wire dead-end only looks more dead-end-ier. The dazzling stranger knows there is no way through, I know there is no way through, even a drunk mole in dark glasses would know there was no way through.

But. I. Have. To. Bag. The. Street.

I keep on running. The bright man stands up, his intentions as unknown to me as mine are to him. I slow as if stopping but don't actually stop. The tension and awkwardness begins to make my skin crawl. I feel him staring as I get ever closer. I feign an exaggerated examination of the massive fence at the end as if I'd only just seen the route ahead blocked. The man has taken a half-step backwards and drawn his hands from his pockets. Oh no...

I reach a thick white line across the road marked with the word STOP written twice. I nod to the stocky middle-aged man some ten metres away, do as I'm told and turn for the open road, sure I'm shortly going to be a story told in the staff canteen. My escape means hot-crossing the bakery bun zone once more.

'Sorry, so sorry, terribly sorry, you're doing a good job, won't keep you, apologies, lovely fork-liftery...'

Running up Clayton Lane at the rear of the vast Manchester City training ground, I reach Ashton Canal. Built in 1796 to enable the coal industry in Oldham and Tameside to access Manchester, it descends for seven miles from Ashton-under-Lyme to Ancoats through 18 locks. Thriving later on connecting to the high peak quarries, it was operational until the 1950's. A period of dereliction and the threat of filling it in were only resolved two decades later, when it reopened in 1974. Many of its bridges and locks are listed buildings.

Crossing into Clayton I reach an eerie, weed-strewn wasteland just south of Ashton New Road. About ten years ago, bulldozers razed fourteen streets of back-to-back terraced houses to the ground for a re-development that failed to happen. Now, the tarmac is cracked, the opportunistic foliage grows high and all is quiet. Running these lost streets, my mind wanders to all the kids chasing balls, all the twitched net-curtains and the scrubbed front steps; all the shouts and arguments, the forehead kisses and looks of love. All the slammed doors and raised voices, the treasured memories, belly laughs and first Christmases, all the rumours, gossip and fears, all the celebrations, joy and tears. All these layers of inconsequential memories of days past hanging around long after everything's gone, people move away and the world moves on.

As the weeds get ever higher and I move further away and out of sight of the main road, my brain helpfully reminds me that this would make a good spot to dump a body. Not so much a note to self for future reference, but rather a horrible thought of what would I do if I stumbled round the next blind corner and encountered such a grisly scene. Call the police obviously, but complete the street I'm on first? Just kidding, we all know what's really important and what's not, so I'd obviously round up to the nearest kilometre before stopping Strava, right?

"The dead body was discovered by a jogger early on Saturday morning and he was understandably upset...at being labelled a 'jogger'. I'm Cindy Falafel-Cakes, RTN News, Manchester."

Up until 1890, this area was once under the township of Droylsden. Then Manchester flexed its civic muscles and the true Victorian spirit of empire by simply moving its boundaries further out, swallowing up Clayton Blackley, Crumpsall, Moston, Openshaw and Gorton. Rule Mancunia! Mancunia rules the Lathes!

Back from this contentious eastern border of the diminished forbidden land of Droylesden, Tameside, I return the way I came, back over the canal to Openshaw. Making short work of a small estate of social housing, I find myself passing Gregg's Manchester Bakery. Stopping on the road outside for a photo of this palace of pies and pasties, I hear a shout from an angry security guard somewhere out of sight to my left. I'm not sure what I'd done wrong, but presumably he thought I was meticulously preparing an Ocean's 11-style heist for a tray of Steak Bakes.

Looping around back past Openshaw Park, I return to several terraced streets surviving from a time when their like filled this area. The Queen amongst which was none other than Weatherfield's star namesake - one of the 73 Coronation Streets found across Great Britain. I speculated to myself that some weirdo soap superfan has visited them all! I mean, fancy going around collecting streets, who would...ah, yeah. Right.

Bouncing back to my car, I was tired but more in my back than my legs. My muscles had stiffened up from the concrete roads the day before, giving me a pleasing, firmer spring in my step and making me feel good, at least on the downhill sections. A few aches and pains are creeping in, but nothing a bit of stretching and recovery won't cure. 64 more streets in the bag, 200 for the week and I even dodged the rain as it started on my drive home. Lovely stuff.

Saturday 28ᵗʰ August 2021 – 9.37km & 3.37km - Operation Openshaw

Tick-tock, tick-tock, tick-tock...

With things going well last week, this week I struggled to squeeze in the midweek runs I had planned. Frustrated with the days slipping by, I decided to live dangerously and run on a Saturday afternoon. Not just any sunny Saturday afternoon either, this was a risky daytime adventure to Openshaw. The inherent danger at hand was the football match happening about a mile away at the Etihad Stadium where Manchester City were entertaining Arsenal. Could I scoot into the area, grab all the streets while they were busy and escape before the football traffic gridlocked the streets? The clock was indeed ticking...

Starting at Delamere Park twenty minutes after the game had kicked off, I headed out onto the wide boulevard of Ashton Old Road. Connecting Ashton-under-Lyne with Manchester, this has long been a main artery between the two areas. A link growing ever more important as the cotton trade transformed both ends in the 18ᵗʰ century, the canal and railway lines only strengthening the flow of trade. In the 19ᵗʰ century, surrounded by heavy industry and its accompanying workforces, the road became the epicentre of the community's downtime. With many pubs and clubs like the grand Halfway House and the Gransmoor Hotel, movies at the Whitehall cinema, talks at the meeting rooms, the Alhambra Theatre with its domed tower or the billiard hall next door, the place would have thrived on an evening and positively buzzed at the weekend.

Sadly, while still busy with shoppers and people at the bus stop, the sense of hubbub and leisure appears lost. Obviously, the draw of Manchester and travel further afield is easier now and the street was always going to decline from its previous grandeur and importance. Yet it's sad to see the pubs have nearly all been demolished or converted to shops and the grand old buildings replaced with modest ones in a mish-mash of economical styles. It is still busy with traffic, nothing is boarded up or neglected and the take-aways, pet shops, hair salons and pound shops here are all still trading but it's obviously no longer the centre of people's lives. Reaching the corner of Fairfield Road, I spy the huge modern Lime Square development opposite with its Morrisons Supermarket, Range store and various coffee and fast food outlets, reminding me that the trade of passing cars is now king. Turning off the main road, I began a technical section of several short back streets with plenty of loops, dead ends and many stops peering blearily at a map on a dazzling screen in the bright midday sun. Losing any sense of rhythm, I sense time passing quicker than I'd like.

Tick-tock, tick-tock...

Away from the main road, I find many people out in the sunshine too; walking, chatting, kids out playing in the suburban closes and cars whizzing around hither and thither. All something I'm plainly not used to, all adding to the feeling that I was not only being glared at but also about to be run over. I needed eyes in the back of my head, every side road requiring a slow, double-check before crossing. I head west to the brand new Youth Close, which is presumably only open to young homeowners, just as the whistle for the end of the first half must have been blown over at the football. Thinking of a refreshing half-time orange, I push on south to Vine Street - which sadly wasn't orange - and after some really awkward parts where I was seemingly constantly changing direction around several small twisting streets, I bounce east towards my car. Passing it and the Park where I began, I push on eastwards towards the border. With the heat and people around, it was a healthy reminder that running through empty streets at dawn is so under-rated.

Tick-tock, tick-tock...

Fifteen minutes into the second-half at the Etihad and...

'Hi, Strava here, it looks like you're in a rush, would now be a good time for me to be a proper technological spanner?'

Me: 'Nooooooooooooooo!'

'Sorry, it's just I thought you'd want to know, I lost signal and stopped back there for about ten minutes, but I'm here now! Don't worry, I've made up for it by drawing a beautiful straight line through all those houses...'

Me: 'Aaaaarrrrrggghhhhh!'

Gormlessly bedazzled and muttering many bad words from my parched lips, I restarted a second run on my watch and diligently went back to complete the last four roads again, thankful it could have been much worse.

Tick-tock, tick-tock...

Finding the Tameside border on Ashton old Road is one of the easiest so far. With its metal flags and its Welcome to (the Forbidden land of) Audenshaw sign, it's safe to say Tameside believe leaving Manchester is something worth celebrating. In the other direction, Manchester has no such sign welcoming people to Openshaw. Make of that what you will. I had for some time thought this was the road furthest east in Manchester, but that honour, as we've already visited goes to Kingsdale Road in Gorton, which is 78 metres further east. Besides, there were no bushes here; it's the little things that matter.

Back along Ashton old Road, I saw the clock was ticking, the calculations in my head constantly working out how long was gone at the match, how long it would take for traffic to become clogged up and how long I dare keep on running. Nudging north of the main road, I enter a brand new estate of simple orange brick houses with dark roofs and dark window frames, but no less charming in the simplicity of their designs. Many of the same road names have survived from when this was two up-two down terracing although the darkly random Ambush Street has gone – I'm betting it didn't see that coming. As I get a bit twitchy about what's around the corner, I spy what I thought read Cheery-bye Street, before a double-take relabelled it Cheeryble Street. Still with 85 minutes played at the football match, I waved cheery-bye to the new estate and bolted due south across the main road and through the park to my car.

Pausing only long enough to sip a little drink and chomp through a protein bar, I swung the car around and made to get out of Dodge! Only as I headed back towards the city centre and closer to the emerging crowds does it dawn on me. I know where I am. The memories of these houses play breathily in my head. I turn off the main road into a housing estate with a familiar layout. I know all these streets, I know all the back streets and run-throughs. I am like a taxi driver with no fear of getting lost, because I've won all these streets the hard way. To paraphrase Emmett 'Doc' Brown, 'where I'm going I don't need main roads!'

52 more streets added today, leaving me with just 1211 streets on my list, less than 20% of Manchester still to do. Incidentally, Manchester City beat Arsenal 5-0.

Sunday 29th August 2021 – 26.92km - The Hills have Hills.

    Crumpsall derives its name from Old English and means 'crooked piece of land beside a river'. That river is of course the Irk, a waterway once so overworked, the New Gazetteer of Lancashire said in 1830, it had more mills upon it than any other stream of its length in the Kingdom. Rising north of Oldham, the river passes through Middleton and North Manchester before merging with the River Irwell in the centre. Socialist critic and philosopher Friedrich Engels was less of a fan; "At the bottom flows, or rather stagnates, the Irk, a narrow, coal-black, foul-smelling stream, full of debris and refuse, which it deposits on the shallower right bank."

    Thankfully the river and these breezy hills are much more affable these days. Buoyed by my successful run yesterday, I headed north back up into the hills up in Blackley and Crumpsall, knowing it was going to be tough, but I hadn't realised how tough.

    Starting at the corner of Marshbrook Drive, I idled north up Slack Road, roaring into Lion Street, before heading back to start proper on Bracklea Drive. Like so many new estates I've run, this reminds me of a second-hand Scalextrix I had as a kid. Like so many of my toys that were lovingly rescued from that 1980's obsession – the jumble sale – it came in a broken box with no instructions and the usual assorted detritus from other toys such as a large jigsaw piece, board game counters, a monopoly hotel and a chewed piece of Lego. Yet what I remember most about this racing car set was all of the straight pieces of track were missing. I had all the bends and no straights. As I curve my way this way and that around this estate, I think a lot about the person designing this estate and wonder if his or her mum also loved jumbles sales.

    Crumpsall's most famous son is probably the singing milkman, Freddie Garrity of 60's band, Freddie and the Dreamers. And the streets were most definitely made for me this morning as I felt great and really positive. It was joyful to reclaim the streets after the chaos of yesterdays midday jaunt with an early morning run beneath cornflower skies and a blinding low sun that kissed everything with its optimistic golden rays. Blasting out the tunes, squinting into the razzle-dazzle sunshine and skimming lightly over the smooth black tarmac like a stone; I was in heaven.

    Delighting in running down Bottomley side, I reach Hexagon Close, which rather aptly is close to Hexagon Tower; the brutalist 14-floor concrete tower block that dominates the skyline around here. Built in 1973 as part of the I.C.I's dye works on the site, it derives its names from the

241

hexagon shape of all its windows, a nod to the chemical compound of Benzene used in the manufacture of synthetic dyes. Sold on in 2008, it's now a multi-level science park filled with laboratories, machine halls and offices. Before construction of the tower in the late 1960's, this site claimed to have the largest concentration of organic chemists in the Commonwealth. Which I have to admit is up there in the top billion most interesting things I've ever read, and instantly forgotten. More interesting, perhaps, is that Johnny Marr used it as a backdrop in the music video for his 2015 song New Town Velocity. A fan of modern architecture, he has also penned Dynamo, a love song to the CIS Tower in Manchester City Centre. Somehow, he's also still cool, which almost seems impossible.

Leaving Crumpsall, I head for the hills in Blackley. Working the steep sloping streets behind St Peter's Church, I then moved down Old Market Street to the wonderful hill of Chapel Lane. It is only 300m, but it winds elegantly up in a wide S-shape and at 8-9% is a healthy lung-buster to get the legs burning and head spinning. I enjoyed it so much, I ran back down to the bottom and did it again. I understand I may be in a minority on that one!

However, after undulating my way along the top of the ridge, I had another Strava fail, leaving me loitering outside Blackley Cemetery. While Strava had me paused like a moody Goth, I'd run on down a side street and back up steep 7% grind of Riverdale Road. Somehow when coach Strava makes you run the same steep hill twice, it's much less fun than doing it voluntarily. Still it's good for the legs, apparently or character or profanity development or something.

Heading south back into Crumpsall, I head for the main reason I'd been putting off this area for so long and not just because of the hills; the sprawling North Manchester Hospital. Exploring the public roads cutting through the site was out of the question at the height of the contagious pandemic. Even now, it still felt a little disrespectful while people inside were fighting for breath and their lives. Sticking to the roads and focusing on being quick, quiet and discrete, I powered along the roads. It's a shame too as the hospital has a fascinating and somewhat interesting history.

Many of the surviving Victorian buildings here didn't start as a hospital at all, but were built as three separate institutions. The oldest was the new Manchester Union Workhouse in 1853, the Prestwich Union Workhouse next door came to be in 1869 and Crumpsall Hospital arrived in 1876, built for the sick of the Workhouses. The two workhouses could house over 2400 inmates, in the cold, calculating way only Victorians could view the world, they were a catch-all place to accommodate the destitute, homeless, elderly, single mothers, orphans, mentally ill and physically sick. The able-bodied would have worked 12-hour days weaving cotton or other menial work to pay their upkeep, the others as much as they could. Workhouses were terrible places to live, often set up to be as much as a deterrent as a means of aid to those that needed it, often with little difference between them and the conditions in prisons. The two workhouses would later merge and house the mental ill before joining the National Health Service in 1948. All three hospitals would merge to become North Manchester Hospital in 1977.

As I stray around the hospital grounds where Jason Orange of Take That fame was born in 1970, I struggle to imagine it as anything but the old workhouses. All around me, the three-storey high accommodation blocks in dark red brick, the chapel and old laundry block with its tall windows. There's something sombre and institutionally unsettling about their drab exteriors when contrasted with the sturdy and formally embellished administration block with its motto carved high overhead for all to see: 'Poor And Needy The Lord Careth For Me'. This heady mix of power and suffering, control and despair shines out from amidst a thoroughly modern hospital with all the blue and white signage and car parks full of shiny cars. Around the corner, I spy the old original entrance to the Manchester Union Workhouse. Now almost stranded in a back car park, hidden from view behind bushes and weeping willows, it's seemingly ignored by all and sundry, yet still has the power to intimidate. Maybe five storeys high but with only three lines of sash windows, it rises high like an impenetrable barrier; a monster that is going to devour all who arrive. A small green roundabout remains in front of the entrance doors as would have been circled by the carriages bringing in the new inmates. Missing now though are the high walls on every side and a porter's lodge at the front where the poor unfortunates would pass through its gated archway. Blocked in on all four sides and met by a number of orderlies, once inside, any panicked hope of escape was already far too late.

A little unnerved by the hospital, I can't wait to escape the long shadows of its history. Spying a shortcut, I divert to an off-road footpath through some woodland beside the Jewish Cemetery, linking Crescent Road back to the valley floor. It sloped gradually away through the thick trees and I picked up speed before it turned and pitched seemingly almost straight down. Eyes darting for safe foot placements amidst the blur, I pivoted and realised I was already going too quickly to stop. Touching 15% in places over tree roots and undergrowth, I barrelled down the narrow, winding track like I'd fled the workhouse, uptight orderlies at my heels with cudgels in one hand and a whistles in the other. Completely out of control beside a high metal fence, I was simultaneously petrified and never more alive. As it levelled off and I reached the safety of the road at the bottom, the adrenaline of what ifs flooded my head. I was lucky not to have tripped and done myself a serious mischief. I decided on this occasion, not to run the same hill twice.

Finishing the hospital area left me with two isolated islands of streets to do across Crumpsall, about half a mile apart from one another, but I decide that's a problem for future me.
A bumper harvest of 85 streets and a metric marathon to boot. Happy running.

Monday 30th August 2021 – 26.13km – Hard to Stomach

Miles Platting isn't named after jazz trumpeter Miles Davis interlacing the strands of his daughter's hair – although the Illinois-born superstar played Manchester three times including a Free-Trade Hall gig so full of complex and daring trumpet solos in 1960 that it is still revered in jazz circles to this day. I digress. No, Miles Platting is named after some boards over a ditch a mile from the centre of Manchester. (Deflated off-key trumpet noises...)

I found this quiet suburb just east of the city centre largely as anonymous as any other as the industry and workers' back-to-back terraced streets are long gone. Now it's mostly modern homes built in the 1960's and 70's and a swish new estate called Platting Village, where I decided to park up. Still with the signs and flags up of its developer, the houses have interesting angular roofs that break up the skyline and the warm terracotta-coloured brickwork contrasting with white or pale blue cladding – this is east Manchester after all. What was once a place few would call desirable is now regenerating and reinventing itself, piggybacking on the designer areas of New Islington, Ancoats and the Northern Quarter just down the road from here, with prices to boot.

Heading east and working the roads just south of the Rochdale Canal, I cross Varley Street and continue up Iron Street – made a hell of a din underfoot – before bagging Energy Street – disappointedly not with go faster chevrons on the road. At the main road, I reach the site of an estate that was once the pride of North-East Manchester, where a strong stomach wasn't required, but strong morals were.

Hemmed in by Hulme Hall Lane, Clifton Street and Lord Street, there's a patch of waste ground covered only by car parks, a wholesale cash and carry and most notably the striking frontage of the Vermillion Asian-fusion restaurant. Yet this area was once entirely owned by the Pendlebury family who ran the United Cattle Products factory and shops nearby. Wealthy from their empire of selling animal stomach linings to those who couldn't afford more expensive cuts of meat, this 1906 diversification into building 400 homes for Manchester's workers was inevitably called the 'Tripe Colony.' Yet far from a get rich quick scheme, only the finest people could move into these substantial terraced homes with inside bathrooms and affordable rents. The company would vet their prospective tenants by visiting their home and making sure they were clean, tidy and upstanding enough to be welcomed into their community. One can only imagine the families turned out in their Sunday best, husband's hair tamed, children threatened and bribed into silence, their home scrubbed and smelling of scouring powder as they anxiously awaited a visit from the 'Man from Pendlebury's'.

In the 1970's the council bought the homes not yet owned by the occupiers, but by the late 80's and early 90's the rot had set in and as people moved away, houses were boarded up and thieves moved in to rob anything of value. By 1994 and in anticipation of a regeneration of the area sparked by the winning of hosting the Commonwealth Games, they sent in the bulldozers. Sadly, that spark fizzled out and the site remains a lifeless plot largely full of weeds and dirt. Running these streets and seeing what looks like an impromptu scrap yard set up on part of it, I feel only sadness. This is another place that once thrived as a community, but is now just another sorry looking scrap of land. A place abandoned because it was easier to erase the problems rather than fix them. One suspects, this area will rise again, although the affordable rents for the finest of the working classes will remain only as a memory.

Pushing further east past the wonderful toasted smell of Fine Lady Bakery, I find a sorry-looking, sturdy old warehouse with bricked up windows and barbed wire fences, a place that helped defend the country not once but twice. Although the original occupiers started production in a mill on Great Ancoats Street in 1910, it was their move here to Newton Heath just three years later that catapulted them into production overdrive, building planes for the Great War. Alliot Verdon Roe and his elder brother Humphrey ran the company, only later did A.V. Roe & Company become Avro, the brothers at the heart of the U.K's fledgling aviation industry. After a struggle through the twenties and divergences into making cars and passenger planes, they returned to military matters in 1938 with a huge order for the Bristol Blenheim bomber. They'd later make key components for the Lancaster Bomber to be assembled elsewhere, places such as Sharston. Avro closed the Newton Heath works in 1947. There's little to see now, no hint of the sandbags and soldiers at the gates, the factory draped in darkness as the local women inside working tirelessly through the night to make the parts that'd bring the war to an end and bring their loved ones home. The time spent toiling, hoping to get through the shift without another air raid, catch some sleep before coming back and doing it all again the following night. It remains in use as a wholesaler's warehouse.

Detouring further up into Newton Heath, where I entertained about five different bin lorry crews with my antics, running past them time and again as I circled around the streets and bumped into them on the way into and out of cul-de-sacs. Nothing was said, but the eyes spoke volumes. Much as must happen on Ten Acres Lane where the National Taekwondo

Centre is based, you know, for Olympic fans of Jade Jones, Bianca Walkden, Bradley Sinden, Lauren Williams and kicking people in the head in general. After crossing the River Medlock, I enjoyed the momentary escapism of an out and back down Bank Bridge Road. With only trees and sky in view, I could briefly imagine running out in the countryside, although another voice in my head said I wouldn't want to be down here after dark with little traffic and no witnesses. It had 'Police Reconstruction' written all over it. Returning hastily to head back west along Cemetery Road, I skirt the edge of Phillips Park Cemetery.

Opening in August 1866 and named after local MP, Mark Phillips, this cemetery beside the River Medlock holds more than 300,000 burials and is deemed full. Although not long after it opened, a disaster led to a macabre sight for those working in the works and factories nearby. Two days of torrential rain – so unlike Manchester – back in July 1872 led to the river swelling and trees and debris swept downstream building up behind a sturdy footbridge nearby. Effectively damned, a great lake built up in the neighbouring Clayton Vale until the sheer weight of the backed-up water grew too much for the bridge. As it inevitably failed, the resulting surge of water washed across the Roman Catholic part of the cemetery, washing more away than just tombstones. The first anyone knew of the problem was in the houses and mills downstream when disinterred bodies and coffins from the graves started floating past in the floodwaters. The papers at the time reported more than fifty swept away, the local gossips said five hundred and the Government enquiry into the matter said the figure was only seventy-six and they'd recovered every single one. Roman Catholic Ministers were somewhat unconvinced, but the government insisted it was the end of the matter, which seems about as open and unobstructive as the damned bridge and as clear and transparent as the water.

Less debatable are the final resting places of Private George Stringer, VC (more on him on 21st September 2021) and Private William Jones, VC. Both earned the highest honour for valour in the presence of the enemy; the Victoria Cross. Jones earned his at Rorke's Drift, South Africa in January 1879 in the Anglo-Zulu war. Whatever your view on Britain's past, it wasn't decisions made by brave men like Jones as he fought for his life and those of his 138 pals as they found themselves defending their outpost against a two-day Zulu attack of 4,000 men. Defending their burning hospital until six of the seven remaining injured soldiers could escape the flames, he remained fighting at his post despite suffering four spear wounds and being shot. Holding off the attack with his bayonet, he retreated only when he saw the seventh patient's bed surrounded by the frenzied enemy. The Zulus withdrew the following morning, the outpost barely defendable. Eleven soldiers earned the VC at Rorke's Drift, the largest amount ever awarded for a single engagement. Neatly the Cemetery is also the 1897 burial site of John Richardson, one of the six hundred light cavalrymen who mistakenly charged the Russian guns at Balaclava in what became known as 'The Charge of the Light Brigade'. It would be a captured gun at Sevastopol later in the same Crimean War, from which all subsequent Victoria Crosses are cast.

Back into Miles Platting, I headed along Bradford Road and completed the side roads along there just as the houses were waking up and people rousing themselves for work. This completed my third long outing in 44 hours and I wasn't at all sure how my body would hold up, but I was surprised at how light, strong and purposeful I felt. So much so, I did far more than I had originally planned and bagged another 69 roads.

Now, I know most runners and readers will understand - because you're awesome and you bought this book - but imagine the faces of regular muggles at work as I try to explain the following:

In under two days, I've covered around 40 miles of tarmac roads in the scenic, soul-lifting environs of Openshaw, Crumpsall, Miles Platting and Newton Heath, clocking up 206 streets in the process. And for all this hard work, I only nudged my target a paltry 3.2% closer to the finish line. They'd be smiling and backing away right up until they bumped into something. To be fair, I don't have to talk about running for that...

Saturday 4th September 2021 – 19.24km – Day Run Believer

Beneath gnarled oyster skies in Openshaw, I go searching for the one cultural pearl hidden at its centre.

Returning to the new houses north of Ashton Old Road where I cut off my previous run around these parts, I looked forward to negotiating my way through another Saturday afternoon. Only this time with the footballers away on an international break, there was no pendulous timer hanging over my head, threatening a tidal wave of traffic. After clocking up so many streets in the previous month, I was both anxious to get back at it, but conscious of the growing niggles needing a little more attention, recovery and stretching. The plan was to take it easy and do a slow and steady 10k. I've never been very good at following plans...

Struggling to settle at a sluggish pace, I found my legs nudging me ever quicker through Openshaw's mix of old and new housing, along busy main roads and into quiet cul-de-sacs. Nonetheless, after clocking up a good number of streets, I found an unassuming building in the corner of an estate by the railway line with an interesting cultural connection.

Varna Street School was a triple storied Victorian giant of education in Manchester, serving 1500 children from the surrounding back-to-back terraces. Dubbed 'the largest school in Lancashire' at the time, that figure seems modest in comparison to some of the big academies across the city now. However, all this largely pales into insignificance compared to its most famous pupil from the 1950s; Davy Jones of The Monkees.

A much sought after child actor and singer, David signed a bumper contract in 1964 to make television shows for Screen Gems, movies for Columbia Pictures and records for Colpix records. Just a year later when aged just nineteen, he released his first single "What Are We Going To Do?" The following year in 1966, inspired by the quirky films of the Beatles, Screen Gems invited him to audition for a part in a U.S television sitcom following the youthful antics of a young band. An instant hit, the four starlets on The Monkees broke the barrier between television and radio, with the show complementing their steady stream of hit singles and albums.

Their success was not without some controversy. When the band learnt the record company had omitted all additional help from session players from the record sleeves, they raged at fooling their fans. They were all musicians in their own right, but not the tight rock and roll band they were playing on screen. Surprisingly, the best singer was Micky

249

Dolenz and the best drummer was Davy Jones, but the producers believed Jones would look lost behind the drum kit, so put him up front and Dolenz had to learn the drums. With twelve-hour days on set and little to do between takes, they would pick up their instruments and practice playing. They had to learn fast as their record company wanted them out on tour. Jones was still touring with the Monkees in the summer of 2011, the year before his death at his home in Florida.

Varna Street has long since closed as a school, but rather pleasingly given its star pupil's artful leanings, Rogue Studios now use this Grade II listed building for budding artists to paint, sculpt, print and perform in its vast rooms and halls.

Daydream believing my way west, I pass the Lime Square shopping complex and head into the neighbouring estate. Not used to running at this time on a Saturday, I got quite an uneasy feeling. This was neither a good area nor bad, simply busy and the kind of area where kids play in the street under the watchful gaze of protective mothers. Anything unusual treated with suspicion. With only one way in and one way out, they were perhaps unused to anyone passing through. I quietly went about my business, moving as swiftly as I felt comfortable, hopefully out of sight before people wondered what I was about. I focused on the far distance and not the eyes of anyone staring or falling quiet as I ran by their house for a second or sometimes third time. All the way round I waited for that shout enquiring what I was doing, but thankfully, it never came.

There were a few unusual street names around here that caught my eye; Bendall Street – where Yuri Geller lives, perhaps -, the peachy Melba Street and Wayne Street – lovely dancer. I also came across Sexa Street and Rock Street, but sadly no Drugs Street or Roll Street. Mercifully, I didn't miss Stray Street, which would have been ironically painful, nor Chariot Street, which I absolutely ran in slow motion.

Although the streets were stacking up, this estate of mistrustful residents was much bigger than I first thought. As the run dragged on, I regretted running without fluids, the dehydration sending me into a bit of a brain fug. Yet, I pushed on. Just a few more kilometres and I'd plugged the Gorton, Debdale, Abbey Hey and Openshaw gap in the eastern part of the map. Only a run or two more further up in Clayton would finish off all of the eastern border.

The highlight of the day came towards the end on an out and back around the Police's Claytonbrook compound where I befriended a rotund ginger tomcat, who rolled over the ground, meowing it was too warm and he was tired. Me too puss cat, me too. Leaving him behind, I headed for the shady sanctuary of my car.

Suffering a little on a run that got way out of hand, I was nonetheless pleased to gather in an impressive 72 more streets. This meant I'd surprisingly hit another significant milestone. I had less than a 1000 roads left to do! As long as I say it quickly, it doesn't hurt my parched brain. The question is; will I reach that finish line by the end of November? I'm a believer.

Sunday 5th September 2021 – 21.76km – Black and Blue in Bradford

Today was an unashamedly blue run this Sunday morning around Clayton, Bradford and Sport City. With humble apologies to any reds fans, but Manchester City's Etihad stadium is the only top-flight football ground actually in Manchester, although United do have history right here in the heart of City territory, more on that later.

I was out before dawn today, reminding myself of all those autumnal and wintry mornings to come, starting out in the darkness and ending in the light. It's always a little unnerving parking up in the dark on a strange side-street, far from home. There's always that frisson of danger, that dark portent of the unknown. What if I've inadvertently parked up outside the area's top gangster's mother's house? Or outside a burglary in progress? What if this is a street under the malevolent shadow of a gang of feral ducks? It's a constant worry. My presence in full running gear seems so illogical and out of context on a dark street on the wrong side of the tracks, I may as well be in a sequinned jump suit or dressed like a Teletubby. Yet even as I nervously endure the initial darkness, I find it worth it to simply run through the dawning of a new day. From the starry dark blue skies to the grubby half-light, the weak grey shadows to the first bleary rays of a sun clambering over the horizon, it can be such a rewarding experience. And with no people around, it's such a fleeting gift of beauty and solitude before the grey clouds swallow our star and the humans spew forth from their homes.

Starting on Bamford Street, just north of North Road, I crept my way around many a dark street, several times unnerved by a local in dark clothing emerging from a house or strutting down the pavement in a hoodie. I tend to eschew stereotypes and defining areas as good or bad, nice or rough, but I'm not naive either. The looks I got told me everyone out and about rather wished they weren't. So I kept my distance, crossed over to other sides of the road and made sure not to accidentally creep up behind anyone unawares. Soon enough the darkness receded and twilight revealed an architectural misfit.

The Droylsden Industrial Co-Operative Society building on the corner of Ravensbury Street and Stockholm Street - with its large tiled lettering, relief emblem and glorious brick and cast-iron crown survives where others have sunk to soot-covered decay. Yet while its conversion to flats means the top floor remains the original brick, the lower floor long ago lost any original features and is simply smoothed over with terracotta coloured plaster. This 1908 store has been saved, but with a rather unsympathetic, featureless facelift. It leaves me torn. It somehow feels like a missed opportunity. With the terraced streets opposite laid with new tarmac and the cleansed brickwork looking pristine and uniform, this Co-op relic could have been the crowning glory of the community.

Leaving the streets of Clayton behind, I hit Bank Street and the first part of why this area is called Sport City; the largest concentration of sporting venues in Europe. Partially hidden behind trees and blue railings is the silver cladded, ultra-modern National Cycling Centre. This side of the building is home of the Indoor BMX track - where Bethany Shriever and Kye Whyte trained for their Olympic Gold and Silver at Tokyo 2020 this summer. On the other side is the impressive curved roof of the giant velodrome, otherwise known as the Gold Medal Factory for the proliferation of precious metal won by the nation's cyclists at every Olympics since Beijing 2008. This is where the likes of Laura and Jason Kenny, Bradley Wiggins, Victoria Pendleton, Sir Chris Hoy, Katie Archibald, Neil Fachie and Dame Sarah Storey all put in the endless laps to perfect their skills.

While the coaches here train their protégés for their own moment of sporting history, football history lies beneath their feet. Here, deep in Manchester City's blue heartlands is the red soil of a former Manchester United football stadium, the Bank Street Ground. After leaving their North Road ground in 1893, Newton Heath F.C. – United's former club name – moved to Bank Street, slowly building stands over the next decade to bring the capacity up to 50,000. It wasn't without detractors though, the pitch being called a 'toxic waste dump' by visiting Walsall Swifts in 1894. By 1910, they had outgrown the place and moved five miles west, out of Manchester into the neighbouring borough of Old Trafford, where they've played ever since. As I cross the canal and enter what in the 20th century used to be called Manchester's engine room, I dare say a few locals might have wished they could move five miles west from here too.

Bradford village was once a rural idyll abuzz with honey production while wolves and eagles stalked the woodland. They've mined coal here as far back as the reign of Elizabeth I in the early 17th century, but it was at the start of our Queen Elizabeth's reign in the 1950's that this area was in its deadly prime. The second Industrial revolution brought with it an insatiable thirst for steel, rubber, power and fuel, and East Manchester had it all. Out of this once verdant arcadia morphed a noisy, smoky place of hellfire and brimstone as a coal mine, brickworks, ironworks, dye-works, gas works, barbed-wire works, rubber works and a colossal electricity power station that made the night skies glow red and turned the land below black. In fact, there was so much heavy industry based here, that in 1959 it had the unenviable status of being the most atmospherically polluted place in the world.

In. The. World. Sure makes you proud.

With industry and homes alike burning the coal from Bradford Colliery, the area spewed around 12 tonnes of soot into the air, every single day. It must have hung thick in the air like a constant volcanic eruption, lining everything from roofs and brickwork to windows and washing. And more importantly, lungs. Retirement years could be counted on the coarse, blackened fingers of one hand in this part of Manchester, if they even lived long enough to choose to stop working. Workers at the nearby gas works, converting coal into Town Gas to be collected in the iconic gasometers – one of which still stands – would be lucky to get too far into their fifties.

Yet, this couldn't last. At the centre of this powerhouse was the colliery, but mining under a city caused subsidence that couldn't be ignored. Much of the land in East Manchester is a metre or more lower than it should be and by the 1960's the shifting ground was causing houses to need repairs or even be demolished. These rising costs for damages and compensation made the pit uneconomic and in 1968 it closed, with vast amounts of premium coal still beneath the city. Modern environmentalists might rejoice, but for Bradford it was devastating. Its heartbeat turned off, the other industries wilted and died, sending the population plummeting. This broken, heavily polluted area was a horrible scar on the city with seemingly no sign of redemption. The catalyst for change and new life would come from sport.

Making a brief dalliance amongst the cones and warning signs along SportCity Way, I felt very self-conscious. The adjacent car park was being used as Covid test and Vaccination centre. Although it had yet to open that morning and I was running on the verge near no one at all, it was the oddest place I'd gone so far. Head down, I got it done fast. Moving South I pass the National Tennis Centre and National Squash Centre to the impressive Etihad Stadium, built directly where the Bradford Ironworks used to be.

The stadium was originally built as an athletics stadium for the 2002 Commonwealth Games - the mascot for which was an Oasis-styled Mad Ferret; playing on the Mancunian phrase 'Mad fer it!'. After the games, Manchester City F.C moved in, ripping out the running track and replacing the temporary stand at one end with a permanent one closer to the pitch. Outside the stadium, there are still a few hints of its running past amongst the football frenzy. The warm-up track for the games still sits beside the stadium and is used for Athletics and other sports. Although when I was there, starlings solely occupied the pitch; the black birds lining up in a somewhat controversial 23-12-16 formation.

As I slowed for my own tour of the huge stadium, shrunk-wrapped with jubilant scenes of recent triumphs and star players, I gatecrashed the big clear up from the previous night's charity Soccer Aid match; the television trucks still packing away their gear and the black bags of rubbish being stacked up. Heading across the car park, I pass the two capped-shafts of Bradford Colliery; The Deep Pit Shaft and Parker Shaft. At over 800m deep, the Deep Pit shaft sunk in 1854 was the second deepest in British coalfields. Unmarked beneath the parking spaces at the Southeast end of the ground, it's a vertiginous thought that on match day, a couple of cars park up above these historic voids plunging down over half a mile into the earth.

I power up and over the elegant footbridge soaring diagonally across the wide road junction. On the other side is the £100 million, 80 acre training complex for the club, with 16 football pitches. It's fronted by yet another stadium - the 7000 capacity Academy stadium - home to the Manchester City Women's team. With the sunshine peeking out between the clouds, I take a last look at the amazing stadium opposite and head for the car.

I really enjoyed this run, with plenty to see and stark contrasts everywhere. The sport city complex might not have rejuvenated the area as intended but it has helped bring in investment and cleaned up that toxic waste dump. Yet, while the Commonwealth Games and City put Manchester on the map, Sport City has also succeeded in largely wiping the suburb of Bradford from it. Maybe some memories are too simply toxic to hold onto.

66 Streets added, a suitable footballing number to finish the day on.

Tuesday 7th September 2021 – 10.96km – Hothouse Flowers

The dragon is slain, but it didn't go quietly...

An early afternoon run today in the hot, dry heat of a blazing summer sun. I would never normally run in such challenging conditions in the heat of the middle of the day, but that roads total needs nibbling at on more than just my days off. The last few runs, I've had that faintest whiff, the merest imagined nose twitch of a finish line somewhere beyond the horizon. The impossible has been tied down and made real, now I just need to slip on the handcuffs and pull off the mask to reveal the owner of the haunted city was...Manchester all along!

'And I would have gotten away with it too, if it wasn't for you meddling roads...!'

With the sun high and fierce, I headed south to Wythenshawe and the hard monotonous concrete streets of Newall Green. Naturally, being closer to the equator, I should have expected Wythenshawe to be a tough challenge, but nonetheless I underestimated how much I'd suffer. For the record, it wasn't that hot. At around 25C, most southern Europeans would be putting on extra layers, Australians would be clinging to radiators and enduring a terrifying cold winter. No, this is solely down to me being a fair-skinned supporter of spring and autumn, a devotee of dappled sunshine and mild temperatures, a fan of frigid dawn sunrises and woolly hats. A distant nuclear furnace frazzling my sweat-soaked neck is less of a personal pleasure. Still sacrifices must be made and thankfully today's run was fairly short.

Some say – mainly me – that Wythenshawe is difficult to write about because it has little history, but today I come armed with a gem that will be bound to inspire and make you say, 'Wow! I did not know that.' So after a warm-up consisting of taking three steps from my car, I start just off Firbank Road, beside Alderman Rodger's Park; a simple dog-walking, playground park with four football pitches. This park is named after Robert Carr Rodgers C.B.E. who was not just a high-ranking councillor but also made Mayor of Manchester for a year in 1963/4. But wait, amongst all his duties and dedication to Manchester, Alderman Rodgers was also a horticulturist, winning a gold medal for his carnations at the 1956 Manchester Flower Show at Platt Fields.

Nothing? No reaction whatsoever, absolutely couldn't care less could you? Well, sorry, there are no refunds at this late stage. I've told you before, we're not talking about that Victorian vice scandal involving councillors at the Town Hall. Flower growing will have to suffice.

Perhaps we'd better move on, and given the other shiny gold disc in the sky, somewhat slowly.

More interesting, architecturally speaking are the homes around here in Newall Green. Built in the late forties by the somewhat unusual builder, British Steel Houses Ltd, this is an area known locally as Tin-Town. Commissioned during the war, over thirty thousand of these prefabricated homes were built across the country. These weren't a short term measure, rather a way to build permanent homes both cheaply and easily when money and labour post-war were in short supply. Way ahead of their time, they use a steel framework clad with corrugated metal walls and roofs, much like modern warehousing, albeit with a brick ground floor and more insulation. Many are now rendered and look much like any other semi in Wythenshawe, if it wasn't for the corrugated metal roofs, although today in the baking sun I imagine they are no place for cats.

As I ran, I saw no animals at all, except a few lobsters in garden chairs wearing sunglasses and flowery dresses. Heading south past the wonderfully named Milky Button park – not named after a Mayor – I work the roads off one side of Greenbrow Road, before crossing over and working back up the other side. As ever, it's not the most interesting of areas for sightseeing, but the past is still there, hidden in plain sight, if you know where to look. Before Wythenshawe became a huge council estate, the land was mainly farmland owned by the Massey family. They tithed out packets of land to farmers and market gardeners in a number of farms still preserved in the fossilized amber of modern street names. Rolling Gate farm, Newall Green Farm, Mill House, White House farm and - the wonderfully named - Knob Hall all have streets, closes and gardens named after them. The latter so named after the knob-like stone balls on all the gables. One still rests atop the concrete street-sign for Knob Hall Gardens.

With a few unexpected little rises sprinkled in across these concrete roads to test the willpower and fatigued legs, overall this was a much harder run than I'd hoped for. Whereas I can normally bound along for hours, this run was seriously draining the power from me after only ten minutes. That I sweated it out for five times as long is something of a miracle. Easily the hardest 10k I've done for a while. For me at least, it was not a day for running.

It was a day for sun worshippers, for not moving and saying 'Isn't it lovely/hot?' to anyone within earshot. Except me. Instead I got the gawp, the look enquiring where I'd escaped from. Perhaps the most awkward was an audience of two at the far end of a cul-de-sac. Wearing the all-white outfits of a bronzed couple recently returned from two weeks in Tenerife, I headed straight towards them like a messenger approaching a King and Queen. Only as I neared, with grave news of yet another defeat in the War of the Carnations, I make a laboured about turn and beat a hasty retreat.

Tough sunny day, but with another 31 streets ticked off, this does mean I have defeated my Wythenshawe nemesis. I've completed the huge area south of the M60, leaving me hot, bothered and incredibly happy.

Wednesday 8th September 2021 – 18km – Collyhurst, there's maybe worse...

"The mother-in-law came round last week. It was absolutely pouring down. So I opened the door and I saw her there and I said, 'Mother, don't just stand there in the rain. Go home."

I find myself just northeast of the city centre today for the veritable delights of Collyhurst. What should be a place of comedy pilgrimage for fans of the late, great Les Dawson - born here Feb 1931 - is instead somewhere I would never normally visit, let alone run through.

Parking up apprehensively just off Oldham Road, this was one of those runs where simply finding somewhere 'safe' to park the car took a bit of research. Even then, I arrived while it was still dark and spent a couple of minutes reading the lay of the land before getting out, putting my drinks belt on and setting off. I had barely started when I encountered a somewhat ominous side road. Dark bushes and fences line either side of the tarmac, three pools of weak, yellow light splashed along its length.

'Nope.' Said every fibre of my being, pointing to every horror film I've ever seen for evidence.

I blinked hard, trying to ignore the imagined newspaper headlines and judgemental voices of practically everyone I know. With a resigned grimace, I worked my way down this maleficent, sinistrous route with a sense of foreboding. Without all my senses yet tuned in, here I was running silently towards a barbed wire gate in No-Thank-You-Ville, Population: all dead. With the weeds, litter and abandoned car vying for my attention, my eyes fall on the small sign on the locked and chained gate: 'HURT' accompanied by a telephone number.

Even more Nope.

Six minutes in Collyhurst and I'd already found a whole clandestine world of Hurt.

It was warm out for six o'clock, warmer still after I engaged the power of spooked. A few minutes and a few more streets away, I settled back down into a good rhythm. Heading northeast, parallel with Oldham Road, around an estate full of building sites, new houses replacing the not so new, I soon come to a railway viaduct to nowhere, part of an old route heading to a Goods Yard and Potato Market nearer the city centre. Now it just stops on one side of Osborne Road looking forlorn and forgotten.

Headed back out to Oldham Road, I find the former site of the Royal Osborne Theatre. Built in 1896, it provided entertainment for the locals in an area until then devoid of public amusements. With an original capacity of three thousand people, in later decades, it would be used as a music hall, cinema, a roller disco and as an acid house club called the Thunderdome; all of which date the changing face of public entertainment. More tellingly, it is now an empty, overgrown lot, demolished in 2010.

Around the corner, past the unmistakeable telephone exchange building is Thornton Street. It's here on one of a crowded grid of numerous terraced streets that comedian Les Dawson was born and raised. The great man, joke-teller and prolific writer describes it thus;

"I was born in Collyhurst, Manchester in the thirties. It was a depressed decade and most of the people who lived in our area were decayed. Our terraced house was so narrow, the mice walked about on their back legs and the kitchen ceiling was so low the oven had a foot-level grill."

It's now a world of spacious long terraces surrounded by areas of grass and patches of wasteland. There is a park, a playground and the houses look relatively modern and well maintained, yet something about the place feels off. I am not relaxed or at home here, I am moving quickly, getting it done and doing my best to garner no attention. Weeds grow at the kerbside, litter remains unpicked and apathy hangs heavily in the air. It has none of the graffiti or sense of threat I've felt in other areas, no anger, it just feels a little neglected and forgotten.

On the corner of Collyhurst Street and Whitley Road – what once was Hamilton Street – was the site of the Collyhurst Picture House. In 1976, the old cinema was converted into one of the rowdiest and influential music venues in the city; the Electric Circus. This somewhat shabby rock venue reflected the drab and broken suburban sprawl outside. The burgeoning punk scene in Manchester rapidly found an affinity with its neglected decay and adopted it as their place. Anyone who was anyone in the rock and punk scene played the Electric Circus through 76 and 77; The Damned, The Stranglers, Siouxsie and the Banshees, The Ramones, The Fall, Joy Division, Talking Heads, AC/DC, Motorhead. Then almost as quick as it opened, the dilapidated live music venue closed, cramming a lifetime of raucous music into two years of memories for the lucky few. Imagine seeing the snarling Sex Pistols here for their third gig here in December 76, supported by The Buzzcocks, Heartbreakers and The Clash, all for a 75p entrance fee!

Of course, Comedian Les wasn't the only notable person from these streets. Footballer Nobby Stiles was born here, in the cellar of his family's Collyhurst terrace home during an air raid in 1942. Twenty-four years later, he was winning the World Cup at Wembley. He's remembered here with a road named after him: Nobby Stiles Drive. Fellow England

260

footballers Stan Bowles and Brian Kidd also come from the area. Not to mention Bruce Jones, the actor best known for playing Les Battersby in Coronation Street.

This area was a hard-man's area of terraced streets that made hardy footballers and unrelenting boxers, but also produced the courageous Henry Kelly (not the presenter of 80's television game show Going for Gold). Our Kelly was born in Collyhurst in 1887, working as a sorting clerk for Royal Mail before enlisting into the army in September 1914. Two years later on October 4th 1916, he would show most conspicuous bravery in an attack at Le Sars, France whilst under heavy fire. Leading three men into an enemy trench, he remained attacking until enemy reinforcements arrived, before carrying his Company Sergeant Major 70 yards back to his trench. Not satisfied with reaching safety, he immediately turned around and climbed back out of the trench while under enemy fire. He returned to no-man's land to carry back another injured soldier, not once but three more times, all while bullets fizzed and cracked through the air around him. For this selfless act, they awarded him the Victoria Cross. He would later receive the Military Cross and bar for two other acts of gallantry, finishing the war as a Major. At the end of the war, he simply returned to Collyhurst and went back to work for Royal Mail. A plaque on a postbox on Rochdale Road rather appropriately commemorates his bravery.

Noting Rochdale Road was getting busier with early rush-hour traffic, I picked up the pace, wanting to be away from here before people started getting up for work. A couple of unpleasant roads reminded me why. One was so full of broken glass, it looked like someone had just started learning to juggle with bottles. The other was way more unnerving. At the end of a close littered with children's toys was a small patch of grass – about the size of a tennis court - surrounded by houses, with several other walkways and cut-throughs leading to it from other closes. On the grass was a blackened patch of ground where a bonfire had been, surrounded by discarded bottles and cans, and like a scene from an apocalypse movie, the ashes were still smoking.

Yet, even more Nope.

Seventy-four minutes in Collyhurst and I felt like I'd tiptoed into the garden of a very urban take on a Hansel and Gretel story. Tiptoeing silently past all the loud toys lest they waken a hungover troll, I made for my pumpkin to get me out of this forbidden forest.

It's little wonder I prefer empty streets, I can't imagine running here at lunchtime or in the evening. Still I'd bagged 59 more streets and as I slowed my racing heart, I knew deep down it wasn't so bad. Sure, I'd got a few wheezy stares from people out early and recognised some illicit aromas here and there, but largely it was just me and some timid cats for company. Yet, as I got back to the car, two police meat wagons and a police car barrelled onto the estate from Oldham Rd, sirens blaring. My cue to head home.

"The wife's run off with the bloke next door. I do miss him."

Saturday 11th September 2021 – 22.82km – The Old, the Brave and the Anonymous

Rusholme. Sage post-work advice I should have taken, but didn't. Instead I pulled up on the border between Longsight and Fallowfield and rushed home much later than planned, but not before I headed for something of a local, if not an international tourist attraction.

Squeezing in another after-work run on tired legs seemed a plausible idea. After my run in Collyhurst, it became apparent how rapidly the nights were growing long and twilight lingering as autumn approached. If I was going to get out early to conquer some areas before people were around, then I'd be enduring more and more running time in the dark. And that'd mean, you know, vampires and werewolves. So, with a gap in my map that needed filling and a chance to sneak it in today, I forced myself out in hope for a distinctly productive weekend.

Southeast of the centre, I would take in four suburbs in an area popular with University students and home to a large multicultural community. Aside from dodging a few cars and people out walking their dogs, I didn't anticipate any problems. It was warm and a bit muggy with a heavy overcast sky trapping the humidity like a blanket, close, but not too sticky. The breeze cooled when it came, but it was all too intermittent and too whispered, like the asthmatic sigh of a migrating swallow. Still, at least it wasn't glaring sunshine.

Setting off from the pretty suburban streets of Collingwood Road, just off Slade Lane with its bay windowed semis and mature brick-walled gardens, I found my way south into the back streets of Levenshulme. Emerging on Albert Road, I make my way to a unique place amongst the roads of Manchester.

Here by Levenshulme Station and the railway bridge over the road is a 160-year-old street with an unusual claim to fame. Leading past the station entrance for about thirty metres, this narrow cobbled road ends at a foot-tunnel heading under the railway. It is nothing notable or picturesque, just a shortcut to nowhere, but it's famed for having no name. At least it didn't until recently. At some fuzzy point in the past, locals began referring to this street with no name as 'The Street With No Name'. Over the decades, the name stuck, then in May 2009, a street sign was put up on the wall of the station and the street with no name became 'The Street With No Name'. So much so, locals are no longer surprised to see people taking pictures and selfies, even Japanese and Chinese tourists as part of their Manchester visit. Still no sign of Bono yet though, perhaps he can't find what he's looking for.

Running west, I still feel okay, tired but thirsty for more roads, so I push on up Birchfields Road, taking a small angled detour beside Birchfields Park to the home of a prestigious Manchester institution; Manchester Grammar School. The school is the largest independent day school in the country and was founded way back in 1515, during the reign of Henry VIII, making it twice as old as the United States of America. And no doubt at least twice as useful in a history quiz. To be fair, I dare say the pupils would thrash us mere mortals in pretty much any kind of quiz. Founded by Manchester-born Hugh Oldham when he was Bishop of Exeter, it was originally located besides the Cathedral, in the buildings now used by Chetham's Music School, before moving to Rusholme in 1931. Some of the more unusual subjects available at the school are: Classical Civilisation, Classical Greek, Electronics, Latin, Further Mathematics and Languages such as Spanish, Italian, Russian and Mandarin.

The alumni of this esteemed establishment call themselves Old Mancunians and include: Cricketer Michael Atherton, Actors Robert Powell and Sir Ben Kingsley, Sports broadcaster Mark 'Chappers' Chapman, Historian Michael Wood, Comic Chris Addison and all manner of Scientists, Writers, Mathematicians, M.P's, Judges, Diplomats and Directors.

Retuning into the back streets, I worked my way methodically along Brynton Road and the roads either side, the distances sapping at my energy. Besides a mosque, it was mainly residential around here and something of a throwback to old communities. With kids playing out on the streets and local grocers, butchers and clothes shops still thriving, it reminded me of my formative years, rather than the supermarkets and screen-obsessed world we occupy now.

At 57 Birch Hall Lane, I come across the former home of Sam Wild, a man who felt so strongly about the rise of fascism in Europe in the late1930's he volunteered to risk his life for a country not his own. The Spanish Civil War was the overthrow of a democratic government by the fascist Franco, backed by German military might. An International Brigade of volunteers stepped up to defend the Spanish people from this tyranny including 2000 Brits of which a quarter would lose their lives in the fighting. 130 of these brave men and women came from Greater Manchester. Sam Wild fought in Spain for two years and was wounded three times. He became the last commander of the International Brigade before they were defeated. Sent back to Manchester to live out his days in Longsight, the people of Spain would later award him the Medal of Valour, their country's highest honour.

264

Other famous people from streets like these in Rusholme include actress Tina O'Brien who plays Sarah Platt in Coronation St and Marc Riley – Former bass player with The Fall and BBC Radio 6 DJ most famous for his comedy partnership with Mark Radcliffe on Radio 1 and known affectionately as Lard. 'Biggedy Biggedy Bong!'

Only as I left Birch Hall Lane, I found I was biggedy biggedy gone. My legs were slowing and all enthusiasm was ebbing away. A planned quick 10-12k run had dragged on, the hole in the map turning out to be a lot larger than I'd hoped. Without fluids or food, I was getting a hunger-knock and everything was beyond hard work. With a simple 'ladder' of short roads to zigzag down back to the car, I had to stop. Leaning on a wall, I had a desperate conference with myself. I could walk 500 metres to the car or run possibly 2-3 kilometres. So close to the end, I really didn't want to return, so I stop-started my way through the last dozen roads, counting them all one-by-one back to the sanctuary of my motor. It was not pretty and I probably looked a bit of a desperate mess, but I fought my way along those roads as if I was ploughing through knee-high sand with weights around my ankles. I'm only surprised I didn't see an oasis or accidentally join the foreign legion.

Sometimes, you get it wrong and that's OK. I'd done too much and my body was pushing back. Taking breaks every few hundred metres and allowing myself to shuffle along in fail-safe mode, I managed the crisis and didn't overdo it once I knew I'd overdone it. Sometimes my brain and ambitions lay plans out in front of me that my body begrudgingly accepts, but it's good to find out in a safe-ish way where the limit is and what the signs are. No harm done, never too old to admit I got it wrong and learnt a lesson.

69 hard-won streets today and at least they all had a name.

Sunday 12th September 2021 – 12.74km – Brunswick and Ardwick Green

Early in the 19th century, Ardwick Green was considered one of the most pleasant and well-constructed suburbs in the whole of the country. Full of elegant mansions and a large green complete with a lake, it was home to wealthy merchants and well-to-do professionals. Wedged between the imposing Manchester University buildings and the swooping commotion of the Mancunian Way, it's now a more humdrum estate but with newer builds replacing some of the old.

After yesterday's struggle, I was somewhat apprehensive although I'd given my body oodles of protein, fluids and a good night's sleep. Although I started a bit awkwardly, I shuffled a while to get some heat in my muscles before stretching out my stride a little and running much of yesterday's stiffness from my legs.

Starting beside the Green, which has lost much of its original splendour of fountains, flowerbeds and bandstands, I spy the brick campanile tower of St Thomas down the street. With its white clock-face, columned belfry and weathervane, this Italianate gem brings a hint of how wealthy this area once was. The more I look, the more I notice some of the terraces of Regency houses remain amongst the sympathetic modern copies. Although now this is the home to Solicitors and Charity offices rather than the homes of Manchester's well-to-do.

This is a place of historical survivors, buildings that have endured changing fashions and changing fortunes, wrecking balls and havoc wreaking bombs. Tanzaro House, stands at one end of the Green on the corner of the wonderfully named Cakebread Street. With its huge windows, tiled entrances and elegant facade, this was once an even grander seven-storey factory with ornate towers and chimneys. Owned by Jewsbury and Brown, they made 'Tanzaro' soft drinks such as lemon barley water, sparkling citrus flavoured drinks and rather less appealing medicinal health drinks such as Magnesia and Potash Waters. Yum! Alas, a devastating fire in 1953 left the top floors in ruins and although the business recovered, almost a decade later it merged with Schweppes, having been in business since 1826. The building remains as a truncated three-storey building used as offices.

Next door is the stone fortress-like building of the Drill Hall, built in 1886 and former home of the territorial army. It was once the home of the 8th Ardwicks who served and died in Flanders, France, Egypt and Gallipoli – a war memorial to their losses sits in the park opposite.

Less evocative but equally telling of the changing political landscape in these parts is the large brick and stone building on higher Ardwick. This club, built in 1878, was once home to a gymnasium, billiard, committee, smoking and card rooms as well as a large upstairs meeting room. This grand, impressive building now looks a little less loved, maybe unsurprising in this staunch labour-supporting city as this was Ardwick Conservative Club.

Still, it's perhaps less surprising than the area's connection to the man once voted the Greatest Briton. After previously becoming a Conservative MP for Oldham in October 1900, this man famously crossed the floor in 1904 to join the Liberal Party. Standing with his new party in the 1906 General Election, he stood for and won the Manchester North West seat aged just 31, holding it for two years before losing it to the Conservatives. His defeat no doubt celebrated heartily at this Ardwick Club. This famous MP for Manchester would later represent Dundee and have a much greater impact on the nation's psyche during the Second World War. He was of course Winston Churchill.

This area of Regency splendour and money was home to many of the movers and shakers in Manchester society. John Rylands - cotton king of Manchester himself - lived in Ardwick Green North in the early 19th century. He became Manchester's first Multi-Millionaire. Despite his philanthropy, at his death in 1888, he left over £2.5m to his third wife. (£289 million in 2021 money). Nathan Mayer Rothschild, second generation of the German banking dynasty settled in Ardwick Green in 1798 aged 21, becoming wealthier as a Textile trader and banker before moving to London. It was such an exclusive area at this time, the Green was only open to residents who had a key to its gates. Wouldn't want any of the riff-raff getting in and interrupting a morning's constitution, would we now?

Much later at the start of the 20th century, after the aristocracy sought views more pastoral and airs less polluted, the area became synonymous with those seeking pleasure. The eastern end of the Green had four large entertainment venues all huddled together; the Empire Music Hall, a Billiard Hall and two picture theatres: the Hippodrome and the Apollo. The latter is the only one still standing and remains a regular tour stop for bands and singers. The Beatles, Stones, Who, Bowie, Springsteen, Queen, Jacksons, ACDC have all played at the Apollo.

Leaving the area and backstreets around the green behind, I turn down the unlikely named Dolphin Street and glimpse yet another view of Manchester's past. Two tall four-storey brick factories flank the road, propelling me from the fledgling dawn light back into the murky, smoke filled shadows of the nineteenth century. With their grubby arched windows, dusty brickwork, faded paint, heavy duty doors and cast-iron cantilever fire escape, these are neither derelict shells nor polished apartments, but something much more real and authentic. It's like time-travel. I can imagine the wide-eyed workers in their simple clothes streaming in with a sigh, their clogs clip-clopping over the cobbles. The owner stepping down from his carriage in his finery, donning his tophat and tapping the pavement with his cane as he strode inside to berate the trembling Manager over the latest accounts.

After a backward glance and a blinking away of my imagination, I pick up the pace and bump straight into the home of deviant pastries.

In the 17th Century, Puritanism was rife across Britain. Fun in any form was an affront to god as the Church of England tried to throw off its Catholic past. Physical pleasures were essentially forbidden, even down to what you ate. Celebrations of Saint's days that had always been community events full of celebrations and dancing soon fell under the Puritan's stern gaze. With one particular Lancashire delicacy labelled as sinfully indulgent, corrupting to the piety of the human soul and prone to inciting revelry in all who indulged. Oh no...not revelry! Everyone stop revelling.

As legend goes, even Oliver Cromwell brought this delicacy to national fame by instating an act of Parliament that threatened imprisonment for anyone found eating one of these deviant pastries or their near cousin; the mince pie. The cause of such ire were small round cakes made from flaky pastry and filled with currants, zested lemon and orange, sugar and spices like cinnamon, cloves and nutmeg. Topped with sugar and browned in the oven, they were, are and always will be utterly scrumptious. They are of course; Lancashire Eccles Cakes, made here at their Hyde Road bakery.

Revelling in the smell of sweet pastry treats wafting outside but thankfully escaping Puritan arrest, I head southwest into neighbouring Brunswick. Bar a few four-storey 1960's maisonettes, almost all of this area is a new estate, part of an ambitious plan to regenerate and rejuvenate the inner city. So much so, I find several roads not even on my map yet. Despite these unborn streets between half-built houses throwing my route out, I rather enjoyed this area. Although the large University buildings dominate the skyline to the west, it looks well planned out and a more inviting place to live than the terraced streets that were here originally.

Amongst its notable past residents were two politicians far removed from the Conservative leanings of the past. Labour MP Ellen Wilkinson was born in Ardwick in 1891 at 41 Coral Street (Now Balsam

Close). Known affectionately as 'Red Nellie' Wilkinson, she was an ardent trade unionist, led a prominent role in the 1936 Jarrow March and became the first woman Minister of Education. She campaigned vociferously for workers rights throughout her life and was the woman who introduced free milk to schools. Less than a hundred metres away and nearly thirty years prior at 5, New York Place, David Lloyd George was born to Welsh parents. He would go on to be Prime Minister from 1916-1922, the last Liberal premier in this country and its only Welsh leader. There is a plaque up on nearby Wadeson Road, but the leader was only in Manchester for the first three months of his life before moving to Pembrokeshire. Still, we all know it must have been the formative ideas conjured from the Mancunian drizzle, the varied colours of his poos and the first grabbing of his mother's finger that set him on his way to liberal fame, right?

At the western fringes of this new estate, I reach a neat little park of grass, trees and playgrounds called Gartside Gardens. It's innocence is deceptive, for one hundred and thirty years this was Rusholme Road Cemetery. Opening in 1821, it became a popular burial spot for the middle and upper classes across Ardwick and the city. John Edward Taylor, the founder of the Manchester Guardian newspaper in 1821 is buried here. He continued to edit the paper until his death is 1844, but his liberal legacy continues at the Guardian newspaper. A little darker and much closer to home was the cemetery's role when the nation's 1837 influenza outbreak reached the city. The poor crowded into their homes and neighbourhoods suffered terribly, but the wealthy soon found money was no cause of immunity. At its worse, this small cemetery conducted 36 burials in one day.

With the morning warming from mild to a drab mugginess, I decide to cut the run short. I still had lots in the legs and felt great, but thought I'd be good to myself and wrap it up early.
52 streets today and now home for wanton revelry.

Tuesday 14th September 2021 – 13.9km – Didsbury Dash

Ah Didsbury, one of the poshest of the 'villages' within Manchester where ladies lunch, dogs are promenaded and there's always a healthy hubbub of people and traffic. It's a place almost without litter or graffiti and even the trees apologetically clear up their leaves each Autumn. Probably. It's also where the seeds were sown for an iconic television series that changed British comedy forever.

Arriving just before one o'clock after an early finish at work, I parked up amidst the grand houses and leafy gardens just north of Barlow Moor Road on Pine Road. Crossing the main road, I enter the warren of pretty terraces and Victorian town-house villas that give this area such character. Windows gleam, alarm boxes flash and the wooden front doors tell you what paint colours are currently on trend. Still, after some of the streets I've run down, I can't deny the pleasure of streets that aren't run down. Here, amidst the polished homes of the middle classes, I can at least relax and not worry about stepping on broken glass or slip on unsanitary unspeakables. No-one here is going to shout an enquiry as to what I'm about or square up to me, I'm more likely to crop up as an A.O.B of some sub-committee or a sternly worded missive to the council.

Emerging from my pleasant daydream of being able to afford any one of these humble abodes, I hit traffic. Like a hermit dropped onto the streets of New Delhi, I am immediately amongst a throng of passers-by, shoppers, buses and shiny cars. This is Wilmslow Road; the main artery and shopping area of this affluent suburb. Lined with thriving pubs, bars, restaurants, shops and boutiques it is busy with people, even at lunchtime on a Tuesday. With everyone at one pace and the cars at another, I weave up and down off the kerb like Gene Kelly Singin' in the Rain. Or maybe Ernie Wise. Completing all the roads, but not necessarily in the right order, I cross the main road and plunge once more into the relative calm of the pristine back streets behind the shops.

The shops on Wilmslow road are the centre now, but it wasn't always so. As I head down Wilmslow Road away from the shops, I head for the original 18th century centre. Before I get there though and even before I reach the gothic sandstone splendour of the former St Paul's Methodist Church, I pass the hugely impressive Lawnhurst. One of Didsbury's, if not Manchester's grandest Victorian mansion houses, it was built in 1892 by German engineer and flour-milling supremo Henry Gustav Simon for his wife and eight children. To give you an idea of the place, after his death, his widow Emily Simon opened up Lawnhurst as a hospital for 100 wounded soldiers during the First World War.

Intellectually and educationally philanthropic in Manchester society, Simonsway in Wythenshawe is named after him.

More recently and more interestingly, it's a small cottage, hidden from view that deserves it's place in the spotlight. The whitewashed Lime Cottage sits beside a larger house, now forming part of the Limes nursing home, but the previous owner rented it out to students at the University. In the mid 1970's, three students from the drama course lived an anarchic life here of wild parties, rebellious ideas, pranks like riding a motorbike up the stairs and the surreal comedic improvisations that would soon bring alternative comedy to the masses. One of these anarchic residents was Rik Mayall. The motorbike's owner was Ade Edmondson's – a friend on the same drama course. These chaotic student digs would form the idea for The Young Ones, the hit television series that changed comedy in the early 80's and even spawned a hit single with Cliff Richard.

I finally reach the centre of the village at the bend in the road by Ye Olde Cock Inn and The Didsbury pubs. The beer garden in front of the Didsbury Inn used to be the village green, back when the pub's name was the Ring O' Bells. The bells in the pub title refer to St James' church at the pub's rear. Its accompanying parsonage - now a wedding venue - swiftly gained such a terrifying reputation for being haunted, servants refused to stay overnight on the premises. So much so, by 1850, it lay entirely empty. Local Alderman - a councillor second only to mayor - Fletcher Moss moved in 15 years later and whatever he encountered within these ghostly walls, he stoutly resided there for over 40 years. Yet the house's reputation lingered on, so much so, that when Moss installed an imposing archway entrance to his gardens, locals dubbed it 'The Gates to Hell!' This area around the church has the highest concentration of listed buildings in all of Manchester.

Heading west past the church into Fletcher Moss Park, I follow the quiet green road of Stenner Lane towards the river and Ford Lane. It retains an interesting place in history, as it led to the only crossing point on the River Mersey between Stockport and Stretford (now the river shallows next to 'Simon's Footbridge' – a gift to Didsbury from Henry Simon). It's believed this was the way Bonnie Prince Charlie led his Scottish troops south towards London to claim the throne as part of the 1745 Jacobite rebellion. Two days after taking Derby and with his support waning, he retreated north, returning once more over the Mersey and on up Ford Lane.

With the River Mersey and an abundance of parks and green spaces, Didsbury is a lovely place for exercise and runners. Obviously not for a tarmac-muncher like me, but for normal people. Overall, I enjoyed

271

running in a place where running isn't an oddity, even if my timing was a little out amongst the crowds. Only 41 roads completed, but never a chance of finding a fly-tipped bugaboo pram, a Peloton exercise bike or an abandoned Emperor-sized mattress. Probably as well, I'd never get it all in my car.

Sunday 19th September 2021 – 23.11km – Crumpsall Soaking

When Manchester was red because of secrets stolen from France...

Today's rain temperature in Manchester was mild with occasional easing into tepid showers. It's been raining most of the night and was still coming down when I drove through the dark at six o'clock, traffic lights gleaming on the shiny streets. Despite the grim start, as I headed to the north of the city, I was feeling good. After chipping away at the total and slowly colouring in areas at random, I was no longer venturing into the unknown but rather plugging gaps and completing whole swathes of the city. Today's run was an ambitious double hit of Lower Crumpsall and a patch of Harpurhey, two holes in the map left from previous runs. And if all went well, my last trip to the hilly north of the city.

Clambering out of the car on Waterloo St, into the sodden Irk valley, I'm close to the meandering river Irk and several ponds and reservoirs amid the woodlands and wild grounds. Serene and full of lush, (well-watered) flora and (well-hydrated) wildlife, these barely hint at the great mills and works once occupying this valley and polluting the water in the pursuit of a particular colour.

In the late 18th century, dyeing fabrics permanently bright red was a problem, the Brits didn't know how. The French and Dutch zealously hoarded the secret for many years against many espionage expeditions and bribes, until Angel Delaunay from Rouen smuggled the secrets out and brought them to Manchester. Setting up business in Crumpsall and Blackley, the area prospered on this forbidden knowledge until the 1920's. For the curious, the process included the delights of rancid milk, cow dung, the dyer's madder (plant), alum, bullock's blood, bleach, chloride of tin and copious amounts of boiling water. I imagine you'd get used to the smell after a few decades, if you were still alive.

Feeling myself very much soaked and - with the steep hills underfoot – reddened in the face, I left the Irk behind and headed west to the workers terraces around Crumpsall Park and on to the edge of Cheetham Hill. The verdant park opened in the 1890s and marks the period in time when green spaces in cities were more than simply places to promenade and walk off one's Victorian lunch. The benefits of being active and the growth in leisure time meant it opened with twelve tennis courts, two bowling greens and two children's playing areas. Although heavily industrialised and crowded in the early twentieth century, the city could at least boast more public parks than any other English city outside the capital. As I work my way around these streets, the heavens open again and the rain grows even heavier. Despite already being soaked to the skin, I somehow proceed to discover a new wetter existence. The water is dripping off my drips and if I fell in the River I couldn't be any worse off.

Squelching back down the hill, the dark clouds skulk off to ruin someone else's washing, the rain first slowing and then stopping entirely. Pushing on past the flowing puddles and gurgling drains, I generate my own breeze, leaving me less of a drowned rat and more of a dampened mouse. Doubling back the way I'd come for a mile or so, I cross Tetlow Bridge over the swollen river, back into Blackley. With the dry refuge of the car within reach, I sigh and turn to head east. Leaving Waterloo St behind me and below me, I clamber up the brutally steep Factory Lane into Harpurhey. Known locally as 'Factory Brew', this hill is blessedly short at only 250 metres in length, but it averages 10% and rises to 15-16% in parts. I love a hill, but this was brutal and left me gasping. At some points, I felt as if I was running hard and still only advancing a few inches at a time. At least there was no danger of stepping in a puddle.

Much warmer, if not drier, I meandered my way around a mainly residential area west of Rochdale Road, the main highlight being the listed buildings of Harpurhey Public Baths and Laundry. Opened in 1910 and only closing as a swimming pool in 2001, it has now been absorbed into the college next door, but the brick and tiled frontage and green window frames and drainpipes remain. Nearly opposite is the former Farmyard Hotel, a huge public house more reminiscent of a busy junction pub or a town centre tavern, rather than up in the suburbs. It's now used as a creative learning centre.

Further up the street and still in use, is something really rather special. Sat on the street outside the beer garden of the Alliance Inn is a very special postbox, though you'd barely notice. Still in its original green and gold Victorian livery, its hexagonal design puts it at somewhere around 150 years old. For context, there have been 37 Prime Ministers since this postbox was first installed and yet it stands unannounced and uncelebrated, resolutely doing what its always done.

Seemingly doing what I've always done, I worked my way up and down several more roads before dropping down the hill on Old Road onto Slack Road. Wet and weary, I finished the streets and slowly walked back to the car. With 77 more streets completed today, I've sailed over another milestone in my journey. I've hit 90% of the city streets completed. It almost feels like a last mile marker, albeit one with 590 streets still to run. Getting there...

Tuesday 21st September 2021 – 12.17km – Plotting Miles in Miles Platting

Miles Platting, like so many of the inner city areas has had mixed fortunes. Centered around the Rochdale Canal, in the late 19th century, the area gained many huge cotton mills; noisily shuttling thread on several floors day after day, the sky thick with coal smoke, the water busy with barges. Soon a timber yard, chemical works, soap factory, tannery and alum works would add to the murmured thrum and acrid aromas filling the air. Such industry tightly packed together led to the large workforce equally packed tight together in row after row of terraced houses on cobbled streets. Large Italian and Irish communities historically populated this area, Catholicism being the cultural glue of a diverse neighbourhood.

With the days cascading from the calendar and the warm summer shaking hands with the inclement autumn, I yet again pencilled in a midweek run. This one not so much on the way home from work as on the wrong side of the city centre. What a strange life I now lead, driving miles out of my way for a run, not at a pretty reservoir, a challenging hilly park or an arboreal riverbank trail, but the random streets of a housing estate in Miles Platting.

Much like Bradford and Gorton, when the industries started closing in the mid-20th century, the area quickly nose-dived into poverty and crime. Thankfully, after a slum clearance and long-term rejuvenation project started in the 1990's, it's a pleasant area of modern and older council houses with much greenery and gardens. As I pull up on Lower Vickers Street, people are out on the large expanse of parkland beside the canal, enjoying the hazy sunshine and feeding the honking geese who roam freely beside the water. Surrounded by modern red brick housing with steeply pitched roofs and dark window frames, there's a hint of old warehouse and wharf buildings about the houses that's rather pleasing.

The regeneration is not without its detractors though. As the council houses are pulled down and the new builds go up, the working class community gets displaced. Many newcomers are banking on the slow creep of the trendy Northern Quarter and Ancoats to fill in the gaps between here and the centre, which would mean even more council houses coming down and their own homes going up in price. They're probably right too. Heading northeast alongside the canal, I close in on a true survivor, the talisman of the suburb that seems to photo-bomb any picture taken in these parts.

Victoria Mill is an old six-storey, cotton-spinning mill built in 1869. Or rather its two mills sat either side of an engine house and a striking octagonal stairwell wrapped around the lower half of the tall mill chimney. With its height and angular features, it seems impossibly large for a brick building and has a real daunting presence in the landscape. One can only imagine what a colossal powerhouse of industry this must have been when the engine was at full tilt and the hundreds of spinning machines were running inside. It's little wonder mill girls across Manchester made up their own rudimentary sign language. The racket and vibrations across the area must have been immense as this castle of wonder and fear appeared to breathe and murmur as if alive.

Deafened now only by the silence, I move past the apartments and offices now filling these floors and pick up the pace. I feel pretty strong and fit, but I'd also rather be at home with a cold drink, so rush around to get this area ticked off sharpish. It was lovely to have empty streets to go at during the day too. As it was so warm and dazzling, there weren't too many people around, certainly no runners, although a few people stared from their sunny gardens as I thundered past, to be fair I'd have stared too. Giving it the beans as they say, I was sweaty, breathing hard and probably looked a bit demented.

Onto Varley Street, I find another stunning relic of the community that used to live, work and worship in these streets. Norbertine Canons from the Belgian Abbey of Tongerlo arrived in Manchester in 1889 to set up a Roman Catholic Priory. They built a large brick and pale sandstone basilica in an Italian Romanesque style. Large and robust rather than outlandishly ornate, it no doubt matched its soot-covered neighbours and formed the heart of the community rather than something lording over it. With emptying streets around it, falling congregation numbers and rising repair costs, the order of Canons closed the basilica in 2007, leaving for Chelmsford the following year. A Grade II listed building; a banqueting company for weddings and special events is the current custodian.

Almost opposite the church, tragedy struck in the Manchester Christmas blitz raids of December 1940. A huge bomb fell on Varley Street destroying several homes and devastating a community in a single moment. This one bomb killed more than twenty people including eleven gathered at number 28 for a Christmas party. A widowed grandmother, her son, three daughters, their husbands and children all lost, three generations of a family wiped out in an instant. Three more bombs scattered across neighbouring streets led to another thirteen funerals. I cannot imagine how frightened and shaken the community must have felt as the war of the newspapers and newsreels came not just to their city, but the very streets they lived on.

After running through several areas of 1960's council houses and past a row of off-white tower blocks, I return to the bright brickwork of the modern estate. Whatever the pros and cons are of the changes around here, I find the naming of three streets after WWI Victoria Cross winners from the Manchester Regiment rather touching. John Hogan VC Road and James Leach VC Road aptly stand beside one another, just as they did back in 1914.

The citation for their medals reads: "For conspicuous bravery near Festubert on 29 October, when, after their trench had been taken by the Germans, and after two attempts at recapture had failed, they voluntarily decided on the afternoon of the same day to recover the trench themselves. Working from traverse to traverse at close quarters with great bravery, they gradually succeeded in regaining possession, killing eight of the enemy, wounding two, and making sixteen prisoners."

Further round the estate sits George Stringer VC Drive, the street-sign aptly decorated with a copy of his medal, which is a lovely touch. His citation in the London Gazette reads:

"For most conspicuous bravery and determination. After the capture of an enemy position, he was posted on the extreme right of the Battalion in order to guard against any hostile attack. His battalion was subsequently forced back by an enemy counter-attack, but Private Stringer held his ground single-handed and kept back the enemy till all his hand-grenades were expended. His very gallant stand saved the flank of his battalion and rendered a steady withdrawal possible."

Humbled by these brave men and a time when war and backbreaking work were the norm, I was glad to read after the run that all three survived the war. No doubt it was a long time before any of them dipped a hand in their pocket for a drink on their return.

Another 42 streets today and all wrapped up in less than an hour. Now for some ice cream in a bowl bigger than my head.

Saturday 2nd October 2021 – 25.05km – The Cardroom, Chips and the Dispensary

Sitting snugly between the Ashton and the Rochdale Canals and close to the River Medlock, the area of New Islington is an area really at the heart of things during the industrial revolution. The busy canals would have brought in coal and raw cotton by the barge-load, before taking out the finished textiles from the numerous warehouses on route to the four corners of the world. The mills would have made a frenetic soundscape to accompany the industrious output of the area. Sadly, the usual story of the rise and fall of the cotton trade hit the area hard.

After the decline and the rot set it, the council redeveloped it into 'The Cardroom' estate in the 1970s - a nod towards the punch-hole cards used to program the looms in the local mills. Alas, this new estate also suffered, slowly falling into a warren of crime and disrepair. The low density design full of dead ends and alleyways was perfect for joyriders and drug dealers, who could melt away at the first hint of trouble. The area needed money and a change of scene.

Last week I had a break from gathering streets and did something I'd not done for a very long time. Before this challenge and indeed before this pandemic, runners of all ages, shapes and paces used to gather in large groups and run a set route for a hunk of metal on a fancy ribbon. We called these strange ritualistic gatherings 'races', the word derived from an old Northern English word meaning 'rapid forward movement'. Such was the spectacle, crowds gathered to watch the active participants stream past in their bright colours. After thrice being postponed over the last eighteen months, a race I'd booked back in November 2019 – four months before this insane challenge began – finally happened. It was emotional, it was brutal and it was amazing. It was the ridiculously hilly Sheffield Half-Marathon.

With 310 metres of elevation to climb in the first 8 kilometres, with long sections at five and six percent, I knew it was going to be tough, but I'm a good climber, just lack the confidence in my pacing. So as I set off in races, I always try to latch onto someone who knows what they're doing. I had a mile to run before the road headed skyward, so I'm there flitting around searching for 'the one'. I'm like a choosy speed-dater; too old, too many water bottles, weird gait. I surge forward and back, drifting left and right; too fast, too breathy, too chatty, too muscly, too...odd. I look up and oh no, the hill's here already! The crowd cheers and applauds as the road clambers up into the heavens and I despair of finding a pilot and begin plodding alone through the maze of slower runners. Then, sliding past like a mountain goat is a young lad in a yellow vest emblazoned with 'Sheffield Fell Runners Club'. Ave Maria! I latched on to him like a car chasing an ambulance through traffic and soared all the way to the top.

A long working week after the excitement of an actual race, and I return to the grind of running to and fro like a kid full of fizz and cake at a birthday party. Today's steady, chaotic meander was just northeast of the city centre and thankfully flat.

New Islington is in a race of its own against competing areas in Manchester's inner city. By the 2010s, millions of pounds have gentrified the area into one fit for professionals, city workers and families with many quirky buildings and ideas. But much like Miles Platting and other areas undergoing investment, you worry problems aren't necessarily solved, just moved on elsewhere. This feels like a place for the Instagram generation with artisan bakeries and hipster bars and restaurants. I definitely felt a stranger without a beard and a flannel shirt. But, it does feel like its reached a tipping point where it's a popular place to live for a certain kind of resident and is finding its own identity accordingly.

Being October and with autumn not just clearing its throat but launching into its opening verse, at six o'clock in the morning it is somewhat dark and uninviting as I park up on Harding Street at the rear of a derelict church in the neighbouring Beswick. It wasn't the nicest of places to be, but having already rejected two other nearby streets, I decided I had to ignore any bad vibes and get on with it. Back onto the busier road, Every Street, I immediately call my lawyer, but sadly he tells me it isn't a loophole and to complete the challenge I must run every street in Manchester, every with a small 'e'. He also asks if I know what time it is, how I have his home phone number and how I know his wife's name, but I haven't got time to answer these questions here, I have a run to report on.

With some tidying up to do on my map, I head east into Bradford, almost immediately hitting more angst as the houses disappear on Gurney Street and I find myself on a dark tree-lined road crossing the River Medlock and lit only by the occasional street lamp. I reassure myself that this is far too scary a place for monsters let alone stray humans and plough on regardless, bravely bouncing down the centre of the tarmac at breakneck speed. Three anxious minutes later and I'm back amongst the slumbering houses on Viaduct Street. At the bottom of the road, I can just make out the end of the abandoned railway viaduct on the other side of Ashton Old Road. Overgrown on top, it remains now as home for garages and similar businesses all the way to the active main line.

After a brief diversion onto an industrial estate, I pass the council's vehicle pound, where men in white coats carrying big-hooped nets bring stray cars and vans after capture. Further still down Rondin Road, I find the Siemens Train Care Facility. With its windows, painted floors and bright lights, it looks more like a Kwik-fit than the greasy, grimy hells of heavy engineering that once dominated Manchester's eastern suburbs. I stare in from the darkness as three shiny modern trains alongside one another sit as if at a gym or exclusive spa. Somewhere at the back of my mind, I can hear a faint childhood echo of Ringo Starr voicing Thomas' distinct displeasure at their special treatment.

Looping north, I head back up Every Street to Holt Town. Now a smattering of faceless, repurposed old factory buildings with bricked up doorways and barred windows, it was once a new venture amidst the fields and besides the babbling River Medlock. Established in 1785 by David Holt, this was the only known factory-colony in the city, finer examples are preserved at Quarry bank Mill at Styal, Cheshire or New Lanark in Scotland. Besides the new cotton mill buildings, Holt built 22 four-storey, back-to-back houses for his mill workers, a reservoir and a large house with conservatory and gardens – presumably for himself. However, competition was rife and within nine years, Holt was bankrupt. Ownership passed to William Mitchell who lived to 1828, his name still (barely) remembered at the corner of Merrill Street and Every Street with the derelict Mitchell Arms Pub. Next to the pub is Holt Town tram stop, which sits over the original back-to-back tenements on the long gone Mill Street and Pump Street.

Crossing the 200-year-old, bridge no.4 over the Ashton Canal on Carruthers Street, one might assume this unassuming and largely hidden listed bridge is of little cultural interest. Yet it and the surrounding area provided the perfect 1970's backdrop for filming of the 2006 hit television drama; Life on Mars. With its dirty, dilapidated and falling down mills, the bridge starred in a car chase scene between a Cortina and a Capri, ending amidst a football match on some waste ground with Gene Hunt his usual charming self. It's all been redeveloped now, the mills replaced with slate grey apartment blocks and the waste ground with sleek grey town houses, the area unrecognisable in just fifteen years. All but for the unassuming and largely hidden listed bridge that's seen it all before.

Much like Miles Platting, New Islington is the old 1960's stock of council houses mixing with the ultra modern and quirky mill conversions, the working class families and social housing tenants rubbing shoulders with the trendy socialites and young professionals. The Stubbs building – originally a late 19th century factory making textile machinery for the mills – has been brought back to life as an impressive apartment conversion. Next door is the wild Chips building. Nine stories high and very long, it's designed to look like three thick chips laying on top of one another, but coloured orange brown and red and covered in large black lettering. In front of the pair and covered in scaffolding – for more than a decade - to stop it falling down is the gothic Ancoats Dispensary and Hospital, built in 1874 and a grade II listed building, it still awaits its turn for regeneration. Such is New Islington, an area of old meets new, of preservation besides conversion and the outlandish opposite the modest; all rubbing shoulders and reflecting the melting pot of ideas amongst its ambitious residents. I can't wait to see what goes up next, but more importantly I can't wait for the scaffolding to come down on the Ancoats Hospital, to see it in all its glory once more.

Another glorious landmark has been revealed too as I peel back the uncompleted roads from this challenge. The gaps in the map are slowly disappearing and with a bumper haul of 98 streets today, I am now way past the 500 streets to go mark, with just 450 streets left to run.

Monday 4th October 2021 – 17.11km & 12.49km – Knives and Forks

"I don't care if the (violent) incidents are unrelated; it is the sheer number that is happening, involving knives, machetes, and a pitchfork."

I try not to read too much about, nor bad mouth individual areas in Manchester, but I'm rather glad I didn't read this 2020 Manchester Evening News story about local thugs in Clayton. I mean a pitchfork? What kind of teen gang threatens someone in a car on Stanton St with a pitchfork?

So early this morning, feeling relatively fresh and ready for a big run day, I obliviously parked my car at the end of...take a wild guess...Stanton St. Thankfully at that time, on the cusp between Nautical and Civil Twilight, there were no unattended youths carrying hay-forks, scythes, sickles or threshing flails. For while the good-for-nothing, toxic wasters of the world will do anything for easy money, cheap thrills or a powerful whiff of fear, they don't tend to do mornings. Nonetheless, even with no solid information, I've been doing this long enough to pick up on things unseen and unsaid, my instincts telling me to be cautious for the first few streets and get up on my toes. Almost immediately though I come across a curiosity.

In the midst of this mix of dark brown semi-detached council houses, red-bricked terraces and modern box houses is a short section of dual carriageway, complete with raised central reservation. This four-lane superhighway leads exactly from nowhere to nowhere through suburbia, but why? The answer is somewhat given away by the street name: Eastern By-Pass. Along with another road with the same name in Openshaw, these are remnants of another failed folly of town planning. Back in 1945, when anything seemed possible but for the fact the country was stony broke, the council proposed a bypass down the eastern part of the city from the junction of Broadway and Oldham Road down through Newton Heath, Clayton Vale, Clayton, Openshaw and Gorton before joining Stockport Road in Levenshulme. It was still on the table in the early 1960's before being abandoned, leaving behind anticipatory white elephants like Eastern By-Pass and the wide expanse between houses on Vale Street.

After the novelty of running both sides of a dual carriageway, I settle into my explore of the streets of Clayton. Like many other notorious areas, it passes largely without a hitch nor a hint of any ne'er do wells or medieval miscreants, only curious bin-men and kids heading to school. My favourite part was an area just off Folkestone Road, which seemingly was the part of the estate the planners named late on a Friday afternoon with the pub calling. We not only get Folkestone Road East and

Folkestone Road West, but also North Crescent and South Crescent and First, Second, Third, Fourth and Fifth Avenue. You just know the same planner probably had a dog called 'Dog'. Still, they were all short streets and they all count the same. In fact, Clayton for me was something of a street-bagging delight. I have never seen so many closes and cul-de-sacs in my life. I've done more U-turns today than a jittery government caught with its pants down and a surprised look on its face.

Yet, despite the area's bad rep, it has an absolute historical gem half-hidden amidst its council houses and terraced streets. Partially screened by trees and the verdant shrubbery in its grounds, Clayton Hall is a 15th century Manor House complete with a (dry) moat and 17th century bridge entrance. Brick-built with some black and white timber framing at first-floor level, it has later renovations but still looks magnificent behind its cast iron gates. Owned by the Clayton family that gave the area its name, then the Byrons - Lord Byron a relative - and finally the Cheethams - of the famous music school and library fame, it's place in Manchester history is secure. I can only wonder if any disgruntled tenant farmer from long ago, ever brought his pitchfork to the gates to have it out with his landlord.

With Clayton disappearing from my rear-view mirror, I headed through the rush-hour traffic for a couple of stops along the way to pick up stray streets I'd missed. First down to Gorton to pick up a couple of roads, including a Close that was seemingly built after the last time I'd run here, I'd swear it wasn't there last time I passed. This was a strange experience, like running an errand but without the parcel to deliver or dry-cleaning to collect. I arrived empty handed, ran around a bit and then left empty-handed. If anyone was tracking my movements, I'd love to see their conclusions.

8.54am: "Subject parked up and ran anti-clockwise around two Closes before returning to the car. No close contacts made. Aborted farming equipment arms deal? Signalling a medieval sleeper cell? Or just out for a 500 metre run?"

8.58am: "Subject returned to car and evacuated the area. Notify Security General. Code Pitchfork."

I'm not sure if they'd think me a spy genius or mentally odd. It's a fine line. One of the roads was named after the recently departed and much loved, long-serving Labour MP for the area, I completed Sir Gerald Kaufman Close and got back into traffic.

Next up was a section of Stanley Grove in Belle Vue that had somehow fallen between two runs. Getting out of the car, a woman at the bus stop pretended she wasn't watching me. I ran past her for two hundred

283

metres, turned around and ran back. Getting back into the car, the woman at the bus stop was no longer pretending, she was just staring with a puzzled frown on her face. I see it from her point of view and realise all my explanations would only make me sound stranger than I appear. I had no defence to the imagined retelling later; "And then blow me down Doreen, if he doesn't get back in his car and drive off...!'

So I got back in my car and drove off.

Now headed for Fallowfield, I went for one last run. Clambering out of the car on Ladybarn Road, between a terrace and a new block of student apartments, I feel much more at ease, even if easing into a run after sitting in rush hour traffic is an awkward process. Rocking along like Tin Man from the Wizard of Oz for a few streets, I eventually find the elasticity returning to my lower limbs and a hint of warmth in my muscles. Deep in student land once more, I'm on familiar territory in these parts, not far from the Fallowfield Loop.

One of the most famous residents who grew up around these parts was drummer with The Smiths; Mike Joyce. After they split up and several lawsuits over royalties, Joyce went on to work with Sinead O'Connor, Suede, Buzzcocks, Public Image Limited and Julian Cope. He now DJ's and presents music shows on the radio.

Heading west for a few uninteresting streets in Old Moat and back along Moseley Road, I slowed and tightened up, this unforgiving additional 12k run beginning to tell on my lower legs. The struggle of pushing myself to the end of yet another dead end and back somewhat grates when you've been at it all morning. Still, these closes and cul-de-sacs must be done, if only once. With very little to see or comment on, I channelled the London marathon inspirations from the day before to pull me through and keep me ticking off fifty metre stretches of tarmac,one-by-one, until my car finally loomed into view.

A really rather ridiculous grand total of 118 streets collected today, with around 20 miles put into the legs. Not as long as a marathon, but with all the slowing down, turning and speeding up again, this certainly felt like a long day out. And despite it being a ridiculous task, I enjoyed it. I have finally sealed the mythical gap between Newton Heath and Gorton, the East of Manchester is complete, Hurrah! The muscles are strong, the fatigue is temporary, but the niggles in my knee, hips and back are starting to stack up. I am pushing my luck a little with my workload, but I'm also very near to the finish. I do sometimes wonder who I am exactly or who I've become. Going by the stairs up to my flat, possibly part-Dalek.

Thursday 7th October 2021 – 25.83km – City Centre Chaos

I knew this wasn't going to be one of my favourite runs. On the one hand, there's much to see in the city centre, much to admire; historical landmarks and hidden treasures, rousing architecture and unmoving statues, skies reflected in glass-fronted towers and the joy of old pubs surviving against the odds. But, I am not alone. Zombie commuters clog up the pavements, coffee in hand, headphones their oblivion. Indifferent cars sweep and swish past, emerging and disappearing into underground parking like rabbits into their burrows. Trams hoot and whistle as they rattle the rails and thunder the ground like impatient dragons. Crossings beep, heels clack, white vans roar and building sites clang and whirr between the earthiest of shouts.

Amongst this battleground of chaos and noise, of commute and computers, of trams and tramplers, I am the stranger. In a telling reflection of my life in general, I am the oddity, the one perpetually going the wrong way, moving in circles and to-ing and fro-ing, back and forth. I am a hive of personal industry, of movement and dynamism, but seemingly to no end, energy spent and little gained. I am but a fleeting nuisance to the rhythms of the city, the buzz of a wasp amongst worker bees, the runner amongst the indifferent, a ghost amongst unbelievers.

Arriving and parking up at six o'clock, it's not just twilight in Ancoats, but dark. The canal is an ominous void at one side of me, the enveloping, inky blackness seemingly wisping from its cold waters and hanging low to mute the glow of the weak streetlights. Somewhat uncomfortable, I get out and stand under a tree, surveying my surrounds, listening, waiting. I've never had any issue but I trust my instincts and every part of me is on high alert. I see nothing untoward, so get up on my toes and walk the first few minutes down the central white lines of the deserted roads. Only once I'm sure I'm alone, do I break into a slow run, an all out sprint just a twitch away.

Settling from whatever or whoever I imagined was watching me or loitering around, I made good progress on my commute to the centre. On my way in, picked up some decidedly sketchy roads around the murky Ancoats Green, crossed the Rochdale Canal and headed on through New Islington towards the Mancunian Way.

Here I find the exciting redevelopment of Mayfield Railway Station and its surroundings. Currently a building site bisected by the meandering River Medlock, this is going to become 1500 new homes and the first new public park in the city for over 100 years. While the freight depot has been revived as an arts, food and concert venue, other relics are being repurposed. The giant Britannia Brewery of the Manchester Brewing Co – once capable of producing 300 barrels of beer a day – is sadly long gone, but in a wonderful revelation, they've rediscovered some of its wells beneath the rubble. Three of which are not only still viable, they're going to use them to water the trees and plants in the newly formed Mayfield Park.

Darting down yet more debatable thoroughfares amidst the building sites and scaffolding that dominates Manchester's centre, I crossed London Road and flitted through the University science and tech campus. I pass the Graphene Engineering Innovation Centre, a reminder that the revolutionary material was discovered here in Manchester. The thinnest, most conductive and strongest material in the world (forty times stronger than diamond) won Professor Andre Geim and Professor Kostya Novoselov of Manchester University the Nobel prize for Physics in 2004. I honoured their achievement by sucking in my stomach and conducting a strong effort up a flight of steps like Rocky. It's something.

Next up were the rather cramped and pungent smelling (take a guess) alleyways of Charles Street and the rather more decadent exterior of the Lass O'Gowrie Pub. Reputedly named after a Scottish poem by a homesick landlord, this 1830's pub retains its beautiful burgundy, amber and forest green tiling and stained glass windows. This gem of a pub is much loved, popular with students, drinkers and office workers alike. So much so, it won national pub of year back in 2012. A plaque on its wall overhanging the Medlock commemorates Manchester's oldest Pissotiere, last used in 1896. Replaced by alleyways it seems.

On through the centre, the sky lightens and the people in suits and raincoats start appearing on the streets. I find my way onto Granby Row, to the shrine of a Manchester institution. Invented in 1908 as a non-alcoholic drink at a time of the Temperance movement by John Noel Nichols, it contains the juice of grapes, blackcurrants, raspberries, herbs and spices. An instant success, it has gone on to be sold worldwide and is manufactured and loved in as far-flung places as Ghana, Nepal, The Gambia and Saudi Arabia. The lovely bottle and fruit monument here on the original factory site pays due homage to what was originally sold as a Vim Tonic, what we now call Vimto. But, this is Manchester, the joyful memories and sweet taste in your mouth must be tainted by a much darker method of Victorian entrepreneurship taken by a William Johnson and William Harrison.

The area opposite the Vimto shrine was once the burial ground of St Augustine's Catholic Church, operating from 1821 to 1908. When in 1854, the neighbouring school on Coburg Street wanted to expand and build new classrooms, the builders found eighteen layers of coffins packed in on top of one another in the tiny space, giving a hint at how busy the undertakers were in the 19th century. The newspapers at the time gave details of a foul stench and 'black unctuous matter' oozing from the excavations. Just a gentle reminder that maybe our jobs aren't that bad after all. Still at least the graves were still there.

During January and February 1824, this graveyard and others in the city were victims of a more abhorrent crime than a horrifying smell. At a time of scientific enlightenment and advancing medical education, Manchester had two highly successful Anatomy schools with a need for dead bodies from the country's prison hangmen. Supply and demand restraints led to the price for a body rising to £10 (£1150 in 2021 money) and the blackest of black markets. Step forward from the shadows William Johnson and William Harrison, Manchester's own bodysnatchers. Digging by faint moonlight and hiding the bodies in cases for shipping to schools in Manchester and London, they were only caught when a nosy neighbour thought they were burglars packing their loot late at night. Caught red-handed, the judge at their trial imprisoned them at Lancaster Castle for fifteen months.

Amidst the growing chaos on the streets and pavements, I repeatedly bounced from kerb to gutter and around the scowls and indifferent stares. No longer able to daydream or drink in the architecture high overhead, I had to focus on not getting run over, knock down a pedestrian or bumping their coffee from their outstretched hand. Despite concentrating on not being a nuisance, I did find much to buoy the soul and keep me amused. I paused at Alan Turing statue in Sackville Gardens, made some noise down Trumpet Street and stuck my nose in the air as I passed the decadent Midland Hotel onto Peter Street. This is tourist-central for visitors to Manchester with the beautiful Library, Peterloo massacre site, Town Hall and the Free Trade Hall all nearby.

The latter is famous not just for speeches by Winston Churchill and Benjamin Disraeli and a play starring Charles Dickens – yes, him again. It was also a concert venue used by the Halle Orchestra and later bands such as Pink Floyd, T-Rex, Genesis and Frank Zappa. Most famously in 1966, it was the scene of Bob Dylan's electric gig when after a break he picked up an electric guitar and was famously heckled 'Judas!' by ardent folk fans. A decade later, it was another rebellious performance making the headlines by the vanguard of the punk movement; The Sex Pistols. A snarling revelation of anger and energy played to a small crowd, it influenced musicians in the audience to go on and form bands such as The Fall, The Smiths and Joy Division.

On to Quay Street, past the glorious Opera House, I take a right and enter the shady canyons between the glass towers of Manchester's money district. This is Spinningfields, the home of offices, suits and the ping of incoming emails. It's eight o'clock and I really shouldn't be here. The coffee shops are busy, the ties are tight, handbags pristine and the shoes polished. I do my best to get through without upsetting anyone, but it wasn't easy. The worst thing about city centre running is that the GPS signal bounces off the hi-rise buildings, meaning some of my lines swirl, loop and curve anywhere but on the roads. On one occasion, I had to run past the same security guard five times while muttering profusely. He watched, I didn't bat an eyelid. My shame-o-meter overheated and seized up long ago. At best, my route through this office district looked like an outpatient searching for the Office of Amnesia Therapy and at worst like forgetful Granddad's in his mobility scooter looking for his lost slippers.

Yet, I still wasn't done. Back across Deansgate, I head for Chinatown – the third largest in Europe - with its traditional Paifang arch over Faulkner Street and plethora of restaurants, laundries and Chinese supermarkets. On through the back streets of Canal Street and the Gay Village, I round Minshull Street with a return to Manchester Crown Court, where I was once detained for a fortnight. Thankfully, only for Jury Service and not whatever you just guiltily imagined.

Find of the day though has to be a few roads close to the Rochdale Canal at the end of Bloom Street. Winser Street, Harter Street and Waterloo Street are lined with five-storey brick warehouses built towards the end of the 19th century. Used for manufacture, storing and packing cotton orders from the nearby mills, these elegant giants with their solid brickwork and large windows make the perfect conversion to designer apartments or offices. More recently, the BBC used them as a location for Season 5 of Peaky Blinders including a dramatic explosive car bomb scene and a horse-drawn funeral procession.

After a brief dalliance with the shoppers near Market Street and through Piccadilly Gardens, I head North-West for Ancoats and a long run home to my distant car. As I pass a huge billboard selling an Italian lager with the tag 'Live Every Moment', I smile at the graffiti beneath showing a crudely drawn figure proclaiming 'I farted in Yoga'. The anarchy of the Sex Pistols lives on...just.

Another 85 crowded, chaotic streets gathered today, leaving just 247 more to complete the full set.

Sunday 17th October 2021 – 19.61km - The Dark Valley and Angel's Meadow

It's been raining all night again and Collyhurst is a shimmering black puddle. Foreboding, quiet and almost brooding, the past here colours the present. It's unfortunate history hangs heavily over the wooded valley and empty streets, the darkness lingering just a little longer around here than elsewhere, the sun in no hurry to chase away the shadows and throw light on what might be best left forgotten. I find it equally unsettling and fascinating.

Working my way up the streets on either side of Rochdale Road, the rain starts up again from the black starless sky. I find myself eyeing passers-by heading through these gloomy back streets with suspicion and mistrust, their tension at my presence only heightening my experience. It doesn't help when you pop in and out of side streets so much, you end up passing them four or five times. Rounding onto Dalton Street, I meander downhill into the Irk Valley. Past the last of three tower blocks and a smattering of social housing, the road bends and offers me a final route of escape. Ahead of me the road descends between portentous dark, dripping bushes and gnarled trees to the broken glass windows of a dilapidated factory. To my left is a long tunnel under the former railway sidings, a relic of when thriving communities on either side would have made this a busy thoroughfare. The worn steps at the far end lay testament to their use for well over a hundred years. The walls of this cut-through are now mossy, covered in graffiti and with three weak lights, look like something lifted straight from a horror movie. I push on into Collyhurst, although maybe not for the better.

The name Collyhurst means wooded hill, and it was this hill made of pinkish-red sandstone that was quarried to build the likes of the Roman fort, Chetham's school, St Ann's Church, the original Cathedral stonework and several bridges over the Irwell. It's also the site of Manchester's plague pits. After suffering outbreaks in the 1580's and 90's, the plague struck Manchester with such ferocity in 1604-05, that simple wooden lodgings were set up in six acres of empty land for the victims in an early form of quarantine, known as pesthouses or fever sheds. One can only imagine the horrifying conditions, prayers and hopelessness of entering these sickly waiting rooms of death. At least two thousand victims lay buried nearby.

Two centuries later and with the dark graveyard of disease and despair next-door long since forgotten, this pastoral idyll become home to a world of beauty and delight. Collyhurst Manor beside the meandering

289

River Irk became the idyllic home of the Elsyian Pleasure Gardens - a paradise of flowers, trees-lined paths, thousands of coloured lights, food, drink and dancing. In the early 1800's, it was a place to promenade and court, see and be seen. Carriages would bring guests from miles around to dance the night away and perhaps find their suitor. A haven of folly and informality, fun and frivolity, this was a place of swishing gowns, coy glances and dashing gentlemen in their finery. It eventually closed in 1852, by when pleasure was the last thing on anyone's mind.

The Industrial Revolution turned the Irk Valley into a powerhouse of factories, dye, paint and chemical works, mines, brickworks, sawmills, gas and soap works. The Manor house went, the gardens filled with spoil from the colliery into a giant hill that still towers over Collyhurst Road now. With this explosion of industry came a huge labour force in cramped, fetid dwellings with disease, dirty water and a toxic atmosphere that rapidly killed workers off almost as soon as they arrived. In 1837, the average life expectancy of the labouring population in Manchester was a paltry 17 years old. Little wonder they rioted, seduced and drank, for tomorrow they may well be dead. When it came to profits for landlords, moneylenders and industrialists, the lives and welfare of their tenants, debtors and workers were of little more importance than that of their workhorses. Death was a constant, but the stream of desperate souls seeking a new life meant everyone was replaceable, within days if not hours.

Running these streets, the slum-houses and most of the industry cleared, I still get a sense of the churning misery that must have hung over this place like a choking smog. It's a place waiting for a cure. Nature has taken over, rewilding abandoned lots and cleansing the river of its toxic past. A few blocks of flats are going up around the edges of the area as it remodels itself as the Northern Gateway. Advanced plans are afoot for major redevelopment for this area and in twenty years time, it'll probably be unrecognisable once more. But, for now, most of it is still empty. Cobbled streets lead nowhere but to the ghosts of the past, great viaducts soaring over the melancholic waste ground below. As I reach Fitzgeorge Street, I realise I've made a terrible mistake.

Ducking under the viaduct, this street is at the heart of the sandstone quarry and plague pits. It later headed up besides a machinery works and past the ends of four steep terraced streets. Now it's Sandhills, a strange country park akin to a roman road meandering up through a steeply sided grassy valley, topped on either side with trees. Only, I'm here too early. I'd planned my run to hit this area and the council estate above at twilight or dawn, but as I peer beneath the railway arches into the gloomy rain at this unlit cobbled road wandering away into the opaque greyness of reflected suburbia, I pause. I'm not one to shy away from running where others wouldn't dare but this had ambush and police tape written all over it. It's one thing running along dark streets through pools of light, quite another blundering into a place where any number of homeless, junkies, or vampires might be hanging out. Or indeed homeless junky vampires. The way ahead makes that tunnel under the railway look like the entrance to a palatial wonderland in comparison.

Weighing up my options and musing that hanging around under the viaduct until it got lighter was no more appealing, I put my brain in neutral and pushed on. After all, this was why I was here, was it not? This was a glimpse of the real Collyhurst, the authentic trudge home from the pub or a friend's house before street-lights were the norm, a journey through a grey, rainy night of fear and trepidation, of moving shadows and imagined foes. I pushed on up the slope through the driving rain, my eyes on stalks and ears straining for anything in the silence beyond the raindrops hitting the cobbles. Four eternally long, wild minutes later, I emerge back into the light of the twenty-first century on Eggington Road, older if not wiser.

I work my way north up the residential streets beside Collyhurst Road and back down Smedley Road, crossing and recrossing the River Irk. The two roads meet in the shadow of a railway bridge that underlines how this valley can never get a break. Here at 7.40am – eerily about the same time I passed underneath - on Saturday 15th August 1953, an electric train heading for Victoria Station missed a danger signal and collided head-on with a steam train headed for Bacup. The front carriage of the electric train crashed through the bridge parapet, teetered momentarily on the edge and then plunged into the River Irk below leaving ten dead and fifty-eight injured. Largely forgotten, there is no memorial or any sign it ever happened, this melancholic valley simply absorbing the tale of ten more sorry souls into its dark history.

Before continuing into the city centre to the Manchester's own version of hell on earth, I divert to something a little more culturally pleasing. Manchester's most famous artist, L.S. Lowry is perhaps most famous for his crowds of matchstick people in an industrial backdrop, but his artistic curiosity also brought him to Collyhurst. Just beyond the large paint factory that still survives on the banks of the river, is a small overgrown alleyway, barely visible from the road. Along here and up some moss and lichen-covered steps is a neglected footbridge soaring over what was once more railway sidings. It's this alleyway and these steps that Lowry painted in his 1938 painting, 'The Footbridge'.

Clambering up the steps to the grassy top with its walls of graffiti and bleak views across the treetops to the tower blocks opposite, I suddenly feel very alone. If I was the last man alive looking out at nature re-greening the scars of humankind, I'd see many a view like across Collyhurst. Then I hear a noise and a groan and glimpse shadows moving on the waste ground beneath the bridge. At which point my imagination points out that this secluded spot is also perfect for those who don't want to be found; the homeless and drug-addled. Or even where gangs dump the bodies of their enemies. Casually and calmly descending the stairs six at a time, I head south out of this shadowy valley for somewhere much, much worse.

Abutting the city centre and the new N.O.M.A. District of redevelopment is Angel Meadow and St Michael's. In the 19th century, this was at the centre of a slum deemed Victorian Britain's most savage. Immigrants drawn to the city by empty pockets and emptier bellies often tumbled onto this top rung of a ladder leading nowhere but down. Many desperately fleeing the Irish Potato famine and ruinous harvests across Britain would become worker fodder for the industrial grinder that forged the prosperous British Empire. Desperately seeking work in the new mills and factories, they might find lodgings in one of the crowded rooms in the dilapidated houses and dirty tenements around here. Families were often split up, many living in cramped windowless cellars in which tenants could only crouch. In this hell of filth, smog and violence, the bankrupt and the mentally-ill rubbed shoulders with deserting soldiers and fallen women. They shared their streets, homes and lives with gangs, thieves, prostitutes and murderers. And if they survived the drunken fights and lack of food and clean water, there was the constant misery of lice, bedbugs, roaches and vermin carrying the full range of highly contagious and highly untreatable diseases.

The burial ground behind St Michael's is possibly the most macabre place in Manchester's history. With a horrifying estimate of 40,000 dead underfoot, the poor were buried here on mass and without ceremony, the pits covered with boards and locked down at night. By 1816, it was full and became an area for illicit pursuits like prizefighting and fighting cockerels. People were so poor and desperate at this time, they would often dig bones after dark, grinding them down to sell to farmers as fertiliser. This horror led to parliament passing a law that flagstones cover all burial grounds. The flagstones over the burial ground at St Michael's became a children's playground and football pitch. L. S. Lowry captured this ghoulish scene in his 1927 work 'The Playground.'

Wandering around this sombre park in the drizzle, the grass luscious green and the trees dropping their leaves, it's almost impossible to imagine all the desperate shuffled footsteps, the prayers and curses, the arguments, fights and horrible screams, the hacking coughs and shuddering fevers that the people endured to try and make it out of this crowded hell. The despair must have been overwhelming, a visible fug of mistrust and helplessness. The irony of such a hellish place being called the heavenly Angel's Meadow, is in itself loaded with the great weight of paternal grief, as a local legend claimed visions of angels here protecting the graves of the children who died very young.

Somewhat low, I look across at the Charter Street Ragged School beside the churchyard, itself overshadowed by two shiny new tower blocks of apartments. A relic of the past and still a charitable mission, it hints at the support some lucky orphans and poverty-stricken urchins got from the more benevolent parts of society, providing hot meals every Sunday and food, clogs and clothing for the thousands of helpless children. Charles Dickens – him again – is said to have been inspired by the area to create his workhouse in 'Hard Times.'

Seeking a lighter - literally - moment in Manchester's past, I leave the dark foreboding clouds behind and hotfoot it across Sadler's Yard to Balloon Street. It was here in May 1785 that England's first aeronaut James Sadler took off from a field in a hydrogen-filled balloon. His cat accompanied him on this, his fourth flight. He landed 10 kilometres away to the north in Radcliffe. The cat's opinions on the flight were not recorded.

64 irksome streets added today and a sense of gratitude I can leave behind places of great sorrow and strife like Collyhurst on the pages of history, if not totally out of my heart. Just 183 left to complete.

Sunday 24th October 2021 – 20.55km - Withington Sunrise

I do have a soft spot for Withington. The manor of Withington with its long lineage of Lordships dating back to the 13th century once stretched from Chorlton to Burnage, from Moss Side and Longsight down to the River Mersey. Now like an older sibling of southeast Manchester, it has to share its room with the show-off Didsbury twins - West and Village. They get all the new toys; the Metrolink, the shiny bars and boutique shops, the love and acclaim, the money and fast cars while Withington has similar impressive Victorian and Edwardian villas and mansions but is a little more reserved and restrained. To coin a sniffy Georgian attitude, its new money vs. old, not that that stops squabbles over where the border is. With money added for a house being in Didsbury, I dare say Withington might continue to shrink bit by bit for the next few years. Then there's the longstanding mutterings of a new Didsbury baby, with money piling into Northenden to become 'Didsbury South.'

It's now late October, the dark mornings grow darker, the air cooler and damper, the trees ever barer. Autumn celebrates its brief seasonal glory with a ticker-tape parade of tumbling leaves, butternut squashes in supermarkets and companies seemingly obsessed with everything pumpkin spice. I love the transitional seasons of Spring and Autumn, but for the early morning runner the former wins over the latter. Especially at the end of October before the clocks lurch back an hour. Out at an almost sensible time of half past seven in the morning, I find myself on the streets of Withington, still enduring the night.

With the drizzle tumbling out of the black skies and the peace only punctuated by the burbling murmur of a thousand raindrops reaching the ground, I set off into the gloom. Starting amidst the drifted piles of leaves on Ballbrook Ave, I picked up the pace to get warm, swiftly crunching and squelching my way over to Wilmslow Road and the respectable glory of Old Broadway. Claimed to be one of Manchester's prettiest streets, I can see why. Built early in the 20th century, each of the grand villas lining the private road has stained glass windows, black and white timbered sections and balconies. The houses are all subtly different to one another, but are collectively in an arts and craft style with hints of art nouveau. It was obviously built with pride and craftsmanship and was said to be popular with doctors who were required to live within four miles of Manchester Royal Infirmary. Once home to the late music producer Tony Wilson and during the 1990's home to chat show hosts Richard and Judy, they are just as desirable today as when built.

Just to the north is Christie's Hospital; the largest cancer treatment and research centre in Europe and source of enormous local pride. Employing over three thousand people, it's been home to many world firsts and treatment breakthroughs since moving to this site from Oxford Road in 1932. The huge hospital is currently a building site as it expands ever further, fighting the good fight against another deadly enemy. As I leave the sci-fi sounding, ultra modern Proton Beam Therapy Centre behind me, I run towards the most glorious of dazzling sunrises.

The fiery yellow skies fill the horizon, seeping skyward through orange and lilacs and chasing away the dulled blues of a lingering twilight. Silhouetting humanity's pathetic boxes, dawn's magnificence gleams along the car windows and paves the damp roads with rose gold. Alone on deserted streets, it feels like a gift, a reward for my early start and the near end of my challenge. I run slowly, agog at this fleeting kaleidoscope of beauty, of half-light and contrast against watercolour skies. Like a total eclipse or rainbow, it can't last, but for a few brief minutes I'm embraced in its soft glow. Within a couple of streets, the magic is gone, the sun clambering up over the tiles and chimneys, dazzling all in its shimmering glare and bringing another day to life.

Working my way west from the Hospital, I gather in several elegant roads of Edwardian houses between Burton Road and Palatine Road, seeing plenty of runners out braving the autumn dreariness. At number 86 Palatine Road, I catch a glimpse over a high hedge of the blue plaque adorning what was Alan Erasmus' house. It was here in 1978 that he and Tony Wilson co-founded Factory Records; the label that would go on to sign Joy Division and the Happy Mondays.

Detouring north off route, I go to see the striking black and white mural of Manchester United striker, Marcus Rashford. Both a footballer and social activist, he is immensely popular amongst the working classes of the city as a local boy who hasn't forgotten his roots. After missing a penalty during the 2020 Euros final and receiving online abuse from moronic keyboard warriors, the mural became a shrine of positivity and messages of support for the three Lions who dared miskick a football. Back onto Wilmslow Road, I pass the last remaining Lion of another trio.

The Red Lion Pub is at least two hundred years old and reportedly the oldest building in Withington. Unlike the Golden Lion and the White Lion in the area - (demolished and converted to a supermarket) - this stout coaching Inn with unusual horizontal sliding Georgian sash windows continues to keep thirsty travellers on this main road fed and watered.

Further south along Wilmslow Rd, back past the Hospital and at the corner of Fog Lane is the former site of Eltville House - home of the

Souchay family. The wife of the German Composer Felix Mendelssohn was a relation of the family and he visited them several times from Germany in the 1840's. In April 1847, he even played a recital on the newly installed organ in St Paul's Church further up Wilmslow Road. A letter he wrote from Eltville House complaining about his health, lack of time and gruelling tour schedule resides in the Music Division of the Library of Congress in Washington DC. Sadly, his ill health didn't improve and just 7 months later he died, aged only 38. Best known perhaps for his music for A Midsummer Night's Dream and many other symphonies, he also was wise enough to corner the Christmas market with his smash hit melody for 'Hark! The Herald Angels Sing.'

From Classical to Classic Album. Leaving Withington behind, I turn up my collar, curl my lip and swagger across into West Didsbury for some rock and roll history. Working back west across Central Road, I return to Burton Road and head south past the shops. After grabbing a couple of stray streets, I continue to a series of small cul-de-sacs on Burton Rd opposite Withington Hospital (Now on West Didsbury's side of the bedroom). One of which is Madchester music scene gold. In the 90s, no.8 Stratford Avenue was the home of Paul 'Bonehead' Arthurs; guitarist with Manchester band Oasis. In 1994, the cover photo for their debut album; 'Definitely Maybe' was shot here in his living room. The band also used a small overgrown courtyard area at the rear for the music video for their second single; 'Shakermaker', which reached no.11 in the UK charts.

Alrite arr kid, so now ya know, rite?! Ee arr, Mendelssohn, don't be snide, play uz out will ya, nice one, top one.

59 more streets today. Just a paltry 124 left to complete.

Sunday 31st October 2021 – 17.2km – The Shock City of Cottonopolis

"Ancoats is to Manchester what Manchester is to England."
Morning Chronicle, 21 Dec 1849.

As I near the end of this challenge, I find myself where not only the city began, but also the Industrialised world as we know it. Ancoats, to the north of the city centre, was a small isolated hamlet before the Rochdale Canal was built, the name literally meaning 'isolated cottages'. But by the late 18th century, large seven and eight storey Cotton Mills were springing up all over Ancoats, the ground and walls vibrating to the clatter of tens of thousands of steam-powered spinning machines and looms. The promise of work brought workers in from the countryside and immigrants from impoverished countries like Ireland, Italy and Poland. The sight of these gigantic, noisy smoke-belching cathedrals to money and power must have been truly terrifying to the newcomers. Unlike anything they'd seen before, their initial wide-eyed wonder must have soon tumbled into one of a bleak, manmade perdition.

With the weather looking grim and getting grimmer, I headed out early in the light rain, the cold wind whipping between the buildings and hinting at winter runs to come. The extra hour of light after the clocks went back helped, but even the sunrise was more shades of grey than any brightness cutting through the thick duvet of clouds.

Cutting through Ancoats, I made for a few streets in and around Piccadilly Station. Despite the weather and early hour, I encountered a smattering of drunk stragglers, spice-heads and randoms hanging around. One kindly offered to fight me for running past him - silly me - I declined with a wave of the hand, his affronted posturing fading away behind me. At the back of the station I find the Store Street Aqueduct, an unimposing tunnel-like stone bridge carrying the Ashton Canal over the street below. Yet for construction and architecture geeks, it is something of a marvel, because this 1798 grade II listed bridge has a skewed arch at a forty-five degree angle to the road. Sadly, render hides the unique spiral construction of its brickwork from view, but it remains one of the first of its kind in Great Britain and the oldest still in use. Nearby is another wonder, this one popular with city centre runners and fitness fanatics. Connecting Ducie Street and Store Street is a short inconsequential road; Jutland Street. Yet this is the steepest street in the city centre, if not Manchester, with an 80m slope, said to be at 33%. I ran up it not once, but twice, because well...when on a roam, do as the roamers do.

Further away from the railway station, on the eastern fringes of the Northern Quarter, I found a few relics of the past, hidden in plain

297

sight. At the corner of Hilton Street and Port Street, there's a small block of Georgian townhouses, shops and weavers cottages hinting at the hardships of spinning Cotton at home. With the weathered brickwork, the Georgian shop fronts with their small windows and the long horizontal windows of the homes, it looks like you could throw down a cinder road and film a Dickensian drama at a moment's notice. These humble weavers rooms hint at the changes to come as the industrial revolution landed nearby and turned the world upside down.

While one person could work one spindle on a spinning wheel in a light and airy attic, just up the road, huge monstrous mills were rising up by the canals. In 1783, Richard Arkwright built Manchester's first cotton mill just west of Ancoats, on Miller Street near the junction with Shudehill. Arkwright was the same man who'd built the world's first water-powered cotton mill in Cromford, Derbyshire just twelve years before. With the introduction of steam-power in the 1790's, Manchester cotton-spinning industry simply exploded. With the canals for transport, an abundance of nearby water, almost limitless supply of cheap coal for the engines and a skilled labour force not held back by Guilds as in other towns, Manchester become a textiles powerhouse.

On Union Street - now Redhill Street - next to the Rochdale Canal, Adam and George Murray built a colossal complex of brick mills through the 1790's and into the 19th century. Eight storeys high and employing about 1000 people, they could simultaneously run 84,000 mechanised spindles and carding machines, becoming the largest mill in the world. Dozens of other massive mills soon surrounded it. The mills brought in supporting foundries and factories making machinery for the Mills, warehouses for storage and food for the workers. By 1816, there were 86 mills in the central area of Manchester, and by 1853 there were 108. This was the area dubbed Cottonopolis - the world's first industrial suburb.

The huge numbers of workers needed to work the mills lived in back-to-back terraces off Oldham Road in shocking conditions. Often, it was one family to a room and many more living like troglodytes in unlit cellars. Communal Privies were the norm, a stinking cesspit shared by a 100 residents. Disease, vermin, animal waste in the streets...Ancoats rapidly became known as 'Stinkopolis' to locals and 'Shock City' to visitors from Europe and America appalled at this 'hell on earth'.

By the 1880's, the Council was shamed into action, demolishing the slums and building the first municipal housing in Manchester; Victoria Square. The grade II listed building was such a success, it's still in use today, the council letting the flats out to the area's older residents. Next to

Victoria Square, the council also built a model street for a new clean city with two rows of terraced houses, each with their own sink and toilet. Imagine...? They called it Sanitary Street. Much later in the 1960's, the residents wanted to rename it, choosing to rub out three letters, leaving it Anita Street - the name it retains to today. It, like Ancoats itself is now a hugely desirable place to live, the mills preserved and converted to luxury apartments and designer office space.

As I run over these old roads between these silent giants, I imagine the masses of workers doing the same, heads down amidst the swirling smoke and acrid rain, summoned to their daily grind at six o'clock in the morning by the wail of the mill siren. Trudging morosely to work for another 12, 14 or even 16-hour day in a hot, damp and dusty mill, I can almost hear their clogs scraping melancholically along the cobblestones. A joke with a friend or neighbour, a hug from a young child, a kiss from a spouse, all before parting into different mills, the deafening clamour within rattling the very thoughts inside their heads.

With unguarded machines whirring back and forth relentlessly and employees fatigued, ill or even malnourished, accidents were common. A moment's lack of concentration and the machinery could take a finger, break a bone or much worse. With no financial safety net or sick pay, not being able to work could have dire consequences. This area and these mills are a healthy reminder that all the employment laws and privileges – sick pay, pensions, holidays, health and safety, employment protections – that we take for granted were earnt in the blood, sweat and sacrifices of those who've suffered before us and fought back against those putting money before people. Reformers at the time lobbying against the factory system in Ancoats even went as far to call it a form of 'White Slavery'.

After six, long, exhausting workdays with only Sunday as a day of rest, it was little wonder workers let off a little steam at the weekend. As I emerge onto Oldham Road, I retrace the route of so many of the mill girls and factory workers of the 19th century, heading for the bawdy pubs and crowded gin houses of Oldham Street. After midnight on a Saturday – sounds familiar – many of those mill workers and girls would be drunk, disorderly and settling old scores with their fists or any weapon that came to hand. The music from numerous bands spilled out into the darkened streets, followed by hollering and cursing drunkards of both sexes in a scene that we take as a norm but must have shocked the 'betters' of Victorian society.

Heading west before I stagger into this haven of alcoholic escapism, I find Victorian society's response in the back streets. Here amidst the car parks and new developments is a relic of justice, albeit in a sorry state. This is what's left of Goulden Police & Fire Station, once the toughest beat of the newly formed Manchester Police. Built in 1872 as a four-storey building and stable yard, complete with 14 bays for rapidly responding horse-drawn police vans, fire pumps or horse ambulances, it was more akin to a windowless fortress than a welcoming civic building. And with good reason. It wasn't just the drunks. Tight communities defended their own and on more than one occasion, arrests led to riots so severe, the rioters stormed the police stations, beat the officers within and forcibly released prisoners. Not to mention the Scuttler gangs openly fighting in the street and all manner of dark corners and unlit alleys. I'm sure I've visited my fair share of those. The Police Station finally closed in 1979.

Then in 2002, disaster struck in the first day of the fireman's strike. A company was storing fireworks in the listed building when it accidentally caught fire. Sometimes a sentence is filled with so much stupidity, I feel the need to go over it one more time in case we missed something. They put fireworks in a listed building, literally tonnes of explosives...inside a historical building. Well, I suppose it at least keeps the true spirit of Guy Fawkes alive. The blaze rapidly devoured the structure and any history left inside. The death of this precious part of Manchester's history must have truly made the strangest of scenes. Army soldiers rolling out hoses from their 1950's 'green goddess' fire engines beside a blaze at an old fire station, as the night sky overhead erupts with a dazzling firework display.

Returning to the wide junction of Oldham Road and Great Ancoats Street, I try to imagine the medieval market cross in the middle of a muddy, dung splattered road. The obelisk here gave this area its forgotten name of New Cross. This wide junction would have been a hive of activity on market days with lines of stalls trailing up Oldham Road and workers haggling over prices and credit. Nearby was the courthouse, stocks, gibbet and cage, where no doubt some of the most rotten of fruit and vegetables ended up. With so many hungry workers to feed in such a small area, there would have been horse drawn carts bringing in produce all the time from the farming villages on the fringes of Manchester. Many of which are now more affluent suburbs. But, with seasonal variations of produce, failed harvests, unjust taxes and profiteering, sometimes food was in short supply and prices soared. When the poorest of workers grafted all day and still found themselves unable to feed their families, anger mounted, the fury contagious.

In April 1812, this area of Manchester was subject to three days of

300

food riots. Up to twelve thousand people descended on the markets around here seeking some retribution. Some intimidated dealers into selling at a fairer price, others pelted merchants with potatoes until they fled and then simply stole their produce. Carters were harassed and their produce tipped onto the streets, women carrying away vegetables in their aprons. One butter-seller's cart was chased for over a mile by 200-300 people until they would sell all they had at a reduced price. The trouble in Manchester sparked similar riots in neighbouring towns and cities across the north-west, cavalry and infantry drafted in to guard grain stores and patrol the streets. Fear of an uprising led to the deaths of several protesters and many more arrested. A timely reminder that not all who have run these streets before me did so for fitness and pleasure. Over two hundred years ago, it was in a most desperate plea for the most basic of needs; food to eat and the right to stay alive.

63 Streets today, leaving me at a grand total of 6214 streets completed and only 61 roads left to run. I'm almost there.

Sunday 7th November 2021 – 15.29km – Northern Quarter Finale

'It is good to have an end to journey toward; but it is the journey that matters, in the end.' Ernest Hemingway.

One last run and this epic travail of Manchester's tarmac can be snugly put to bed. While that filled me with some relief, it was tinged with sadness, like the last sunset of a glorious holiday. I wish I could enjoy it all again afresh, but I also am so in need of a rest. So, with mixed emotions I headed to the bohemian Mecca of the Northern Quarter.

Just north of the centre, during the turmoil of the industrial revolution, this area found itself southwest of the Ancoats mills and south of the worst slums around Angel Meadow and Shudehill. In the early 19th century, it became an area for warehouses, shops, merchants and traders selling their wares, many living on-site. This commercial chaos rapidly developed into Smithfield Market, a sprawling four and a half acre site. At the height of empire, people could buy fish, meat, fruit and vegetables here from around the world. The Italian community in nearby Ancoats even made ice cream to sell in the market and on the streets. It was so large, it even had its own police force; Manchester Market Police. It sadly closed in 1972, when the shopping zeitgeist moved to the new Arndale centre and underground market. The future was here and it was inside, warm, bright, sterile and boring. The Northern Quarter with its heart ripped out retired to two decades of further neglect and unseen decay as an unsafe place best avoided.

It was the early 80's when one of these warehouses opened as Afflecks Palace; a counter-culture bazaar born in response to the Arndale centre, tapping into the punk and anti-Thatcher youth culture. This, along with cheap rents and fresh ideas, started a change that led to the area becoming a haven for the disenfranchised and freethinkers. Much like Prague in the original Bohemia in Czechia, this is a place for the unconventional wanderers; the musical, artistic and literary vagabonds who seek freedom of thought and spirit. Yet, just like Prague, it has more recently suffered from its own success. The bars and money have become more important than the ideas born within them. Painted adverts for soft drinks and high street stores join the large cultural murals and street art that decorate the area's blank walls. The large multinational corporate brands circle the small shoal of independent shops, boutiques, bars and cafes, desperate to crash the party and return more lost revenue to their faceless offshore headquarters. The council walks the tightrope of development and gentrification without losing the creative spark that makes the area a special place to live and work.

In the early morning gloom, I worked my way through Ancoats and on down Lever St, Spear St and some questionable alleyways with even more questionable aromas. Then on Dale St, I find a cafe selling bacon butties from a trestle table on the street at 7am. The heavenly aroma...oh the moneyless torture. I could have easily stopped and eaten five in a row. Then I recalled Friedrich Engels 1840's description of nearby Withy Grove in 'The Condition of the Working Class of England'; "dirty, old and tumble-down...with pigs walking about in the alleys, rooting in offal heaps."

Hmmm, maybe later.

Heading on to Tib St, which is now a back street mix of shops, pubs, hairdressers, florists and apartments, but back in the 19th and much of the 20th centuries, it was the go to attraction of the area. Often having a footfall of 10,000 people in a day, its shops opened beyond midnight, all because, Tib Street was a pet shop paradise. Lined with shop windows full of kittens, puppies, rabbits, birds and more exotic creatures, children would press their noses to the glass and pester parents as families promenaded this free zoo. A zoo of another kind came as the area declined in the 1970's as the secluded nature of the street made it an ideal place for adult shops and an unofficial red-light district.

Moving swiftly on, I round the haven of the alternative; Afflecks Palace and reach the wonderfully named Short Street at its rear. It is indeed short, but more importantly home to a famous Mancunian mosaic. The artwork proclaims 'On the sixth day god created MANchester', perfectly summing up the proud cockiness and dry humour that the city's inhabitants use to get through life's trials and tribulations.

I make short work of the grid-like streets with their bars, boutiques and old warehouses. It has such a distinct atmosphere and unspoilt architecture, its often used as a stand-in for old New York in TV and movies. Alfie, Morbius, Captain America: The First Avenger and Guy Ritchie's Sherlock Holmes were all filmed here.

Leaving the Hollywood Northern Quarter behind, I head west for a few final streets around Parsonage Gardens and St Ann's Square. The Christmas markets are up, sadly missed last year with lockdown, just awaiting our European friends to bring us their goodies; handcrafted toys, gluhwein and bratwurst...back off Engels, don't ruin them as well.

The market is apt, as before St Anne's Church was built in 1712, the field beside it was used for an annual fair dating as far back as the 13th century. The magnificently understated tower and nave rose up over Manchester when it was little more than a village of timber-framed houses surrounded by fields. I'm guessing it'd be less impressive to run those muddy streets...in a single morning, but I'd give it a go. The tower would be visible to visitors to Manchester for miles around, surveyors using it to measure distance to other locations. It still marks the centre of the city, to this day.

It also marks a fitting place to draw my challenge to a close. It's taken the best part of 20 months to complete the 6275 streets of Manchester. After starting on 313 roads, I've completed the remaining 95% of the roads in 103 runs, covering a further distance of 2018 kilometres/1254 miles. Using my averages, I can say I've run all of Manchester's streets in approximately 110 runs, covering 2124 Kilometres/ 1320 miles.

61 streets completed. 0 streets left to do.

'I may not have gone where I intended to go, but I think I ended up where I intended to be.' Douglas Adams.

Sunday 14th November 2021 – 0km - All Roads Lead to Home

The drinks have been drunk, the whoops whooped and hangover endured. A week after ticking off the final street in Manchester I find myself reflecting on just what I've achieved. I've no doubt someone could do it quicker, more efficiently and in fewer total runs, but as far as I am aware, I am the first to run all the streets in the city. It's not been the search for a life-saving vaccine, the road to an Olympic Medal or a trek across the Antarctic, but to me it's been a special adventure. An expedition around my home like no other. It seems strange to be able to say I've run past every front door or front gate of the 555,000 inhabitants in the city, past all the pubs people drink in, in front of their workplaces and the shops they visit. I've visited all the hospitals and cemeteries, all the churches and factories, sports grounds and parks.

Visiting each road just once has also given me a real sense of how fleeting history can be in such a dynamic city. Industries, houses and shops come and go as the tides of progress build up and wash away thriving communities. A feeling no better exemplified than by the Failsworth Industrial Society Co-operative opened by bands and a procession through Newton Heath in 1898. On one run, I saw this huge building - said to be one of the first in Manchester to have electric light - wrapped in scaffolding awaiting redemption. Some months later when I visited for an adjacent run, I found it had been deemed unsafe and razed to the ground. Another connection to our collective past gone, the carefully aligned bricks, mortar and slates reduced to a mound of rubble and dust. It made me think of the elderly slowly losing their connections to the present, as we bulldoze all the buildings from their memories. Bit by bit we erase them from the community too.

I've seen and discovered so many stories in my travels of places disappearing, of the wealthy and well-connected shaping this great city as it stepped out into the industrial unknown. The rivers of money pouring into so few hands as the labours of many helped clothe the world. But it's the vast swathes of terraced streets that used to crowd this city with sooty red brickwork, corner shops and uneven cobblestones that hide the truth. The untold tales of simple, hardworking families born here and drawn here from all around the world lining every street. The generations of people who built this city, stood together and made it their home.

I'd be lying if I said I'd loved every minute of my adventure, but for every crunch of broken glass underfoot there's been a magnificent sunrise, for every downtrodden Estate there's been a historical survivor cherishing its second life. For every abandoned mattress, there's been a

305

mural of public art. All human life is here; good and bad, rising and falling, mourning and celebrating, living small and dreaming big.

Dream big my friends. Be awesome and dream big.

Acknowledgments

I could never have achieved this great challenge and written this book without some help along the way. My thanks in the first place must go to all the badass women and supportive men in the RBR Running group, without which this would never have happened. The selfless encouragement, appreciation and support for my weekly runs and accompanying write-ups on Facebook helped get me out the door in the rain and dig ever deeper in my research. This book would never have existed without you.

My family, brother and most friends were supportive when I shared in passing what I've been doing, although during 2020-21, everyone understandably had more pressing matters on their mind. Some of my running friends Andy Martin, Dave Jones, James Dean and Steph Hertel listened to my random missions to the darkest areas of Manchester and offered interest and sage advice beyond psychiatric help and a suit of armour.

My good friend Meg Holmes, who through the years has always believed in my writing even when I've had my doubts and celebrates every win as if one of her own. Gwen Mackie and Narnold T Rockstar Bear who both offered sage advice and assistance when the right words eluded me or I was in urgent need of snackages. Sue Knowles Leary who listens patiently to my ramblings after a run and keeps me going when writing my novels too. Caroline Findlay for teaching me new swearwords and a shared love of the general public.

Just going to keep adding people now so it looks like I have more friends. Sarah Harley, Rose Rencius, Michele Grabowski, Jackie Parkins; thank you for your friendship and kind words through the start of this most troublesome of decades.

While I've endeavoured to cross reference information and stories to multiple sources where possible, any errors I've made in writing this book are entirely my own. I am a runner and a writer, not a historian, so prefer a good historical yarn and a ghost story to a long list of names and dates. Thank you to all the amateur and professional historians doing an astounding job keeping the past alive.

My thanks also go to Manchester bands; the Stone Roses, Courteeeners and Doves, all of whom have dragged me through many a long run with their upbeat songs. I only mention them here as I have my doubts anyone gets this far. They deserve a mention if only to fool people skimming this page into thinking I have a much more exciting, star-studded life than I do.

When in reality, I'm already back at it, collecting the streets across the neighbouring boroughs of Trafford and Salford for a sequel. There are so many more stories to be told...

Bibliography and Further Reading

Some books I've read, some I've skimmed and some I've avoided until I'm done for fear of being overawed by the research, understanding and dedication of real historians. Not an exhaustive list, but for those who want to dive a little deeper, these will slake that thirst.

Angela Buckley, *The Real Sherlock Holmes - the Hidden Story of Jermone Caminada,* Pen and Sword, 2014

Kathryn Coase, *2000 Years of Manchester,* Pen & Sword History, 2019

Andrew Davies, *The Gangs of Manchester,* Milo Books, 2009

Paul Doraszczyk and Sarah Butler, *Manchester: Something Rich and Strange,* Manchester University Press, 2020

David Ebsworth, *The Jacobites' Apprentice,* Silverwood Books, 2012

Friedrich Engels, *The Condition of the Working Class in England,* Penguin, 2009

Ed Glinert, *The Manchester Compendium: A Street-by-Street History of England's Greatest Industrial City,* Penguin, 2009

Nick Holland, *In Search of Anne Bronte,* The History Press, 2017

Michala Hulme, *Bloody British History: Manchester,* The History Press, 2016

Stuart Hylton, *A History of Manchester,* The History Press, 2003

Alan Kidd and Terry Wyke, *Manchester: Making the Modern City,* Liverpool University Press, 2016

Mike Nevell, *Manchester: The Hidden History,* The History Press, 2008

Glynis Reeve, *The Illustrated History of Manchester's Suburbs*, DB Publishing, 2015

Again, not an exhaustive list of the websites, newspapers and internet rabbit holes I've tumbled down in the last few years searching for interesting Mancunian stories, historical nuggets and cultural treats.

100 Halls Around Manchester – 100hallsaroundmanchester.wordpress.com
About Manchester – aboutmanchester.co.uk
BBC Manchester Archives – bbc.co.uk
EatMcr –eatmcr.co.uk
Facebook History pages –facebook.com
Gorton Monastery – themonastery.co.uk
Gorton Manchester blog –gortonmanchester.wordpress.com
Historic England – historicengland.org.uk
Manchester City Council –manchester.gov.uk
Manchester's Finest – manchestersfinest.com
M.E.N. - Manchestereveningnews.co.uk
The Friends of Baileys Wood – facebook.com/BaileysWoodFriends
The Friends of Marie Louise Gardens –marielouisegardens.org.uk
Withington Girls School Archive – wgs.org.uk

The Hannah Curious Series - Young Adult Fantasy Fiction
Also by Neil Scott

Hannah Curious and the Darkhive of Lost Words

When fifteen-year-old Hannah Darnell receives a peculiar parcel from Alex, the half-forgotten imaginary friend from her childhood, her curiosity leads her on a perilous adventure where getting back home runs a distant second to simply staying alive.

Ambushed at their reunion by shady agents in raincoats and fedoras, her supposedly make-believe companion rushes her through a hidden doorway into the clandestine world of Lexica; a dizzying, fantastical place of alphabets harvested from swaying fields, industrious Words toiling at their desks and ruthless Languages plotting against one another.

Trapped five hundred floors beneath the streets of London in a Language whirling in grammatical turmoil, Hannah finds herself in a holding camp amongst a ragtag bunch of kindhearted revolutionaries. As she hears their stories and of the lack of political guidance from either the House of Commas or House of Words in Wordminster, she learns of a shocking secret that threatens all their futures. With Alex at her side, Hannah must attempt an unprecedented escape through all the mysterious quirks, peculiar characters, fiendish riddles and figments of the imagination within this strange world. Not just to free herself, but to save from erasure every story ever written.

Hannah Curious and the Last Knight Watchman

When Hannah Darnell discovers the fight for the English Language's future is all but lost, she takes an unimaginable journey to risk everything she has to save everything she loves. With the Darkhive Prison emptied and Old English Words corrupting books, newspapers and the internet, Lexican chaos is rapidly spilling over into Hannah's world.

Seeking a reclusive Captain who doesn't want to be found and a Letter Well in a notorious den of rogues, wastrels and drunken scoundrels, she relies on her imaginary Nouner friend Alex more than ever. Their quest for a highly secret and terrifyingly powerful solution finds them battling questioning Whyjackers, cursing Vulgars and sharp-suited Slangsters, all while avoiding armies of Author-tarian Guards and nefarious Blondeshirts. With every weary step through a cursed world of wonders, they must make deadly decisions, hoping each one won't be their last.

Fugitives of Lexica, Hannah and Alex are a blot of ink on nefarious leader Millard Bellwether's meticulous plans and he pursues them with all the forces at his disposal. Having captured and erased all but one of the Shrouded Guild's Knight Watchmen, he will stop at nothing to have the last Word.

Printed in Great Britain
by Amazon